Windows 98

for Busy People

Second Edition

Make Your Work Go Faster with These Speed Techniques

Save time—start your favorite program at the same time that you turn on your computer (pages 129-131).

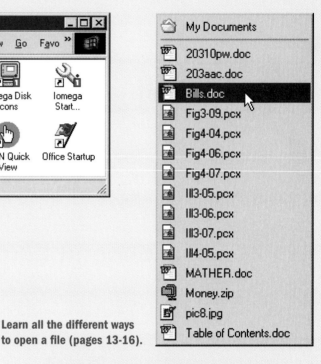

Learn all the different ways to open a file (pages 13-16).

Click a shortcut icon to go straight to where you want to go—a file, a program, even a site on the Internet (pages 46-47).

See what's in a file before you open it (page 62).

Organize Your Work—and Yourself

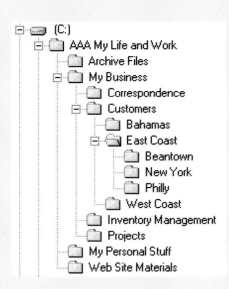

Devise a strategy for storing your work so you can open, back up, copy, and delete files quickly (pages 30-31).

Can't find a file? Discover all the ways to look for missing files with the Find command (pages 64-70).

In Windows Explorer and My Computer, locate, copy, move, rename, or delete files and folders (pages 58-64).

Find out the different ways to select files—and be able to move or copy them faster (pages 71-75).

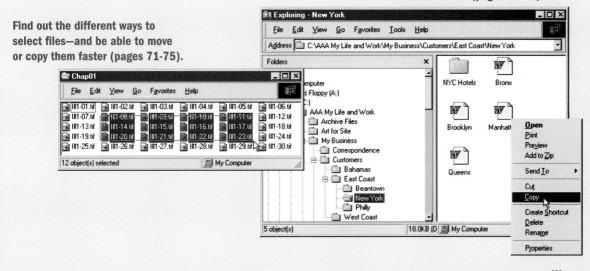

Make Your Windows Desktop Look Just So

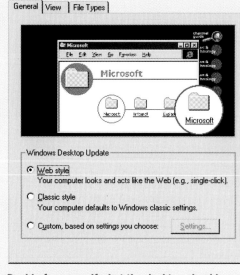

Decide for yourself what the desktop should look like and whether you want a Web-style or Classic-style desktop (pages 140-141 and 50-51).

Keep shortcut icons in a desktop folder so they don't crowd the screen (page 49).

Learn how to prevent eyestrain as you work (pages 141-143).

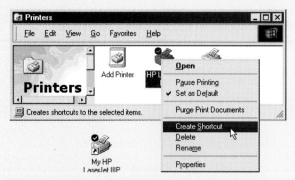

Speed up printing by creating a printer shortcut, and then print files by dragging them over the printer shortcut icon (pages 186-188).

Make Windows 98 Work Your Way

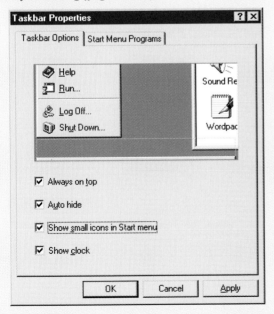

Decide for yourself how loud your computer is (pages 241-242).

Change the command menus around so that you can open programs quickly (pages 134-139).

Tame the Taskbar and make it do your bidding (pages 42-46).

A graphics file doesn't open in your favorite graphics program? Tell Windows which program opens which kind of file (pages 131-134).

Cruise the Internet with Internet Explorer 5

Don't waste time searching for stuff on the Internet. Learn how to surf the Internet quickly and productively (pages 152-154).

Lost on the Internet? Return to a site you visited before by clicking the Back or History button (pages 154-157).

Bookmark your favorite Web sites so you can visit them quickly (pages 157-158).

The Internet is a jungle, and sometimes finding your way around is hard. Take advantage of this book's techniques for getting around and marking your path on the Web with Internet Explorer 5 (pages 150-157).

Copy pictures, photos, and text from the Internet (pages 164-165).

Send and Receive E-Mail Messages

Send e-mail messages—even files—over the Internet with Outlook Express (pages 176-177).

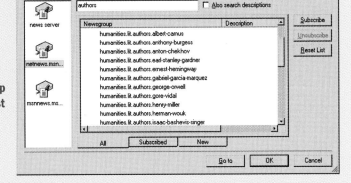

You can also use Outlook Express as an Address Book to stockpile the addresses of friends, family, clients, and customers (pages 171-174).

Outlook Express is also a newsgroup reader. Use it to find, visit, and post messages to newsgroups on the Internet (pages 181-183).

Be a Web Developer—Create Web Pages of Your Very Own

Be sure to put hyperlinks on your Web page to make it fit snugly on the Internet. You can also link Web pages you've created and in so doing create a Web site (pages 205-208).

History of Peruvian Vampire Movies § Mexican Vampire Movies
Peruvian Vampire Film Festival § Other Peruvian Vampire Movie
Sites
Origins of the Vampire Myth

Decorate your Web pages with clip art images, pictures, photos, or drawings (pages 201-203).

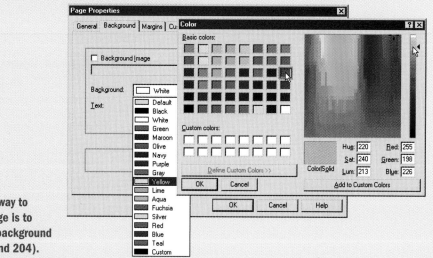

Maybe the easiest way to decorate a Web page is to give it an enticing background color (pages 203 and 204).

Maintain Your System and Make It Run Better

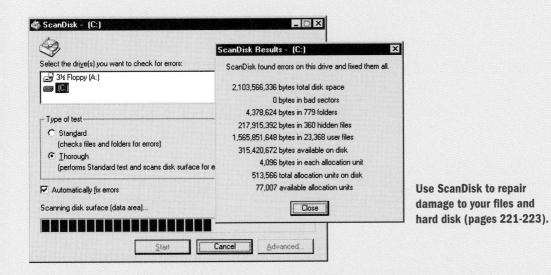

Defrag Legend

Unoptimized data that:
- □ Belongs at beginning of drive
- ▤ Belongs in middle of drive
- ▥ Belongs at end of drive

- ▤ Optimized (defragmented) data
- □ Free space
- ▣ Data that will not be moved
- ◪ Bad (damaged) area of the disk
- □ Data that's currently being read
- ▤ Data that's currently being written

Each box represents one disk cluster.

[Close]

Defragmenting Drive C

3% Complete

[Stop] [Pause] [Sho...]

Defragment your hard disk
so that files load faster and
programs run more smoothly
(pages 219-220).

Disk Cleanup for (C:)

Disk Cleanup | More Options | Settings

You can use Disk Cleanup to free up to 231.01 MB of disk
space on (C:).

Files to delete:

☑ 📁 Temporary Internet Files		40.50 MB
☑ 📄 Downloaded Program Files		0.00 MB
☐ 📄 Offline Web Pages		0.01 MB
☐ 🗑 Recycle Bin		17.22 MB
☑ 📄 Temporary files		0.37 MB

Total amount of disk space you gain: 40.88 MB

Description

The Temporary Internet Files folder contains Web pages
stored on your hard disk for quick viewing. Your personalized
settings for Web pages will be left intact.

[View Files]

[OK] [Cancel]

Use the Disk Cleanup utility to wipe your disk
clean of temporary files, temporary Internet
files, downloaded Internet programs, and other
jet trash from the Internet (pages 218-219).

ScanDisk - (C:)

Select the drive(s) you want to check for errors:

- 📁 3½ Floppy (A:)
- 💾 (C:)

Type of test
- ○ Standard
  (checks files and folders for errors)
- ● Thorough
  (performs Standard test and scans disk surface for e...

☑ Automatically fix errors

Scanning disk surface (data area)...

[Start] [Cancel] [Advanced...]

ScanDisk Results - (C:)

ScanDisk found errors on this drive and fixed them all.

2,103,566,336 bytes total disk space
0 bytes in bad sectors
4,378,624 bytes in 779 folders
217,915,392 bytes in 360 hidden files
1,565,851,648 bytes in 23,368 user files
315,420,672 bytes available on disk
4,096 bytes in each allocation unit
513,566 total allocation units on disk
77,007 available allocation units

[Close]

Use ScanDisk to repair
damage to your files and
hard disk (pages 221-223).

Windows98

for Busy People

Second Edition

The Book to Use When There's No Time to Lose!

Ron Mansfield and Peter Weverka

OSBORNE

Osborne/**McGraw-Hill**

Berkeley / New York / St. Louis / San Francisco / Auckland / Bogotá
Hamburg / London / Madrid / Mexico City / Milan / Montreal / New Delhi
Panama City / Paris / São Paulo / Singapore / Sydney / Tokyo / Toronto

A Division of The **McGraw·Hill** *Companies*

Osborne/**McGraw-Hill**
2600 Tenth Street
Berkeley, California 94710
U.S.A.

For information on translations or book distributors outside the U.S.A., or to arrange
bulk purchase discounts for sales promotions, premiums, or fund-raisers, please contact
Osborne/**McGraw-Hill** at the above address.

Windows 98 for Busy People, Second Edition

234567890 DOC DOC 90198765432109

ISBN 0-07-212203-X

Publisher   Brandon A. Nordin
Associate Publisher and
Editor-in-Chief   Scott Rogers
Acquisitions Editor   Joanne Cuthbertson
Project Editors   Madhu Prasher and Mark Karmendy
Editorial Assistant   Stephane Thomas
Technical Editor   Greg Guntle
Copy Editor   Claire Splan
Proofreader   C^2 Editorial Services
Indexer   Valerie Robbins
Graphic Artist   Robert Hansen
Computer Designers   Mickey Galicia and Gary Corrigan
Series Design   Jil Weil
Cover Design   Damore Johann Design, Inc.
Cover Illustration/Chapter Opener Illustration   Robert deMichiell

This book was composed with Corel VENTURA.

For Marie, Noriko, and Tom
—P.W.

For Bivian Marr, N.P. and Dr. Amy Rosenman, M.D.
Your alertness and loving care saved Nancy's life.
—R.M.

CONTENTS AT A GLANCE

CONTENTS

Acknowledgments

We are very grateful to everyone at Osborne/McGraw-Hill for their excellent work on our book.

Thanks go especially to Joanne Cuthbertson, who helped develop the Busy People series and who made many excellent suggestions for improving this book. We would also like to thank copy editor Claire Splan for probing so tenderly with the editorial scalpel, and editorial assistant Stephane Thomas and project editors Madhu Prasher and Mark Karmendy for making sure that manuscripts always landed in the right place.

Greg Guntel poured over the manuscript to make sure that all the instructions on these pages are indeed accurate, and we thank him for that. Thanks as well go to the indexer, Valerie Robbins, for her excellent work, to Jil Weil for her new Busy People series design, and to Robert deMichiell for the witty pictures you will find on the pages of this book.

These Berkeleyans at Osborne/McGraw-Hill gave their best to this book, and for that we are very grateful: Micky Galicia, Gary Corrigan, and Bob Hansen.

Finally, thanks to Publisher Brandon Nordin and Editor-in-Chief Scott Rogers for their continuing support of the Busy People series.

Introduction

Windows 98, the newest version of the Windows operating system, takes off where Windows 95 left off and is more complicated than ever. A browser, Internet Explorer, comes with the software. And Microsoft has also included an e-mailer and newsgroup reader called Outlook Express, as well as FrontPage Express, a program for creating Web pages and Web sites. Those are the major changes, but hundreds of other alterations have been made to Windows as well. You will find new utility programs in Windows 98. All across the board, little but very important things have been done to make the software run more efficiently and make connecting to the Internet easier.

This book is your key to understanding how Windows 98 works and how you can use Windows to the best advantage. Everything that is essential and helpful in Windows 98, everything that might be of use to a busy person, is explained in this book. And it is explained in such a way that you understand how to make Windows 98 serve you. I don't describe *what* Windows 98 does in this book—I'm not interested in that and I assume that you aren't either. In this book, you learn *how* to make Windows 98 work for *you.* In other words, you learn how to make the hours you spend in front of the computer more productive and enjoyable.

If you're looking for a gee-whiz computer book with a yellow-and-black cover and lots of cute but indecipherable headings ("Hey! Where'd That Darn File Go?"), you came to the wrong place. And this isn't an 850-page monster volume, either. I do not cover every nook and cranny of Windows 98 because, frankly, I think you have better things to do than toy with a computer operating system. All this book does is teach Windows 98 quickly and thoroughly so you can get more out of your computer.

In Chapter 9, *"Windows Update: Getting an Up-to-Date Copy of Windows"* explains how you can download Windows 98, Second Edition from the Internet if you are a registered user of the first edition.

Whom this book is for

This book is for users of Microsoft Windows 98 Second Edition, the very latest version of the Windows operating system. It is for busy people who want to get to the heart of Windows 98 and its many excellent features without having to spend a lot of time doing it. Microsoft made many minor improvements to the Second Edition of Windows 98, and they are covered in this book.

By reading this book, you will learn how to do tasks well. Topics are presented in such a way that you can look up instructions in a hurry. You will find lots of numbered lists and labeled figures so you know exactly how to complete a task or solve a problem. This book is loaded with cross-references, too, so you know where to go if one part of the book doesn't completely explain how to do a task.

What's in this book, anyway?

Chapter 1 explains the basics that you need to know each time you run Windows 98. It tells how to start computer programs, open files so you can work on them, open and close windows, shut down Windows 98, and use the Windows 98 Help program. In Chapter 2, you learn the dozen tasks that you can do right away to make your work in Windows 98 more productive. It explains how to open files quickly, create shortcut icons, handle the Taskbar, make the screen look just right, and manage one or two Windows 98 Internet features.

In Chapter 3, you learn everything you need to know about files and folders—how to create them, move them, delete them, and copy them. You also find out how to find missing files, recover a file you deleted, and share data between files. Chapter 4 takes on the setup work you have to do in Windows 98. It describes installing and uninstalling software and hardware and how to establish a rock-solid connection between your computer and the Internet.

Chapter 5 explains how to work faster in Windows 98. You learn how to supercharge the mouse and keyboard, how to customize the menu system, how to make your favorite program start when you turn on your computer, and how you can avoid eyestrain by taking advantage of the many features for changing the screen's appearance.

Chapters 6 and 7 describe how to use Internet Explorer and Outlook Express to surf the Internet, view Web pages offline, copy pictures and photos from the Internet, send and receive e-mail, and visit newsgroups. You also learn everything you need to know about printing files.

Chapter 8 explains how to create Web pages and Web sites with FrontPage Express. You also learn how to upload your Web pages to an Internet Service Provider so that others can view your Web pages on the Internet.

In Chapter 9, you discover how to use the Windows 98 system tools to make your computer run faster and more smoothly. This chapter also explains how to use the Backup program to back up files and how to update your copy of Windows 98 from the Internet.

Chapter 10 explains how to play and record sounds, as well as play .avi and .mpeg video clips. You also learn about Imaging, the Windows 98 graphics program. Last but not least, Appendix A tells how to install Windows 98 and reinstall the operating system so that only the components of Windows 98 that you really want are on your computer.

Getting the most out of this book

This book was designed and written to take you, busy person that you are, straight to the instructions you need. In that spirit, you will find the following elements in this book. They point to important things you should know about in the text.

INFORMATION THAT IS EASY TO LOOK UP   The editors and I took great pains to make sure that the information in this book is easy to look up. You are invited to turn to a chapter, thumb through the pages, and find out by reading the headings which strategies are available for completing a task. The descriptive headings help you find information quickly. The bulleted and numbered lists make it easy to follow instructions. The tables make options easier to understand. I want you to be able to look down the pages and quickly find the

Throughout the book, you'll see cross-references in the margins, where it is easy to see and read them.

SHORTCUT

In Windows, there are often two ways to do things—the fast but dicey way and the slow, thorough way. I explain fast-but-dicey techniques in Shortcuts like this one, which appear in the margin of the book.

TIP

Look for Tips in the margin. They appear throughout the book to offer handy bits of advice that will make you a better user of Windows 98.

DEFINITION

To help you understand Windows and computer terminology, Definitions of important terms appear in the margins of the book.

topics that concern you. You don't have to slog through a morass of commentary to find the information you need in this book.

BLUEPRINTS   The Blueprints at the very front of this book are like previews of coming attractions. While you are waiting for the movie to begin, look at the Blueprints. The page numbers on the Blueprints tell you where to turn in this book to learn more about a topic that has aroused your curiosity.

FAST FORWARDS   Each chapter begins with a handful of Fast Forwards. Fast Forwards are step-by-step, abbreviated instructions for doing things that are explained more fully later on. Each Fast Forward is cross-referenced to pages in the chapter that you may turn to for all the details. You might not need the details. You might be savvy enough to learn all you need to know from a Fast Forward.

ANNOTATED FIGURES   Most of the figures (not the illustrations) in this book are annotated. They are thoroughly annotated, in fact. A savvy Windows user can simply look at the figures to figure out how to do tasks.

EXPERT ADVICE

Where you see an Expert Advice box like this one, prick up your ears and read attentively, because that is where you will find time-saving tips and techniques for becoming a better Windows 98 user.

We'd like to hear from you

If you have a comment about this book or a shortcut that you would like to share with other readers, please write an e-mail message. Peter Weverka and Ron Mansfield are being held hostage at Peter_Weverka@msn.com. All inquiries and comments are welcome, as they help us pass our dreary days in captivity.

By the way, although this book was written by two people, we opted not to use the word "we" on the pages of this book when explaining what we think you should do to get the most out of Windows 98. "We" seemed a bit pretentious, like the royal "we" ("We are not amused," Queen Victoria once said about her awe-inspiring royal illustrious self). No, the authors are not Siamese twins. Instead of "we," we opted for the first-person singular, "I."

CHAPTER 1

The Bare Essentials

INCLUDES

- Starting Windows 98
- Starting and quitting computer programs
- Switching back and forth between programs
- Opening, closing, saving, and naming files
- Minimizing and maximizing, moving, resizing, and scrolling in windows
- Shutting down Windows 98

Start Windows 98 ➥ pp. 4–5

Flip the switch to turn on your computer or press CTRL-ALT-DEL. Network users and people who share their computers with others sometimes have to enter passwords to start Windows 98, but with luck you can press ESC or click OK in the Password dialog box and forge ahead.

Start a Computer Program ➥ pp. 8–10

- Click the Start button (or press CTRL-ESC) to open the Start menu, slide the pointer over Programs, and click the name of the program you want to start on the Programs menu or one of its submenus.
- Double-click a shortcut icon on the desktop.

Switch to Another Program You Are Running ➥ pp. 11–12

- Click a program button on the Taskbar.
- Press and hold down the ALT-TAB keys. Keep pressing TAB until, in the dialog box, the square appears around the program you want to switch to, and then release the ALT and the TAB keys.

Quit a Program ➥ p. 12

- Click the Close button (the X) in the upper-right corner of the program window.
- Choose File | Exit (or File | Close).
- Right-click a program button on the Taskbar and choose Close on the shortcut menu.

Open a File ➥ pp. 13–16

- Choose File | Open and, in the Open dialog box, find the folder in which the file is located, double-click the folder, click the name of the file, and click the Open button.
- Click the Start button, choose Documents, and click the file's name on the Documents menu.

Manipulate Program Windows
Onscreen ➡ pp. 18–23

- Click the Minimize button to collapse a window onto the Taskbar, the Restore button to shrink a window to the size it was before you minimized it, the Maximize button to enlarge a window to full-screen size, or the Close button to close the program window and the program as well.
- To minimize all the windows on the desktop at once, click the Show Desktop button on the Quick Launch toolbar or right-click on the Taskbar and choose Minimize All Windows.
- To move a window, click its title bar and drag it elsewhere.
- To change the size of a window, move the mouse pointer over a border, and when the pointer changes into a two-headed arrow, click and drag.

Shut Down Windows 98 ➡ pp. 23–26

1. Click the Start button (or press CTRL-ESC) and choose Shut Down.
2. In the Shut Down dialog box, choose Shut Down.
3. Click OK.
4. After you see the "It's now safe to turn off your computer" message, turn off the computer's power switch and the monitor.

Windows 98 is different from a standard computer program because you run Windows 98 whenever you start your computer. To get technical about it, Windows 98 is an *operating system.* Computer programs run on top of Windows 98 and Windows 98, like a symphony conductor, runs the programs so that they work harmoniously. With Windows 98, you can run several programs at once, cruise the Internet, and print files all at the same time.

Chapter 1 explains the bare essentials of running Windows 98. In this chapter, you learn the five or six things that you do whenever you sit at your computer. This chapter describes how to start Windows 98, start and close computer programs, open and close files, manipulate windows, and shut down Windows 98.

Starting Windows 98

All you have to do to start Windows 98 is turn on your computer, or, if your computer is turned on but asleep, press CTRL-ALT-DEL. If all goes well, you shortly see some technical gibberish, hear a *Ta-Da!* sound, see the "Microsoft Windows 98" opening screen, and then see the *desktop.* The Windows 98 desktop looks something like Figure 1.1. In the figure, two programs have already been opened. Their names appear on buttons on the *Taskbar* along the bottom of the screen.

Two or three obstacles can keep the desktop from appearing right away. You might accidentally have left a floppy disk in the A drive or you might be connected to a network:

In Chapter 5, "When People Share a Computer: Using User Profiles" explains how to handle passwords for different users.

- **Disk in Floppy Drive**   Try to start Windows 98 when a disk is shoved in the floppy drive and you get a confusing "Invalid system disk" message. The message says to "Replace the disk, and then press any key." Translation: "Replace the disk" means to eject the floppy disk. "Any" is not a particular key

Icons and shortcut icons

Desktop

Channel bar

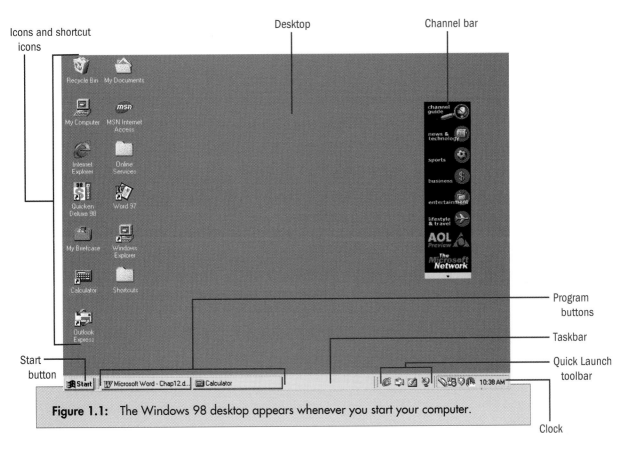

Program buttons

Taskbar

Start button

Quick Launch toolbar

Figure 1.1: The Windows 98 desktop appears whenever you start your computer.

Clock

on the keyboard. Look for a key labeled "Any" and you will look in vain. Simply press any key whatsoever to make Windows 98 start.

- **Connected to Network**   Network users have to enter a user name and password, and sometimes a domain name as well. If you don't know or can't remember this important stuff, ask the network administrator. With luck, you can sometimes click OK or press ESC and start Windows 98 without a password.

- **Shared Computer**   You might have to enter a password to start Windows 98 if others share your computer or you are a member of a workgroup. Press ESC or click Cancel in the Enter Password dialog box.

A Brief Geography Lesson

Before you take the leap of faith and start using Windows 98, you might as well look around and find out what's what. Following is a short geography lesson that explains the different parts of the screen. Glance at Figure 1.1 to find out precisely where the regions in this geography lesson are located.

DESKTOP   "Desktop" is the catchall name for the part of the screen where all the work is done. When you open a program or file, it appears in a window on the desktop.

SHORTCUT ICONS   A *shortcut icon* is an image you can double-click to open a program, open a file, or even connect to a Web site. A handful of shortcut icons appear on the desktop automatically, and you can create shortcut icons of your own, as "Create the Shortcut Icons You Need" in Chapter 2 explains. A small arrow appears in the lower-left corner of shortcut icons.

CHANNEL BAR   The Channel bar is a brazen attempt on the part of Microsoft to plug you into corporate Web sites, including Disney's, MSNBC's, and AOL's. Does that appeal to you? Perhaps you want to keep the Channel bar from squatting on the desktop and taking up valuable space. If so, turn to "Get Rid of or Display the Channel Bar" in Chapter 2.

TIP

If you can't see the Taskbar, someone has either dragged it offscreen or instructed Windows 98 not to display it. See "Learn How to Handle the Taskbar" in Chapter 2.

TASKBAR   The Taskbar is the stripe along the bottom of the desktop. Names of computer programs that are running appear on buttons on the Taskbar, as do the Start button and the Quick Launch toolbar. You can burden the Taskbar with all kinds of stuff and change its size as well, as the following grotesque illustration shows.

PROGRAM BUTTONS The names of programs that are currently running appear on buttons on the Taskbar. To switch to a different program, click its button.

QUICK LAUNCH TOOLBAR The Quick Launch toolbar is one of several toolbars you can tack onto the Taskbar to either make your work go faster or make the Taskbar more crowded, depending on your point of view. A *toolbar* is a set of buttons. By clicking a button on a toolbar, you can perform a task or open a program.

CLOCK The clock, located in the lower-right corner of the desktop, tells the time. And if you slide the mouse pointer over the clock, you can also find out today's date and the day of the week.

> Wednesday, June 23, 1999
> 11:46 AM

EXPERT ADVICE

To find out what something is in Windows 98, gently slide the mouse pointer on top of it. If you're lucky, a box appears with an oh-so brief explanation of what the thing is. For example, slide the mouse pointer over the Start button and Windows tells you to "Click here to begin." Truer words were never spoken.

Starting, Closing, and Switching Between Programs

The desktop, the Taskbar, and all the other gizmos are nice, but what really matters is starting programs and getting down to work. To that end, the following pages explain how to start programs, close programs, and switch between the programs that are open. You also learn how to run old-fashioned DOS programs, in case you still use those clunkers.

The Four Ways to Start a Computer Program

Windows 98 offers no less than four different ways to start a program. Such an embarrassment of riches! You be the judge of which technique works best. The four techniques are:

- Clicking the name of a program on the Programs menu or one of its submenus.
- Double-clicking a shortcut icon.
- Clicking a file on the Documents menu.
- Using the Run dialog box.

Figure 1.2 demonstrates the standard way to start a program—from the Programs menu. At the top of the Programs menu are submenu names, not program names. Notice the little arrows to the right of the submenu names. When you click or move the mouse pointer over a submenu name, a submenu appears beside the arrow. The program you want to open may be on a submenu. If it is, click it on the submenu to start it.

Starting a Program with Its Shortcut Icon

Probably the fastest way to start a program is to double-click its shortcut icon. When you install a program, a shortcut icon is sometimes placed on the desktop as part of the installation procedure. Sometimes you have to create the shortcut icon yourself. Anyhow, nothing could be easier or faster than double-clicking an icon to start a program (or clicking it if you opted for a "Web-style" Windows screen).

Starting a Program from the Documents Menu

Another fast way to start a program is to click a filename on the Documents menu. The Documents menu is located on the Start menu. To see it, click the Start button (or press CTRL-ESC) and either

In Chapter 5, "Starting Your Favorite Program When You Start Windows" explains how to start programs automatically each time you turn on your computer.

If you opt for Web-style pages, shortcut icons work like hyperlinks and you click instead of double-click them. See "Decide Whether You Like the Classic-Style or Web-Style Motif" in Chapter 2.

In Chapter 2, "Create the Shortcut Icons You Need" explains how to create your own shortcut icons.

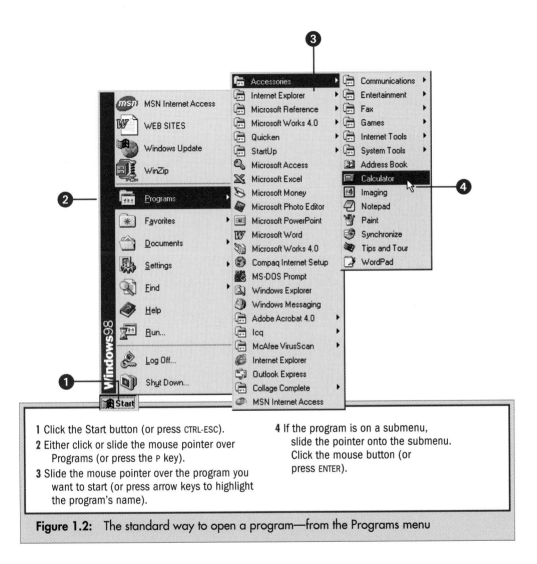

1 Click the Start button (or press CTRL-ESC).
2 Either click or slide the mouse pointer over Programs (or press the P key).
3 Slide the mouse pointer over the program you want to start (or press arrow keys to highlight the program's name).

4 If the program is on a submenu, slide the pointer onto the submenu. Click the mouse button (or press ENTER).

Figure 1.2: The standard way to open a program—from the Programs menu

click or slide the mouse pointer over the word "Documents." The Documents menu lists the last 15 files that you worked on. By clicking a file, you not only reopen it, you also open the program with which it was created. In effect, you kill two birds with one stone when you open a program from the Documents menu.

In Chapter 5, "Adding a Program Name to a Menu" explains how to put stray programs on the Programs menu where you can find and start them without having to negotiate the Run dialog box.

Starting a Program from the Run Dialog Box

Finally, you can open a program by way of the Run dialog box. Use the Run dialog box as a last resort if the program you want to open isn't listed on the Programs menu or doesn't appear as an icon on the desktop. Follow these steps to start a program with the Run dialog box:

1. Click the Start button or press CTRL-ESC to see the Start menu.

2. Choose Run. You see the Run dialog box.

3. Click the Browse button. You see the Browse dialog box.

4. Using the same techniques you would use to find and open a file in the Open dialog box, find the program you want to start. To do so, you likely have to click the down arrow to open the Look In drop-down menu, choose the C drive, double-click a folder or two, and then click to select the .exe file of the program you want to open.

5. Click the Open button. Back in the Run dialog box, you see the path to the program you want to open.

6. Click OK.

Running a DOS Program

Not so long ago, PC users ran DOS programs, not Windows-based programs. Instead of clicking icons, you had to know and be able to type esoteric command names. Legions of nerds rose up to interpret and give DOS commands, but with the advent of Windows, the nerd legionnaires have become Web site developers.

If you are cursed and still rely on a DOS program, follow these steps to run it in Windows 98:

1. Click the Start button or press CTRL-ESC to see the Start menu.

2. Choose Programs.

3. On the Programs menu, choose MS-DOS Prompt. You see the black-clad screen and the familiar spindly letters:

4. Type a command or do whatever you have to do in DOS.

5. To close the MS-DOS window, click the Close button (the X) in the upper-right corner.

Switching Between Programs

In Windows 98, you can run more than one program at the same time. In fact, you can run several programs. You can run as many programs as the memory in your computer allows. To switch to a new program, click its button on the Taskbar:

In the illustration shown here, Quicken is the active program. To switch to another open program, all you have to do is click its button on the Taskbar.

Laptop users and others who are fond of keyboard techniques can also switch between programs by pressing ALT-TAB and holding down the ALT key. When you press ALT-TAB, a box appears with icons that represent each program that is running. A square appears around the active program:

DEFINITION

Active program: The program that is currently in use. On the Taskbar, the active program is the one whose program button appears to be "pressed down."

Quicken Deluxe 98 - QDATA - [Quicken Reminders]

Still holding down the ALT key, press TAB until you can read the program's name and the square moves to the program that you want to switch to, and then release the ALT key and the TAB key.

Closing Programs That Are Open

Windows 98 offers as many ways to close programs as it does to start them. Let me count the ways to close a program:

- Click the Close button (the X) in the upper-right corner of the program window.
- Choose File | Exit (or File | Close).
- Press ALT-F4.
- Right-click a program button on the Taskbar and choose Close from the shortcut menu.
- Either double-click the Control menu icon in the upper-left corner of the window that the program is in (you'll find the icon to the left of the program's name), or click the icon to open the Control menu and then choose Close.

TIP

By right-clicking a program button and choosing Close, you can close a program without having to display its window onscreen.

EXPERT ADVICE

If a program freezes and you can't close it, press CTRL-ALT-DEL. You see the Close Program dialog box and its list of open programs. Make sure that the program you want to close is highlighted in the list and then click the End Task button. Being a cynic, right after I encounter a program that has frozen, I like to gracefully close the other programs that are open and restart the computer.

Opening, Saving, and Closing Files

In computer land, nothing is more important than files. Computer programs are stored in files. Data is stored in files. To start working, you open a file. When you are finished working, you save and close your file. Following are instructions for opening, saving, closing, and naming files.

EXPERT ADVICE

Occasionally, you try to open a file and you see the Open With dialog box. This dialog box is Windows' way of saying, "I don't know which program was used to create that file. Which program should I use to open it?" In the list of programs in the dialog box, click the name of the program that can open the file, and then click OK. In Chapter 5, "Telling Windows Which Program Opens a File" explains how to specify once and for all which program opens a certain kind of file.

Different Ways of Opening Files

I have good news and bad news. The bad news is that opening a file can be difficult if you aren't sure where it is located on your computer. The good news is that Windows 98 offers many shortcuts for opening files. Read on to learn the ins and outs of opening a file.

Speedy Ways to Open Files

First, the shortcuts. If you can use one of these techniques to open a file, go for it! Otherwise you have to use the dreary and forbidding Open dialog box, which is explained in the next section of this book. Here are the fastest ways to open a file:

- **Documents Menu**   The last 15 files you worked on are listed in alphabetical order on the Documents menu. To open one of these files, click the Start button (or press CTRL-ESC) and choose Documents on the Start menu. Then, on the Documents menu, click the name of the document you want to open.

- **My Computer and Windows Explorer**   Double-click a filename in Windows Explorer or My Computer to open it. Doing so opens the file as well as the program with which it was created. "Rummaging for Folders and Files with Windows Explorer and My Computer" in Chapter 3 explains the two programs.

- **Shortcut Icon**   Besides shortcut icons to start programs, you can create shortcut icons to open files. The icons lie on the desktop. All you have to do to open a file for which you've

My Journal

created a shortcut icon is double-click the icon (or click it if yours is a "Web-style" screen). See "Create the Shortcut Icons You Need" in Chapter 2.

- **File Menu** In many programs, names of the last four files you opened appear at the bottom of the File menu. To open one of these files, open the File menu and click the filename.

My Documents

- **My Documents Folder** When you choose File | Open, the Open dialog box appears and lists the files that are in the My Documents folder. One way to open files quickly is to keep the files on which you are currently working in the My Documents folder where you can get at them. See "Learn to Take Advantage of the My Documents and Favorites Folders" in Chapter 2 for further instructions.

Favorites

- **Favorites Folder** Another strategy is to place shortcuts to the files you use often in the Favorites folder. To open these files, click the Start button (or press CTRL-ESC), click Favorites on the Start menu, and click the name of the file you want to open. In some programs, the Open dialog box offers a button called "Look in Favorites." By clicking this button, you can quickly see and open the files in the Favorites folder.

EXPERT ADVICE

The Documents menu lists the last 15 files you opened, but suppose you don't want anyone to know what you've been doing with your computer. To keep Sherlock Holmes and other sleuths from finding out, empty the Documents menu: Click the Start button, choose Settings, and choose Taskbar & Start Menu. You see the Taskbar Properties dialog box. Click the Start Menu Programs tab, click the Clear button, and click OK. You can also delete a filename on the Documents menu by right-clicking it and choosing Delete.

Opening Files with the Open Dialog Box

If you can't open a file by any other means, you have to resort to the Open dialog box. Follow these steps to locate a file and open it:

My Documents

1. In the program in which you are working, choose File | Open or press CTRL-O. You see the Open dialog box.

   If you already opened a file since the last time you started your computer, the dialog box opens to the folder where the last file you opened is kept. Otherwise, the dialog box opens to the My Documents folder.

2. Find and select the folder in which the file is located. The Open dialog box offers strategies for doing so:

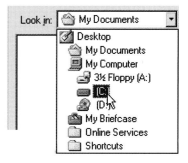

- Open the Look In drop-down menu and choose a drive or folder. Go this route when you want to start looking from the top of the folder hierarchy downward. At the beginning of Chapter 3, "How the Folder Hierarchy Works" explains how folders and files operate in Windows 98.

- Double-click a folder to open it and see its contents. As shown in Figure 1.3, the Open dialog box lists the folders and/or files in the folder you double-clicked. Keep double-clicking folders until you can see the file you want to open. The name of the folder you are looking in always appears in the Look In box.

Double-click to see the contents of folders.

Click here to move up the folder hierarchy.

Double-click the file you want to open.

Figure 1.3: Windows offers many ways to help you find the file you want to open.

- Click the Up One Level button (or press BACKSPACE) to close a folder and move up the folder hierarchy.

3. Click to select the file you want to open.

4. Either double-click the file or click the Open button.

If you have trouble finding the file you want to open, try these techniques for examining files in the Open dialog box:

- Click the Details button. As the next illustration shows, you see how large the files are, what type of file you are dealing with, and when you last modified the files.
- Open the Files of Type drop-down list and choose an option, as shown in the illustration. Choose files of a certain type to shorten the list, or choose All Documents (or All Files) to see all the files in the folder, no matter which program was used to create them.

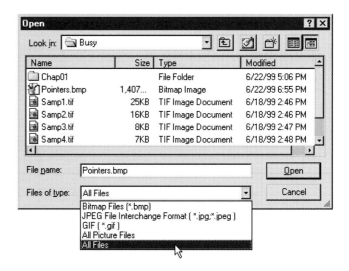

Saving a File

Saving the file from time to time as you do your work is essential. When you save a file, the program takes the work you did since the last time you saved the file and stores the work safely on the hard disk. Until you save your work, it rests in the computer's electronic memory (RAM), a tenuous place at best. If a power outage occurs or someone trips over the computer's power cord, you lose all the work you did since the last time you saved your file. Make it a habit to save files every ten minutes or so or when you complete a tedious task that you couldn't bear to do all over again.

Saving a file is pretty darn simple:

Save

- Click the Save button.
- Choose File | Save.
- Press CTRL-S.

Saving a File for the First Time

When you save a file for the first time, a dialog box appears and invites you to give the file a name and to tell Windows 98 which folder to keep it in. So the first time you save, you do two things at once—you save your work and name your file. Figure 1.4 shows how to save and name a file. Be sure to choose names that you will remember later. Filenames can be 255 characters long and can include numbers, characters, and blank spaces. However, these characters cannot be part of a filename:

/ ? : * " < > |

Closing a File

Congratulations! You finished working on your file, you saved it, and now you are ready to close it and go to lunch. Use one of these techniques to close a file:

- Choose File | Close.
- Double-click the Control menu icon in the upper-left corner of the file window. The icon is located on the title bar, to the left of the filename.
- Press ALT-F4.

TIP

Before you close a file, be sure to save it. Most programs offer a safeguard to keep you from closing a file without saving your work. Usually, a message box asks if you want to save the changes that you recently made to the file before closing it.

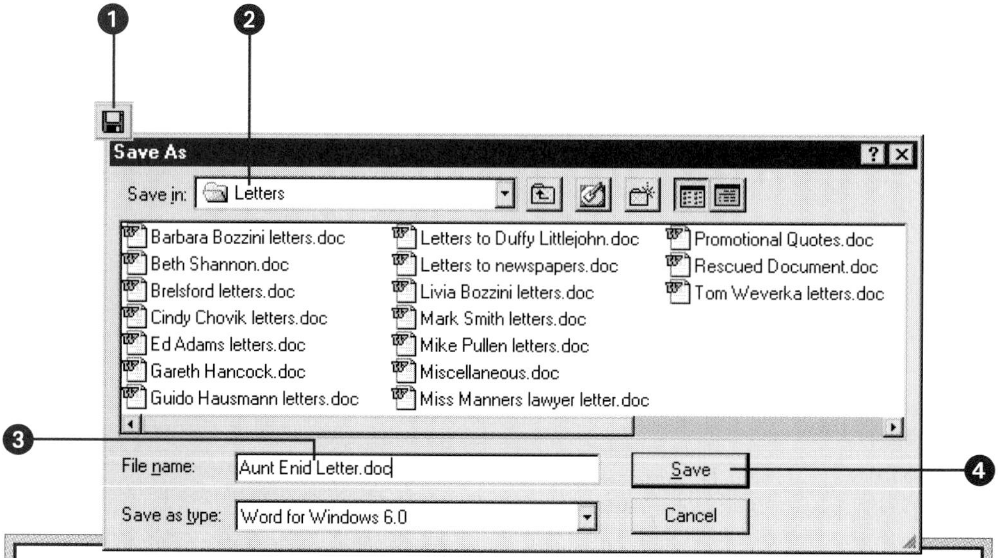

1 Click the Save button, choose File | Save, or press CTRL-S. You see the Save As dialog box.

2 Locate and select the folder in which to store your new file. Use the same techniques you use to find the file you want to open in the Open dialog box.

3 Enter a descriptive name in the File Name text box. Be sure to observe the rules for naming files.

4 Click the Save button.

Figure 1.4:   The Save As dialog box is where you give new files a name and tell Windows 98 which folders to store them in.

All About Windows

Windows are so important in Windows 98, Microsoft named the operating system after them. Clicking buttons is also important, but Microsoft rejected the name "Buttons" for its operating system. "Buttons" sounds like the name of a kitten or clown, whereas "Windows" has a futuristic ring and is appealing to voyeurs.

When you open a file or start a program, it appears in a window like the one in Figure 1.5. Learn how to manipulate windows on the desktop and you will go a long way toward working faster and better. On the following pages are instructions for minimizing and maximizing windows, arranging windows onscreen, moving windows,

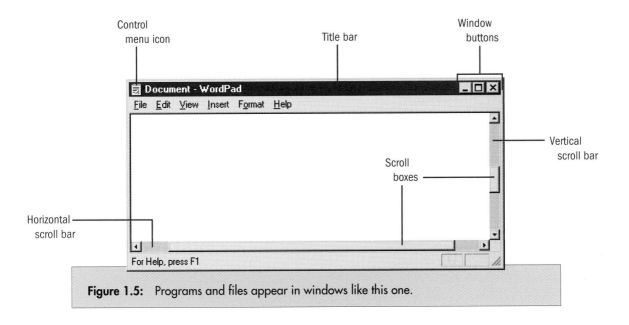

Figure 1.5: Programs and files appear in windows like this one.

changing the size of windows, and scrolling in a window. Refer to Figure 1.5 if you get stumped by arcane window terminology.

Minimizing, Maximizing, and Closing Windows

Slide the mouse pointer over the three square buttons in the upper-right corner of a window and you see the words Minimize, Restore (or Maximize), and Close. Clicking the window buttons is the cleanest and surest way to change the size of or close windows.

MINIMIZE BUTTON Collapses the window and makes it disappear. Clicking this button by no means closes the program. To see a program window after it has been minimized, click its button on the Taskbar or press ALT-SPACEBAR-N.

RESTORE BUTTON Shrinks a window to the size it was before you maximized it last time. After you click the Restore button, it changes names and becomes the Maximize button. You can also double-click the title bar to restore a window or press ALT-SPACEBAR-R.

MAXIMIZE BUTTON   Enlarges a window to full-screen size. After you click the Maximize button, it changes names and becomes the Restore button. You can also double-click the title bar to maximize a window or press ALT-SPACEBAR-X.

CLOSE BUTTON   Closes the program window and the program as well. You can also press ALT-F4 to close the program window.

Besides minimizing, maximizing, restoring, and closing windows by clicking window buttons, you can also click the Control menu icon and choose Minimize, Maximize, Restore, or Close from the Control menu.

EXPERT ADVICE

To minimize all the open windows on the desktop at once, click the Show Desktop button on the Quick Launch toolbar. Click the button again to bring all the windows back. You can also minimize all the windows by right-clicking on the Taskbar and choosing Minimize All Windows on the shortcut menu. Right-click again and choose Undo Minimize All to see the windows.

Changing the Size and Location of Windows

Sometimes minimizing and maximizing windows is not enough and you have to change a window's size and position on your own. And to really change the way that windows are arranged onscreen, you can try out two unusual commands, Cascade and Tile. Use these techniques to move and change the size of windows:

- **Changing a Window's Size**   To make a window larger or smaller, move the mouse pointer over a border of the window. When the pointer changes into double-arrows, click and drag the border. The bare outlines of a new window show how large the window will be when you are done changing its size. When the window is just-so, release the mouse button.

Drag a corner of the window to change its size but keep the window's proportions. Drag a side to make it wider; drag the top or bottom to make it taller or shorter.

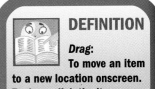

- **Moving a Window**   To change the location of a window onscreen, click its title bar and start dragging. As this illustration shows, the bare outlines of a window appear. When the window outline is where you want the window to be, release the mouse button.

DEFINITION

Drag:
To move an item to a new location onscreen. To drag, click the item you want to move, hold down the mouse button, slide the item to a new location, and release the mouse button.

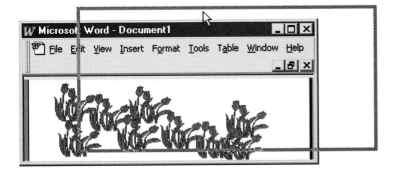

The Cascade and Tile commands are not for everybody and you can experiment with them as you will. To test these commands, right-click the Taskbar and choose Cascade Windows, Tile Windows Horizontally, or Tile Windows Vertically from the shortcut menu:

- **Cascade**   The Cascade command puts all the open windows onscreen in a fan-like arrangement, as shown in Figure 1.6. To work on a particular file, click its title bar to move it to the front of the line.
- **Tile**   The Tile commands open all the windows at once. You see a small portion of each open window. To make the window you want to work in fill the screen, click its Maximize button.

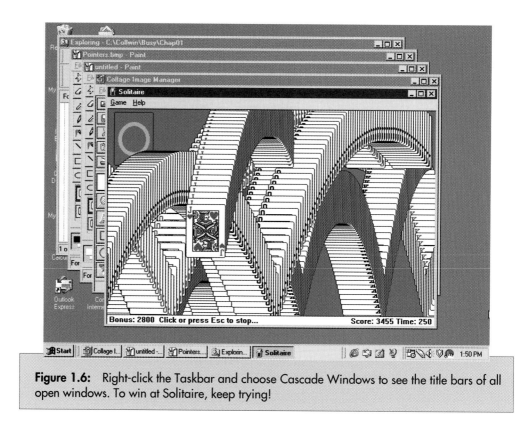

Figure 1.6: Right-click the Taskbar and choose Cascade Windows to see the title bars of all open windows. To win at Solitaire, keep trying!

Right-click the Taskbar and choose Undo Cascade or Undo Tile if you regret choosing either command.

Scrolling in a Window

By manipulating the scroll bars, you can change your view of a file. Use the scroll bar on the right side of the window (or press PAGE UP or PAGE DOWN) to move to the top or bottom of a file; use the scroll bar along the bottom to move from side to side. In the case of scroll bars, a figure is worth a thousand words. Figure 1.7 demonstrates how the scroll bars work.

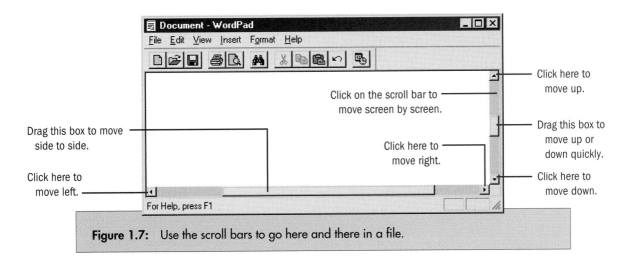

Click here to move up.

Click on the scroll bar to move screen by screen.

Drag this box to move up or down quickly.

Drag this box to move side to side.

Click here to move right.

Click here to move left.

Click here to move down.

Figure 1.7: Use the scroll bars to go here and there in a file.

Shutting Down Windows 98

Shutting down Windows 98 is always a glorious moment. It means your work is done and you can go treetopping or do whatever it is you like to do. However, you have to follow a specific procedure to shut down Windows 98. Read on to see how to shut down and what to do if your computer hangs and you can't shut down the proper way.

EXPERT ADVICE

Whatever you do, don't close Windows 98 simply by turning off your computer. Doing so can do serious damage to the hard disk. Be sure to follow the standard shutdown procedure. If worse comes to worse, your computer hangs, and turning off your computer proves the only way to shut down, wait a half-minute before turning your computer back on to allow the hard disk to stop spinning.

Shutting Down the Right Way

Follow these steps to shut down Windows 98:

1. Click the Start button (or press CTRL-ESC) and choose Shut
    Down, the last command on the Start menu. You see the Shut
    Down Windows dialog box:

2. Choose a shutdown option (most likely the second):

    *   **Stand By** Puts your computer in Standby mode and shuts
        down the monitor and hard drive. To arouse your computer
        from its slumber, jiggle the mouse or press any key on the
        keyboard. (If you choose this option, do not follow step 5
        and turn off your computer's power switch, or you'll lose
        unsaved data in files that were open when you shut down.)

    *   **Shut Down** Shuts down Windows 98.

    *   **Restart** Shuts down Windows 98 and restarts the program
        right away. Choose this option when you are running low
        on memory or you have reconfigured your system.
        Restarting Windows 98 clears the computer's memory
        banks and makes programs run faster. When you fiddle with
        display settings or install new software, you usually have to
        restart your computer.

    *   **Restart in MS-DOS Mode** Restarts the computer in
        MS-DOS mode so that technicians can run DOS
        disk-checking commands. I hope you never have to choose
        this option.

3. Click OK.

4. Stare patiently at the "Please wait while your computer shuts down" screen. *Do not* turn off the computer's power switch yet.

5. Turn off the monitor (and the printer and scanner and copy machine and coffee maker as well, if they are running). Turn off your computer's power switch as well if you so choose.

EXPERT ADVICE

Many people simply leave their computers on, the idea being that turning a computer on and off too often sends electrical jolts through the system and can do damage. Decide for yourself whether or not to turn off the power when you are finished with your computer. Leaving a computer on uses electricity. And the hard disk and fan never get a rest, so they wear out faster. If you decide to leave your computer on, be sure to choose the Stand By option when you shut down—it saves electricity.

Shutting Down When the Computer Freezes Up

What happens if your computer goes berserk, freezes, and refuses to do anything more? When this happens, your only recourse is to try to gracefully shut down Windows 98 and then restart your computer. And if you can't gracefully shut down, you have to clumsily shut down, lose unsaved data in the files you are working on, and risk doing damage to your hard disk.

Follow these steps to handle a stubborn computer that has stopped working:

1. Press CTRL-ALT-DEL. With any luck, you see the Close Program dialog box shown in Figure 1.8.

2. Click the name of the program that is "not responding."

3. Click the End Task button. Again with any luck, the program you were working in when the computer froze shuts down. Save all open files, close all programs, and restart your computer.

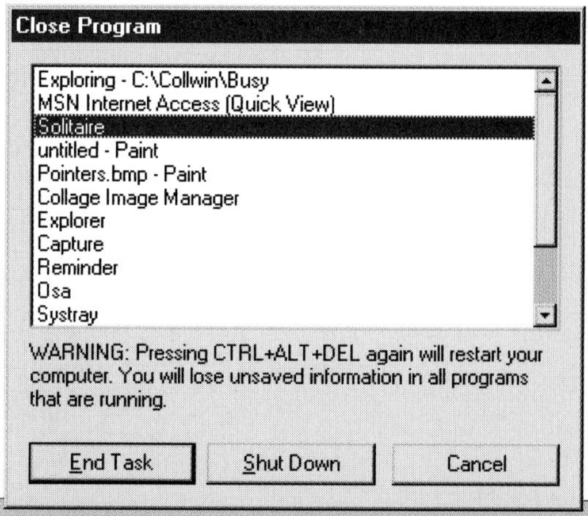

Figure 1.8: When your computer freezes, see if you can handle the problem in the Close Program dialog box.

4. If your computer still doesn't budge, click the Shut Down button or press CTRL-ALT-DEL again. With any luck, your computer shuts down and restarts.

5. If you continue to suffer bad luck, turn off the computer's power switch.

6. Wait a full minute before turning your computer on again. If you turn it on before the platters stop spinning, you could harm the hard disk.

When you turn your computer back on, Windows 98 runs the ScanDisk utility program to see if any damage was done to the hard disk. Chapter 9 explains how ScanDisk works.

Stuff to Do Once to Make Your Life Easier

Open a File Quickly in the My Documents or Favorites Folder ➥ pp. 31–34

- **My Documents**   Double-click the My Documents icon on the desktop or choose File | Open to see the Open dialog box, and then double-click the name of the file you want to open.
- **Favorites**   Click the Start button, choose Favorites, and click the name of the file. You can also open the Favorites menu in Windows Explorer or My Computer and select the file there.

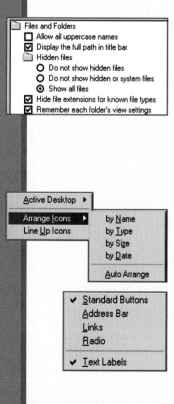

View Files in Different Ways ➥ pp. 35–36

- Click the down arrow next to the Views button and choose an option: Large Icons, Small Icons, List, or Details.
- After choosing Details, click the Name, Size, Type, or Modified button to arrange files in alphabetical order by name, size, type, or date of modification.

Decide How to List Files and Folders in Windows ➥ pp. 37–38

1. Click the Start button, choose Settings | Folder Options, and click the View tab.
2. Check or uncheck the Hide File Extensions for Known File Types check box to hide or display file extensions.
3. Select either the Do Not Show Hidden Files or the Show All Files option button to hide or display hidden file types.

Rearrange Icons on the Desktop ➥ pp. 38–39

- Right-click and choose Arrange Icons | Auto Arrange to display icons with the same amount of space around each one.
- Right-click and choose Line Up Icons to put icons neatly in rows.

Remove or Display a Toolbar ➥ p. 42

- Choose View | Toolbars and click the name of the toolbar you want to see or hide.
- Right-click anywhere on a toolbar or menu bar and click a toolbar name.

Create a Shortcut to a File, Program, Folder, Printer, or Whatnot ➡ pp. 46–47

1. In Windows Explorer or My Computer, right-click the item you want to create a shortcut to and choose Create Shortcut.
2. Drag the shortcut item onto the desktop.
3. Right-click the icon, choose Rename, and enter a descriptive name.

Choose the Kind of Desktop You Want—Web Style or Classic Style ➡ pp. 50–51

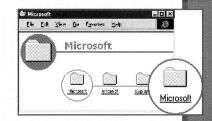

1. Click the Start button and choose Settings | Folder Options.
2. On the General tab, click the Web Style or Classic Style option button.
3. Click OK.

Get Rid of or Display the Channel Bar ➡ pp. 51–52

1. Right-click the desktop and choose Properties.
2. Click the Web tab in the Display Properties dialog box.
3. Uncheck or check the Internet Explorer Channel Bar check box and click OK.

In every computer program, you can put your best foot forward by learning to do three or four important things right from the start. Windows 98 being an operating system, all the features are connected to one another. That means you can get a good start by doing a dozen or so things, not three or four.

This chapter explains the dozen things you can do in Windows 98 to make the hours you spend at the computer more rewarding and enjoyable. You learn strategies for organizing your work on disk, how you can save time by storing files in the My Documents and Favorites folders, and why you should devise a strategy now for backing up your work. This chapter shows how to control what the screen looks like, how to handle toolbars, how to manipulate the Taskbar, and how to create shortcuts to the files and folders you want to work with. You also learn how to settle a few important Internet issues from the get-go and how to control the way that files are displayed in windows and dialog boxes.

Devise a Strategy for Storing Your Work on Disk

In Chapter 3, "How the Folder Hierarchy Works" explains how folders are stored in Windows 98. "Organizing and Managing Files and Folders" explains how to create and move folders.

Most people mistakenly believe that the files created with a program have to be stored on disk either in the same folder as the program itself or in a nearby folder. Nothing could be further from the truth. Files created in Microsoft Word, for example, need not be stored deep in the folder hierarchy where the Microsoft Word program is. You can store Microsoft Word files and the files you create yourself anywhere you want. And you should store them in a convenient place where you can find them easily.

Figure 2.1 demonstrates one strategy for storing personal files on the hard disk. In this strategy, all personal files are stored directly on the C drive in a folder called "AAA My Life and Work" and its subfolders. This user put the letters "AAA" in the name so that her personal folder would be first in the list of folders on the C drive, where she could find it easily. Inside the AAA My Life and Work

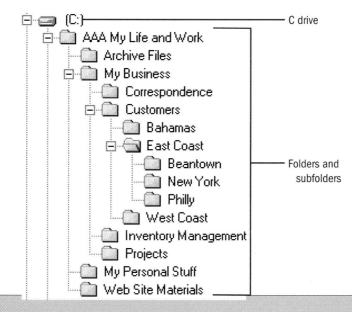

C drive

Folders and
subfolders

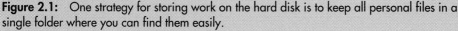

Figure 2.1: One strategy for storing work on the hard disk is to keep all personal files in a single folder where you can find them easily.

folder are subfolders for storing archive files, files that pertain to a business, personal files, and Web site materials. Inside the My Business subfolder are more subfolders for storing files that pertain to various aspects of the business.

As a Windows 98 user, one of your first jobs is to devise a strategy for storing your work on disk. Create folders for the different kinds of work you do and arrange the folders on disk in such a way that you can find them easily. When you want to create a link between files or open, back up, delete, move, or copy a file, you will know exactly where it is if you carefully devise a strategy for storing your work on disk.

Learn to Take Advantage of the My Documents and Favorites Folders

Windows 98 offers two speedy ways of opening files and folders: the My Documents folder and the Favorites folder. These convenient folders are easy to get at. Instead of tunneling through the folder hierarchy to find and open a file, all you have to do is click a couple of times to open the My Documents folder or Favorites folder, and then open the file from there.

My Documents: For Storing Your Current Work

Maybe the fastest way to open a file you are working on is to keep it temporarily in the My Documents folder. That way, all you have to do to open your file is open the My Documents folder and take it from there. The My Documents folder is by far the easiest folder to open in Windows 98. Here are two methods for accessing the folder and opening a file:

My Documents

- Double-click the My Documents icon on the desktop. My Computer opens to show the contents of the My Documents folder, as shown at the top of Figure 2.2. Double-click the file that you want to open.

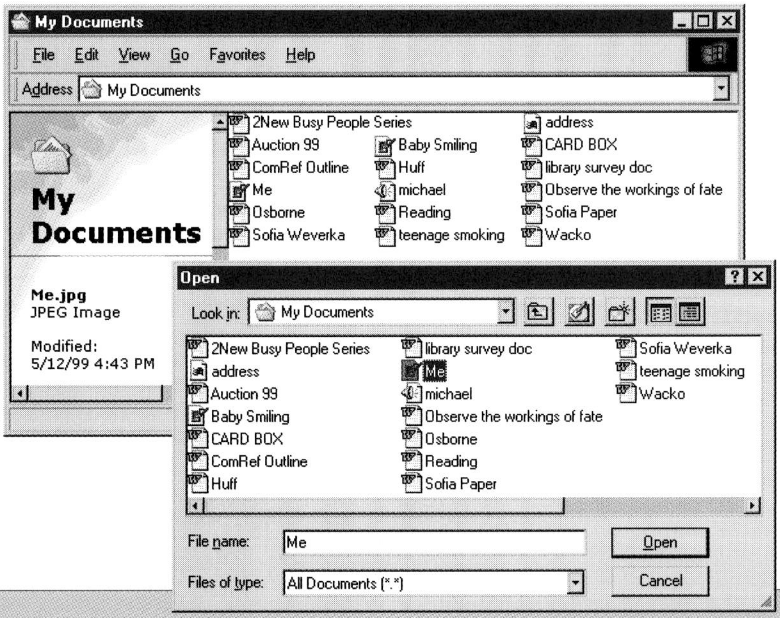

Figure 2.2: Double-click the My Documents icon on the desktop to open the My Documents folder in My Computer (left), or choose File | Open to see the My Documents folder in the Open dialog box (right).

- Choose File | Open. As shown on the bottom of Figure 2.2, the contents of the My Documents folder appear in the Open dialog box. Select a file and click the Open button. (You don't see the My Documents folder if you previously opened files in a different folder. If the My Documents folder doesn't appear, click the down arrow in the Look In box and choose My Documents.)

By the way, don't confuse the My Documents folder with the Documents option on the Start menu. When you click the Start button and choose Documents, you see a list of the last 15 files you worked on, not the contents of the My Documents folder. However, you can choose My Documents, the topmost option on the Documents menu, to open the My Documents folder in My Computer.

Favorites: For Files and Folders You Go to Often

Windows 98 is very fond of the Favorites folder. When you bookmark a site on the Internet, for example, a shortcut to the site is placed in the Favorites folder. Shortcuts to channels are kept in the Favorites folder as well. You can also put your own shortcuts in the Favorites folder. Some programs even have a Look in Favorites button in dialog boxes so you can see the contents of the Favorites folder, go to the folder quickly, and open a file.

Favorites

Put shortcuts to your most important folders and files in the Favorites folder and you can get to those folders and files very, very quickly. The Favorites folder is located on the C drive at C:\Windows\Favorites. To work with the Favorites folder:

Later in this chapter, "Create the Shortcut Icons You Need" explains how to create a shortcut.

- Click the Start button, and from the Start menu, choose Favorites. On the Favorites menu, click a folder icon to open the folder in My Computer; click a file to open a file.
- Choose File | Open and click the Look in Favorites button in the Open dialog box. Then select a file and click Open. (The Look in Favorites button is available only in Microsoft computer programs.)

- Open the Favorites menu in Windows Explorer or My Computer, and then double-click the item that you want to access.

Decide When and How to Back Up Files

Computers are fabulous machines until they break down. A broken computer is worse than useless. The data stored on the hard disk is trapped inside and will never be of use to anyone. Unless someone had the foresight to back up the data, no one will ever be able to see or use it again.

In computer lingo, *backing up* means to make a second copy of a computer file and store it in a safe place where nothing can harm it. How to back up a file to a floppy disk is explained in Chapter 3 ("Making Backup Copies to a Floppy Disk"), and how to back up many files at once is a subject of Chapter 9 ("Backup: Backing Up Files and Folders on the Hard Disk"). For now, you need to devise a backup plan. Answer these questions to get started:

- *Which of my files are important or irreplaceable and therefore need to be backed up?* Losing a client database, an address list, or a novel-in-progress is gut wrenching and can have tragic consequences.
- *How often should I back up my important files—daily, weekly, monthly?* The answer depends on how much trouble reconstructing a file is. If reconstructing a file is any trouble whatsoever, back it up.
- *How should I back up my files?* To back up a few small files, copy them to floppy disks. To quickly back up many hundreds of files, copy them to a tape drive or zip drive with the Windows 98 Backup utility.
- *Where should I store the backup copies of the files?* Store disks or tapes where they are safe from floods, wildfires, earthquakes, power outages, burglars, disk failures, and children with grubby hands or glasses of apple juice. Since no such place exists, do your best under the circumstances.

Learn the Ways to View Folders and Files

Because finding the folder or file you want to open can be difficult, Windows offers different ways of viewing folders and files. No matter where you go in Windows—Windows Explorer, My Computer, the Recycle Bin, the Open dialog box, the My Documents folder, or the Find window—you can choose a View menu option to get a better idea of what is in the folder you are rummaging through. Folders and files can appear as large icons, as small icons, in a list, or in a detailed list. And if you opt for a detailed list, you can arrange the list by name, file type, size, or the date on which the file was last saved.

Figure 2.3 shows different ways of viewing folders and files. Follow these steps to change views:

1. Either click the down arrow next to the Views button to see the Views menu or click Views on the menu bar.

2. Choose an option: Large Icons, Small Icons, List, or Details.

TIP
You can also change views by clicking the Views button until you arrive at the view you want.

Figure 2.3: Large Icons, Small Icons, List, and Details

Figure 2.4 shows how to rearrange files and folders in Details view so you can find what you're looking for. If I were you, I would fold down the corner of this page. These same techniques work in Windows Explorer, My Computer, the Recycle Bin, the Open dialog box, the Find window, and other places where files are sometimes hard to locate.

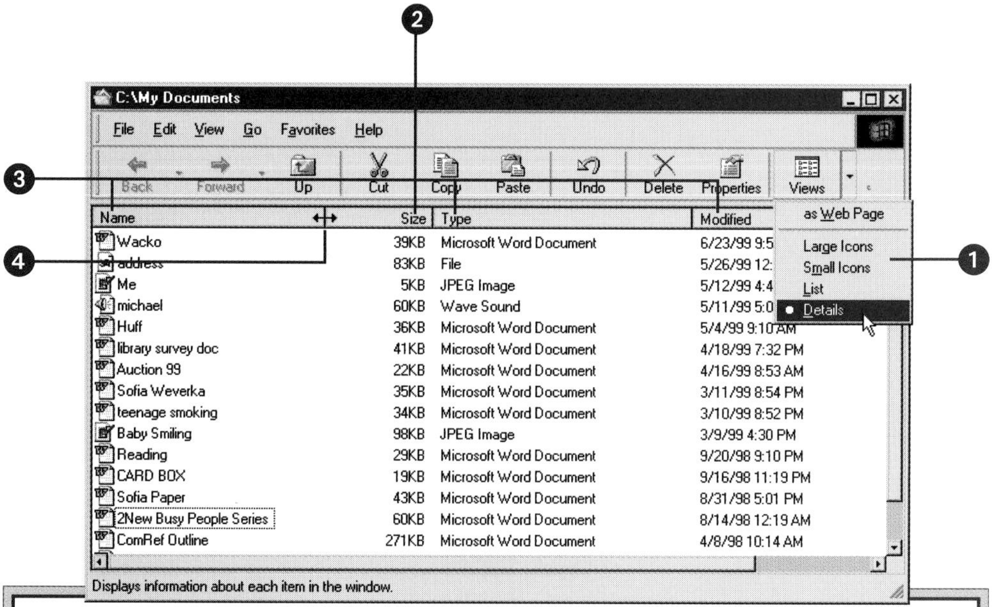

1 Choose Details on the Views drop-down menu (or click the Details button in some dialog boxes).

2 Click a button—Name, Size, Type, or Modified—to arrange the files, respectively, in alphabetical order by name; from smallest to largest in size; in alphabetical order by type; or in date order by the day and time on which the files were last saved.

3 To arrange the files the opposite way, click the same button—Name, Size, Type, or Modified—again. Clicking a button a second time reverses the order of the files.

4 If necessary, drag the border between buttons to widen columns and read filenames, file sizes, and so on.

Figure 2.4: Arranging files by name, type, size, or date.

Decide How to List Files in Folders and Dialog Boxes

Unless you tell it otherwise, Windows does not show file extensions in dialog boxes and folder windows. Hidden files are not shown either. But not being able to see file extensions can be a handicap when you are working with different types of files because the extension identifies the kind of file you are working with. In graphics and desktop publishing programs, where files of different types are often jumbled together, being able to identify files by their three-letter extensions is a must.

Follow these steps to tell Windows 98 how to display filenames in windows and dialog boxes:

1. Click the Start button and choose Settings | Folder Options. If you are starting from a folder window, choose View | Folder Options.

2. In the Folder Options dialog box, click the View tab.

3. Under Files and Folders in the Advanced settings part of the dialog box, check or uncheck the following options, and then click OK:

   - **Display the Full Path in Title Bar** Lists the path to the file you are working on in the title bar. I find this option very nice. In Windows Explorer, My Computer, and other windows where files are manipulated, all you have to do is glance at the title bar to see precisely where files are located on your computer:

DEFINITION

File extension: A three-letter designation at the end of a filename that describes what type of file the file is. The extension comes after the filename and is separated from the name by a period. Paint.exe, for example, is an .exe (or executable) file, also known as a program file. Sunset.gif is a .gif file, a kind of graphics file.

DEFINITION

Path: A list of the successive folders in which a file is located.

C:\AAA My Life and Work\My Business\Customers\East Coast\Philly

- **Hidden Files**   Check the first option, Do Not Show Hidden Files, to keep the background files that programs need from appearing in dialog boxes. Click the second option, Do Not Show Hidden or System Files, to keep Windows system files from appearing as well. Click the third option to see all files in every folder.
- **Hide File Extensions for Known File Types**   Uncheck this box if you want to see file extensions as well as filenames in windows and dialog boxes where files appear.

EXPERT ADVICE

The only drawback to displaying file extensions is that you have to know and enter an extension whenever you save and name a file. For example, instead of naming a Microsoft Word file *Addresses*, you have to type *Addresses.doc* in the Save As dialog box, "doc" being the three-letter extension for Word files.

Make the Desktop Look Just So

In Chapter 5, "Making the Screen Easier to Look At" explains other ways to change the appearance of the screen.

Since you have to stare at the Windows 98 desktop as you work, you might as well stare at a pretty face as an ugly one. The next few pages explain how to display and rearrange icons on the desktop, pick a screen saver, and choose a screen size and screen resolution for your monitor.

Displaying Icons on the Desktop (and in Folders)

Later in this chapter, "Keeping Shortcut Icons in a Desktop Folder" explains a technique to keep the desktop from getting crowded with shortcut icons.

Icons on the desktop and icons in folder windows tend to jumble together when you do a lot of moving and copying and pasting. To prevent icons from jumbling together, right-click a blank place on the desktop or in a folder window and choose one of these commands:

- **Arrange Icons | Auto Arrange**   Arranges icons in military fashion, with the same amount of space around each one.
- **Line Up Icons**   Lines up the icons in rows but does not close empty space between icons.

EXPERT ADVICE

To make desktop and folder icons larger so you can see them better, right-click a blank place on the desktop and choose Properties. In the Display Properties dialog box, click the Effects tab, check the Use Large Icons check box, and click OK.

Selecting a Screen Saver

In the old days of computer technology, monitors suffered from burn-in if they were left on too long. The onscreen image would eat into the monitor's phosphorous lining and damage it. To prevent burn-in, screen savers were developed.

Although screen savers aren't necessary anymore, since they don't save the screen from damage, they are fun and worth using if only because they burst onscreen when you've been idle too long and remind you to go back to work. Figure 2.5 shows how to select a screen saver of your very own.

Choosing a Screen Size and Screen Resolution

In computer lingo, *resolution* describes how clearly images and letters appear onscreen. Resolution is determined by the number of colors, 16 or 256, that are used to display images and the size of the screen in pixels. The more pixels, the larger the screen appears to be. The more colors used in a display, the clearer the pictures look. If you work with

DEFINITION

Screen saver: A moving image that appears automatically onscreen when the computer has been idle for a certain period of time.

DEFINITION

Pixel: A dot in a grid of thousands of dots that, together, make an image. On a monitor screen, the image you see is composed of thousands of pixels. The term stands for "picture element."

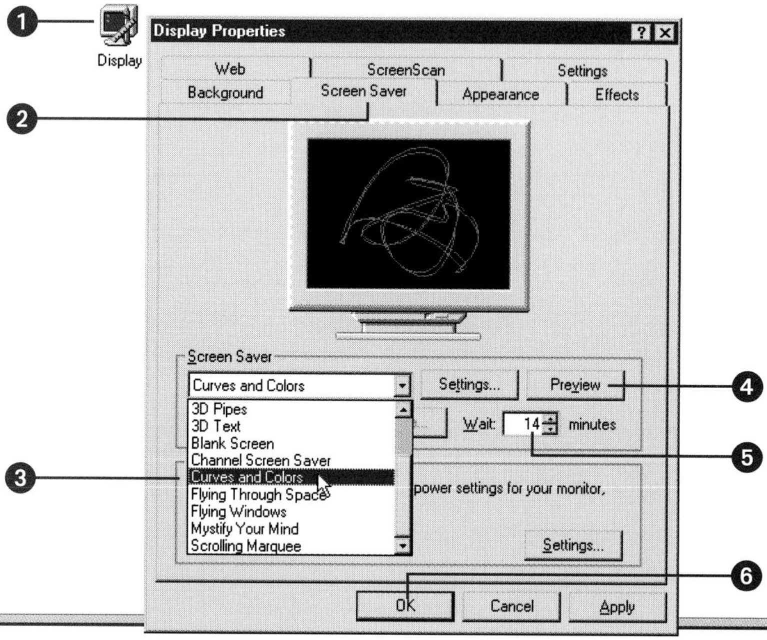

1 Either click the Start button, choose Settings | Control Panel, and double-click the Display icon, or right-click an empty part of the desktop and choose Properties from the shortcut menu.

2 Click the Screen Saver tab in the Display Properties dialog box.

3 From the Screen Saver drop-down menu, choose a screen saver and glance at the sample monitor to see what it is.

4 Click the Preview button. The screen saver fills the screen. Jiggle the mouse to see the Display Properties dialog box again.

5 In the Wait box, enter how many minutes should elapse before the screen saver kicks in. If you're lazy, enter **1**—the screen saver will burst onscreen after every minute you waste by dreaming.

6 Click OK.

Figure 2.5: The screen saver you choose in the Display Properties dialog box will appear onscreen if you neglect to touch the computer for a certain number of minutes.

graphic images or photographs, you owe it yourself to display pictures in 256 colors. At 16 colors everything is a smudge.

Figure 2.6 describes how to choose a screen size and screen resolution. Depending on which option you choose, you might have to restart your computer before the settings take effect.

❶ Display

Display Properties ? X

| Background | Screen Saver | Appearance | Effects |
| Web | ScreenScan | Settings **❷** |

Display:
NEC MultiSync XV15 on S3 Trio64V2-DX/GX (775/785)

Colors

High Color (16 bit) ▼

16 Colors
256 Colors
High Color (16 bit)
True Color (24 bit)

❸

Screen area
Less ─────┤────── More
800 by 600 pixels

❹

into this monitor. Advanced...

❺

OK   Cancel   Apply

1 Either click the Start button, choose Settings | Control Panel, and double-click the Display icon, or right-click a blank spot on the desktop and choose Properties.

2 In the Display Properties dialog box, click the Settings tab.

3 From the Colors drop-down menu, choose a new color setting.

4 Under the Screen area, drag the slider to 640 by 480 pixels, 800 by 600 pixels, 1,024 by 768, 1,600 by 1,200 pixels, or another size. The sample monitor gives an inkling of what these settings look like onscreen.

5 Click OK.

Figure 2.6: Experiment with the Screen Area and Colors settings until you concoct a screen you are happy with.

EXPERT ADVICE

Some monitors can't display at 1,024 by 768 or 1,600 by 1,200 pixels. Other monitors do not offer 256 colors. If you choose a setting in the Display Properties dialog box and nothing happens, blame it on your monitor or video card, not on Windows 98.

Learn How Toolbars Work

DEFINITION

Toolbar:
An assortment
of buttons for performing
tasks.

Knowing how to display and remove toolbars is worthwhile, because toolbars take up valuable space onscreen. Fortunately, removing them and getting them back is as easy as right-clicking or choosing options from the View menu, as the next illustration shows. A check mark next to a toolbar's name on a menu means that the toolbar is displayed. Display or remove toolbars as you need them.

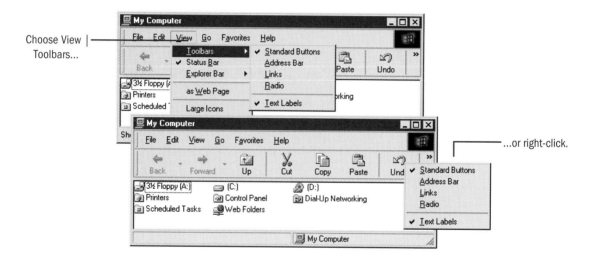

Choose View | Toolbars...

...or right-click.

Do the following to display or remove toolbars:

- **With the View Menu**   Choose View | Toolbars and click the name of the toolbar you want to see or hide.
- **By Right-clicking**   Right-click anywhere on a toolbar or the menu bar and click a toolbar name.

DEFINITION

Taskbar:
The stripe along
the bottom of the screen.
Names of programs that are
running appear on buttons
on the Taskbar.

Learn How to Handle the Taskbar

Microsoft introduced the Taskbar in Windows 95. In Windows 98, Microsoft has burdened the Taskbar with additional cargo, so learning how to pilot the Taskbar is worthwhile. These pages explain how to change the position and size of the Taskbar, handle the toolbars on the Taskbar, and remove and display the Taskbar.

Techniques for Managing a Crowded Taskbar

As you surely know, Windows puts a new button on the Taskbar when you open a new program. By clicking a Taskbar button, you can start working in a different program. That's fine and dandy, except when six or eight programs and a toolbar are open, the Taskbar gets very crowded, and you can't tell what's what:

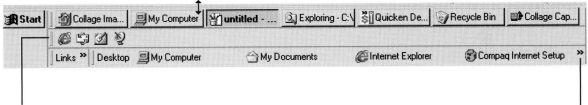

> **TIP**
>
> The next section in this chapter explains Auto Hide, a technique for making the Taskbar appear onscreen only when you click the bottom of the screen.

One way to solve the overcrowding problem is to enlarge the Taskbar. Gently move the mouse pointer over the top of the Taskbar, and when you see the double arrows, click and drag the Taskbar up the screen. You can make the Taskbar as large as you want, and when you want to shrink it down to size, move the pointer over the top of the Taskbar again, and click and drag—but this time drag down the screen.

To move a toolbar, slide its border.　　　　　　　　　　Click to see more buttons.

When Windows can't display all the buttons or toolbars, double arrows and slider-borders appear on the Taskbar. Click a double arrow to see more buttons. To move a toolbar left or right on the Taskbar, drag its slider-border left or right.

Some people solve the crowded toolbar problem by dragging the toolbar from the bottom of the screen to the side of the screen. To take this drastic measure, click a blank space on the Taskbar, drag toward the upper-right or upper-left corner of the screen, and release the mouse button. Do the opposite to return the Taskbar to its home port along the bottom of the screen.

Auto Hide: Playing Hide and Seek with the Taskbar

Don't panic if the Taskbar disappears. It disappeared because somebody turned on the Auto Hide option, you shrunk the Taskbar to minuscule proportions, or someone has instructed Windows to put the Taskbar behind open windows. To find out where the problem lies, move the mouse pointer to the very bottom of the screen:

- If the Taskbar suddenly reappears, Auto Hide has been turned on.

  The Auto Hide option is a very convenient way of grabbing more room for programs onscreen. When Auto Hide is turned on, the Taskbar does not appear. To see it, move the mouse pointer to the very bottom of the desktop—the Taskbar comes out of hiding, ready for you to click a button. Figure 2.7 explains how to turn on Auto Hide.

- If you see the top half of a double arrow, you shrunk the Taskbar. Click and drag upwards to see the Taskbar again.

- If nothing happens, the Always on Top option that tells Windows to place the Taskbar in front of open windows has been turned off. Click the Start button and choose Settings | Taskbar & Start Menu. Then check the Always on Top option in the Taskbar Properties dialog box.

Introducing the Toolbars on the Taskbar

Earlier in this chapter, "Learn How Toolbars Work" explains how to remove and display toolbars.

As if the Taskbar isn't crowded enough, you can place a total of four different toolbars on the Taskbar. To display or remove a toolbar, right-click a blank space on the Taskbar (search carefully to find it if you must), choose Toolbars on the shortcut menu, and click a toolbar name:

- **Address Toolbar** Presents a text box so you can type Internet addresses. Either type an address or click the arrow to see addresses you entered in the past and perhaps choose one. Press ENTER to start Windows Explorer and either display a Web page onscreen or go on the Internet and retrieve a Web page.

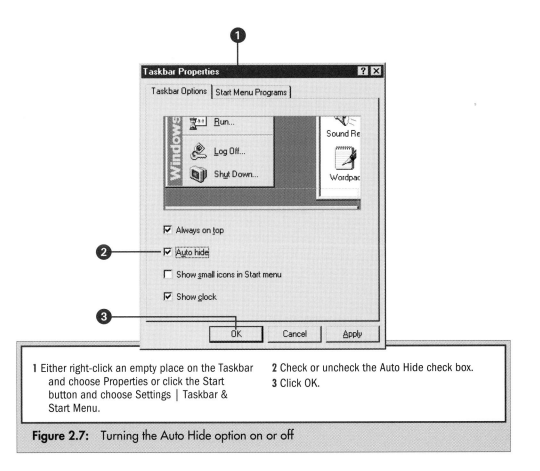

1 Either right-click an empty place on the Taskbar and choose Properties or click the Start button and choose Settings | Taskbar & Start Menu.

2 Check or uncheck the Auto Hide check box.
3 Click OK.

Figure 2.7: Turning the Auto Hide option on or off

- **Links Toolbar**   Puts buttons for each Internet site you bookmarked on the Taskbar. Rather than burden the Taskbar with this one, click the Start button and choose Favorites | Links. The Links toolbar gets its buttons from the Favorites\Links subfolder.
- **Desktop Toolbar**   Collects all the icons and shortcut icons on the desktop in a toolbar. Don't bother with this one. If you need to see desktop icons in a hurry, simply click the Show Desktop button on the Quick Launch toolbar.
- **Quick Launch Toolbar**   Offers the all-important Show Desktop button and buttons for quickly connecting to the Internet.

EXPERT ADVICE

You can launch your favorite programs from the Quick Launch toolbar. To do so, create a shortcut icon for each program you want to launch. Then drag the shortcut icons onto the Quick Launch toolbar—that's right, simply drag them on. To remove an icon from the Quick Launch toolbar, drag it onto the desktop.

Create the Shortcut Icons You Need

In my opinion, shortcuts are one of the best things going in Windows 98. Instead of burrowing into the Programs menu to open a program, you can double-click its shortcut icon. Create a shortcut to a printer and all you have to do to print a file is drop it on the shortcut icon. You can create shortcuts to your favorite folders to open them quickly in My Computer. And creating shortcuts is easy.

Calculator

Probably one or two shortcuts are already on your desktop. To distinguish a shortcut icon from an icon, look for the little arrow in the lower-left corner. The arrow tells you that the icon is a shortcut icon. When you double-click a shortcut icon, a program, file, folder, printer, or network location opens onscreen. Herewith are directions for creating shortcuts, naming shortcut icons, and deleting, moving, and copying shortcuts. You also learn how to tidy the desktop by keeping all shortcut icons in a desktop folder.

Creating a Shortcut Icon

In Chapter 3, "Rummaging for Folders and Files with Windows Explorer and My Computer" explains how to find items with those two programs.

Figure 2.8 demonstrates how to create a shortcut icon. Figure 2.9 shows how to create a shortcut icon for an item on a Windows menu. Some Windows menu items—the Calculator and the CD Player, for example—deserve shortcut icons, since opening them from the Windows menus is such a chore. If I were you, I would double-click shortcut icons after creating them to make sure they take you where you want to go. If you ever doubt where a shortcut leads, right-click it and choose Properties. The Shortcut tab of the Properties dialog box lists the path to the file, folder, or whatever.

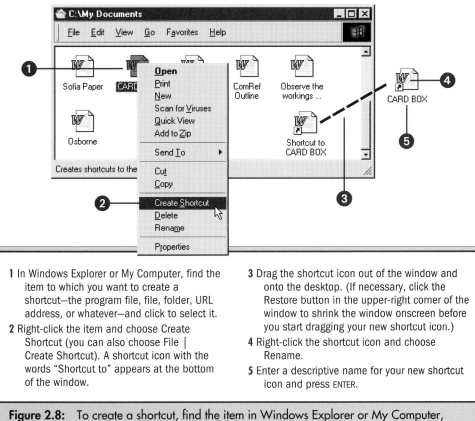

Figure 2.8: To create a shortcut, find the item in Windows Explorer or My Computer, right-click it, and choose Create Shortcut.

1 In Windows Explorer or My Computer, find the item to which you want to create a shortcut—the program file, file, folder, URL address, or whatever—and click to select it.

2 Right-click the item and choose Create Shortcut (you can also choose File | Create Shortcut). A shortcut icon with the words "Shortcut to" appears at the bottom of the window.

3 Drag the shortcut icon out of the window and onto the desktop. (If necessary, click the Restore button in the upper-right corner of the window to shrink the window onscreen before you start dragging your new shortcut icon.)

4 Right-click the shortcut icon and choose Rename.

5 Enter a descriptive name for your new shortcut icon and press ENTER.

Copying and Moving Shortcuts

After you've created a shortcut, you can move or copy it here, there, and everywhere. Some shortcut icons beg to be put in several different places. For example, shortcuts to your favorite programs belong on the desktop and on the Quick Launch toolbar. A shortcut to your favorite folder belongs in the My Documents and Favorites folder. Here's how to copy or move a shortcut icon:

- **Copying** Hold down the CTRL key as you drag the icon to a new location—into a folder window or onto the desktop, for example. As you drag, a plus sign appears below the pointer so

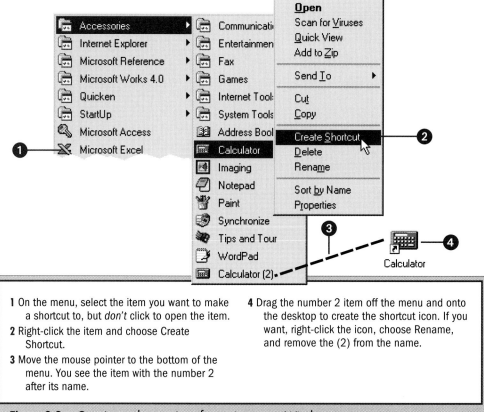

1 On the menu, select the item you want to make a shortcut to, but *don't* click to open the item.
2 Right-click the item and choose Create Shortcut.
3 Move the mouse pointer to the bottom of the menu. You see the item with the number 2 after its name.
4 Drag the number 2 item off the menu and onto the desktop to create the shortcut icon. If you want, right-click the icon, choose Rename, and remove the (2) from the name.

Figure 2.9: Creating a shortcut icon for an item on a Windows menu

you know that you are copying the shortcut, not moving it. You can also right-click the shortcut icon, choose Copy from the shortcut menu, and then right-click where you want to place the copy and choose Paste.

• **Moving**   Drag the shortcut icon to a new location. You can also right-click the shortcut icon, choose Cut from the shortcut menu, and then right-click where you want to move the shortcut icon and choose Paste.

Another way to move or copy a shortcut icon is to drag it while holding down the right mouse button. When you release the mouse button, a menu appears with options called Move Here and Copy Here. Choose one or the other.

Deleting Shortcuts

Deleting a shortcut icon is easy: Right-click it and choose Delete from the shortcut menu. Then click Yes when Windows asks if you really want to delete your shortcut icon. Don't worry about deleting the file or folder that the shortcut goes to—you are merely deleting a shortcut when you delete a shortcut icon. To delete several shortcut icons at once, hold down the CTRL key and click them before you right-click and choose Delete.

Shortcuts, like files and folders, land in the Recycle Bin after they have been deleted. You can revive a shortcut if that proves necessary (see "Recycle Bin: Recovering Deleted Files and Folders" in Chapter 3).

> **CAUTION**
> Before you delete a shortcut icon, examine it to make sure a little arrow is in the lower-left corner. If the arrow isn't there, you are about to delete not a shortcut icon, but a folder or, worse yet, a program.

Keeping Shortcut Icons in a Desktop Folder

The Windows desktop can get mighty crowded with shortcut icons. One way to practice crowd control is to create a desktop folder and put shortcut icons inside it. When you want to take a shortcut, double-click the desktop folder to see the shortcut icons inside and then double-click a shortcut icon. *Desktop folders* stay on the desktop beside My Computer, My Documents, and the other major-league icons.

Follow these steps to create a desktop folder for your shortcut icons:

1. Right-click a blank place on the desktop and choose New | Folder. A new folder appears.

2. Type a name for your folder (I suggest "My Shortcuts") and press ENTER.

3. Double-click your new desktop folder to open it in My Computer.

4. Drag the shortcut icons that litter the desktop into your new folder.

My Shortcuts

When you need to double-click a shortcut icon, you will know where to find it—in your Shortcuts folder on the desktop.

Decide Whether You Like the Classic-Style or Web-Style Motif

TIP

No matter which style you choose, you can see a folder in Web or Classic style by opening the Views menu and checking or unchecking the As Web Page option (see Figure 2.11).

People who are at home on the Internet will be glad to know that they can make the Windows desktop and folders look and work like Web pages. Figure 2.10 demonstrates how to choose the Web style or Classic style for the desktop and for folders. Figure 2.11 shows the difference between the Web style and the Classic style. Windows makes the following changes to the desktop and to folders when you choose the Web style:

• Icon names look like hyperlinks. The names are underlined and the mouse pointer changes to a gloved hand when you move it over an icon.

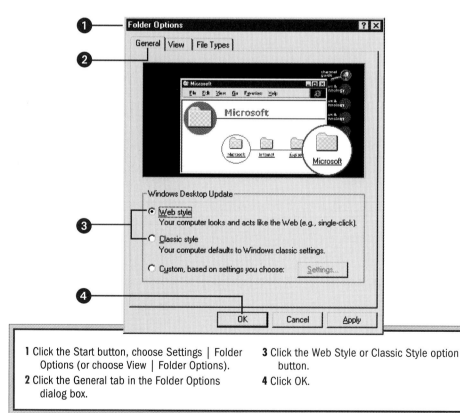

1 Click the Start button, choose Settings | Folder Options (or choose View | Folder Options).

2 Click the General tab in the Folder Options dialog box.

3 Click the Web Style or Classic Style option button.

4 Click OK.

Figure 2.10: Choosing the Web style or Classic style for Windows desktop and folders

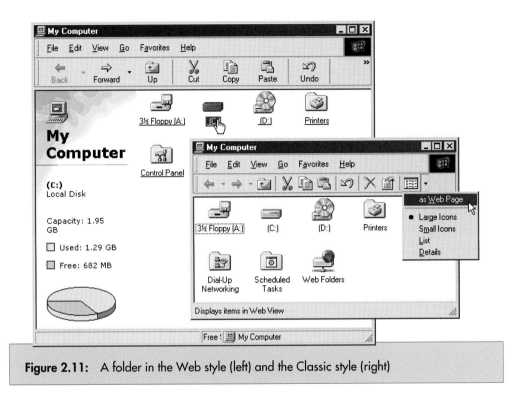

Figure 2.11:   A folder in the Web style (left) and the Classic style (right)

- Instead of double-clicking icons, you single-click them.
- To select an item, you move the pointer over it instead of clicking it. You can still use the CTRL-click and SHIFT-click techniques to select more than one item at the same time, but instead of clicking, hold down the CTRL or SHIFT key and slowly point to the items you want to select. "Selecting Files and Folders" in Chapter 3 explains all the selection techniques.
- You can read a description of a drive, folder, or file by moving the pointer over it. In Figure 2.11, I have moved the pointer over the C drive icon, and the folder tells how much used and free space is on the C drive.

Get Rid of the Channel Bar

What's that monstrosity that occupies so much space on the right side of the desktop? It's called the Channel bar. Before you decide whether channels are for you or learn how to download infomercials from a channel, you might as well get rid of the Channel bar. Follow these steps:

1. Right-click an empty place on the desktop and choose Properties from the shortcut menu.
2. In the Display Properties dialog box, click the Web tab.
3. Uncheck the Internet Explorer Channel Bar check box (if you can't uncheck it, check View My Active Desktop as a Web Page first).
4. Click OK.

Create an Emergency Startup Disk

When you installed Windows 98, you created an emergency startup disk. Do you still have it? Floppy disks have a habit of disappearing, but keeping an emergency startup disk on hand is absolutely necessary. If something evil this way comes and your computer dies, put the emergency startup disk in the A drive and push the computer's reset button. With luck, your computer will start in MS-DOS mode. From there the neighborhood computer guru might be able to fix your computer.

Follow these steps to create an emergency startup disk if yours has run away:

1. Put an empty disk with at least 1.2MB of disk space in the floppy drive.
2. Click the Start button and choose Settings | Control Panel.
3. In the Control Panel, double-click the Add/Remove Programs icon.

Add/Remove
Programs

4. Click the Startup Disk tab in the Add/Remove Programs Properties dialog box.
5. Click the Create Disk button.
6. Follow the onscreen directions.

When the deed is done, label the disk and put it in a safe place.

CHAPTER 3

Working with Files and Folders

INCLUDES

- Peering into a computer with Windows Explorer and My Computer
- Finding a folder or file with Windows' Find command
- Selecting, creating, renaming, copying, moving, and deleting files and folders
- Recovering files you deleted
- Copying and moving data from file to file

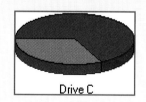

Find Out How Much Free and Used Space Is on Your Hard Disk ➥ pp. 63–64

1. Open My Computer or Windows Explorer and click the (C:) drive icon.
2. Choose File | Properties.

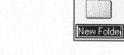

Search for a File or Folder with the Windows Find Command ➥ pp. 64–70

1. Click the Start button and choose Find | Files or Folders.
2. Enter criteria for the search on the Name & Location, Date, and/or Advanced tabs.
3. Click the Find Now button.

Create a New Folder ➥ pp. 70–71

1. In My Computer or Windows Explorer, locate and select the folder in which to put your new folder.
2. Choose File | New | Folder, type a name for the new folder, and press ENTER.

Select Files in Windows Explorer and My Computer ➥ pp. 71–72

- CTRL-click to select various files.
- Click the first file, then SHIFT-click the last file to select neighboring files.
- Press CTRL-A or choose Edit | Select All to select all the files in the folder.

Move or Copy Files to New Folders ➥ pp. 72–75

1. Open My Computer or Windows Explorer, then locate and select the files you want to move or copy.
2. To copy the files, click the Copy button, choose Edit | Copy, or press CTRL-C; to move the files, click the Cut button, choose Edit | Cut, or press CTRL-X.
3. Display and click the folder that is to receive the files or folders.
4. Click the Paste button, choose Edit | Paste, or press CTRL-V.

Rename a File or Folder ➜ pp. 75–76

1. In Windows Explorer, My Computer, or the Open dialog box, find and click the file or folder you want to rename.
2. Right-click and choose Rename from the shortcut menu.
3. Type a new name and press ENTER.

Delete Files or Folders ➜ p. 77

1. In Windows Explorer, My Computer, or the Open dialog box, find and select the folder(s) and file(s) you want to delete.
2. Press the DEL key, choose File | Delete, or right-click an item you selected and choose Delete from the shortcut menu.
3. Click Yes in the message box that asks if you want to delete the items.

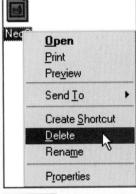

Recover a File You Deleted Accidentally ➜ p. 78

1. Double-click the Recycle Bin icon on the desktop.
2. Select the files and folders you want to restore and choose File | Restore.

In this installment of the Windows 98 saga, you discover how to peer into your computer. You learn how to find out precisely what's inside and rearrange it, if you want to. You learn the various and sundry ways to manage and organize files and folders with Windows 98.

This chapter starts by demystifying the folder hierarchy by which folders and files are stored. Then it describes two gadgets that you can use to inquire into your computer system—Windows Explorer and My Computer. You learn how to locate files and folders and how to select, copy, move, rename, and delete them. For the mistake-prone, this chapter explains how to recover a file or folder that was deleted accidentally. And you also learn how to copy and move data from one file to another.

How the Folder Hierarchy Works

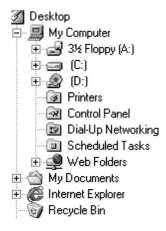

By now you must have noticed that your computer system is littered with folders. Files are kept in folders. Sometimes folders hold other folders. When you save a file for the first time, you are asked which folder to save it in. When you install new software, the installation program informs you that your new software will be kept in the such-and-such folder.

What you may not realize is that Windows maintains a structure, or hierarchy, for folders so that data is well organized and easy to get at. Yes, there is a method in this madness. At the top of the hierarchy is the Desktop folder. Inside it are the A drive, C drive, D drive—the *root directories*—and the other major-league folders. As you dig deeper into the hierarchy, you encounter more folders.

Figure 3.1 shows where customer information files—Bronx, Brooklyn, Queens, and Manhattan—are kept on a computer. The

Path to the
open folder

Folders and files in
the open folder

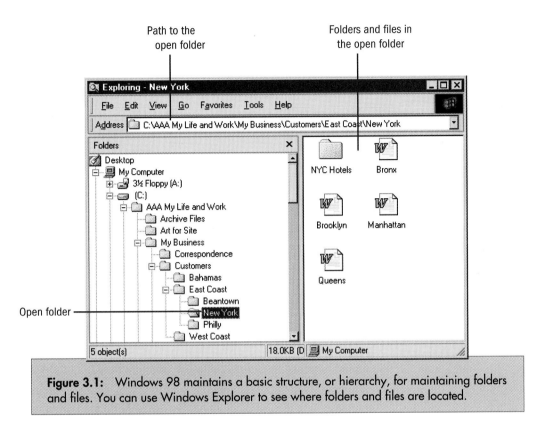

Open folder

Figure 3.1: Windows 98 maintains a basic structure, or hierarchy, for maintaining folders and files. You can use Windows Explorer to see where folders and files are located.

files are stored five layers deep—five folders deep—on the C drive in a folder called New York. In Figure 3.1, I used a Windows program called Windows Explorer to locate the files, which appear on the right side of the window.

Altogether, the five folders add up to the *path* that is shown in the Address bar in Figure 3.1: C:\AAA My Life and Work\My Business\Customers\East Coast\New York. By organizing folders this way, you can open files quickly. When you want to move, delete, or copy a file, you know precisely where to find it. Throughout this chapter, you learn how to locate, manipulate, and organize the files and folders on your computer. As you manage your files and folders, remember how the folder hierarchy works.

DEFINITION

Path:
A list of the successive folders in which a file is located. Also called the pathname. The path is listed in the Address bar of the Windows Explorer and My Computer windows.

Exploring Your Computer System

In Chapter 2, "Learn the Ways to View Folders and Files" explains different ways of displaying stuff in folder windows, including Windows Explorer and My Computer.

Before you can arrange, delete, move, or copy files and folders, you have to find them. Before you can create a new folder, you have to find the folder in which to put the new one. To create a shortcut icon, you have to find the file to which the shortcut goes. Windows 98 users spend a lot of time rummaging in their computers. Knowing what's there is essential, so Windows 98 offers two programs for peering inside a computer: Windows Explorer and My Computer.

The following pages introduce these venerable programs and explain how to use them to get from folder to folder. These pages also explain how to find out how much disk space you have and how to see what's in a file without opening it.

Rummaging for Folders and Files with Windows Explorer and My Computer

My Computer and Windows Explorer work similarly. Both were designed for the same purpose—to manage folders and files. The programs look very much alike. The chief difference between them is that you stay in one window in Windows Explorer. In My Computer, you open a new window each time you visit a new folder.

Personally, I prefer Windows Explorer to My Computer. In Windows Explorer, you get a bird's-eye view of the folders on your system, whereas My Computer myopically shows each folder in its own window. However, My Computer has won several beauty contests at which I wasn't the judge, so the following pages explain how to use both programs.

SHORTCUT
To quickly open Windows Explorer, right-click just about anything in Windows 98—a program icon, a folder in the Open dialog box, a folder in a My Computer window—and choose Explore from the shortcut menu. You can also hold down the SHIFT key and double-click a folder.

Windows Explorer: Investigating Folders and Files

As Figure 3.1 shows, you always know where the folder you are examining is located on your computer when you use Windows Explorer. In the Windows Explorer window, drive icons and folders appear in the window pane on the left; the window pane on the right shows the folders and files in the folder you are currently visiting. Folders and files are listed in alphabetical order.

To start Windows Explorer, click the Start button (or press CTRL-ESC) and choose Programs | Windows Explorer. You see the Windows Explorer window. Follow these instructions to find folders and files:

- **Finding Folders in the Hierarchy**   On the left side of the Windows Explorer, click the plus sign (+) next to a folder you want to investigate. The folders inside that folder appear below it. Click a minus sign (–) to keep the folders inside a folder from being displayed.

- **Seeing the Contents of a Folder**   Click the folder's name or icon (not the plus sign beside the name and icon). The files and folders in the folder you clicked appear on the right side of Windows Explorer in alphabetical order, with the folders first. Instead of a folder icon, you see an open folder icon beside the folder's name.

- **Finding Folders and Viewing Their Contents**   Double-click a folder's icon or name when you want to see the folders below it in the hierarchy (on the left side of the window) *and* display its folders and files (on the right side of the window). Double-click a second time to hide the folders inside the folder you clicked.

That's about all there is to know, except that you can drag the boundary between the two sides of the Windows Explorer window to give more room to either window pane. And, besides clicking folder names or icons to go from folder to folder, you can use the techniques in Table 3.1.

My Computer: Peering into Your System

The My Computer program is a bit like a Web browser: Each time you visit a new folder, the My Computer window shows the contents of that folder and none other as shown in Figure 3.2. However, you can click the Back, Forward, and Up buttons to go backward or forward to the different folders you have visited.

My Computer

To start My Computer, double-click the My Computer icon on the desktop. The top-level drives and folders on your computer appear in the My Computer window, as shown at the top of Figure 3.2.

Navigation Technique	Description
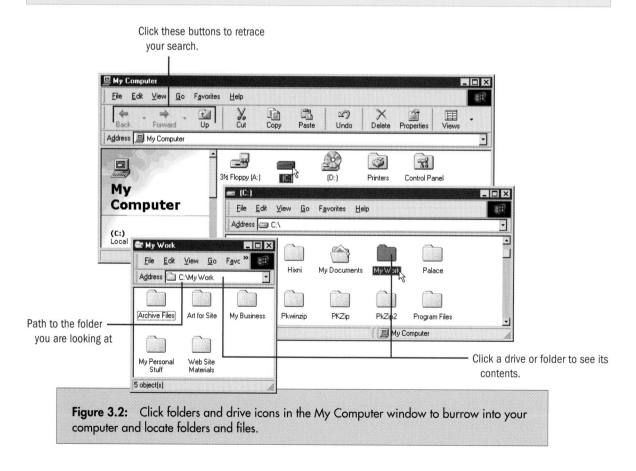 Back	Click the Back button (or press ALT-LEFT ARROW) to revisit a folder you saw earlier. You can also click the down arrow beside the button to see a list of the folders you visited and click a folder's name to visit it again.*
Forward	Click the Forward button (or press ALT-RIGHT ARROW) to return to a folder you viewed earlier. You can also click the down arrow to see a list of folders and click a folder's name.
Up	Click the Up button (or press BACKSPACE) to see the folder you previously visited.
Address	Open the Address drop-down list and click a folder to see its contents.**

* If you don't see the Up, Back, or Forward button, choose View I Toolbars I Standard Buttons.
** If you don't see the Address drop-down list, choose View I Toolbars I Address Bar.

Table 3.1: Going from Folder to Folder in Windows Explorer and My Computer

Click these buttons to retrace
your search.

Path to the folder
you are looking at

Click a drive or folder to see its
contents.

Figure 3.2: Click folders and drive icons in the My Computer window to burrow into your computer and locate folders and files.

Wherever your adventures in My Computer take you, you can look in the Address bar to see the path to the folder you are visiting (choose View | Toolbars | Address Bar to see the Address bar).

Follow these instructions to use the My Computer program to search for a folder or file that you want to move, copy, delete, or torture somehow:

- **Visiting Folders and Viewing Their Contents** Double-click a drive icon (for example, [C:]) or a folder (if you chose a Web-style Windows 98, click rather than double-click). A new window appears with the folders and files in the drive or folder you double-clicked (see Figure 3.2).

- **Navigating Amongst Open Windows** My Computer offers a bunch of techniques for going from folder to folder, as described in Table 3.1. In My Computer, you can also go from folder to folder—that is, from window to window—by clicking buttons on the Taskbar.

- **Seeing the Folders and Files in a Window** To see all the items in a window with many folders and files, use the scroll bar or click the Maximize button to enlarge the window. You can also change the way in which folders and files are displayed in a window. See "Learn the Ways to View Folders and Files" in Chapter 2.

- **Arranging Windows Onscreen** You can move windows to different places by dragging them by the title bar. And you can resize them as well by dragging their borders. Click a window's Maximize button to make it fill the screen. If you no longer need to see a window, click its Close or Minimize button.

> **TIP**
>
> In a long search, the screen quickly fills with My Computer windows. To close a succession of My Computer windows all at once, hold down the SHIFT key and click the Close button in the last window.

EXPERT ADVICE

If you prefer to see one My Computer window at a time, choose View | Folder Options, click the "Custom Based on the Settings Options You Choose" option button on the General Tab of the Folder Options dialog box, and click the Settings button. Then, in the Custom Settings dialog box, click the "Open Each Folder in the Same Window" option button and click OK.

The Quick Way to See What's in a File

Machete in hand, you traveled deep into your computer with Windows Explorer or My Computer to retrieve a file. You found it at last—you think you found it, anyway. How can you tell for sure? One way is to double-click the file and open it, but that means opening the program with which the file was created, too. You don't have time for that! What can you do? As Figure 3.3 shows, Windows offers one or two techniques for finding out quickly what is in a file in the Open dialog box, the My Computer window, or the Windows Explorer window.

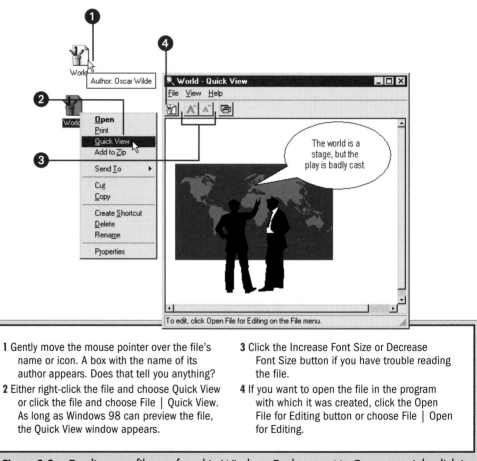

1 Gently move the mouse pointer over the file's name or icon. A box with the name of its author appears. Does that tell you anything?

2 Either right-click the file and choose Quick View or click the file and choose File | Quick View. As long as Windows 98 can preview the file, the Quick View window appears.

3 Click the Increase Font Size or Decrease Font Size button if you have trouble reading the file.

4 If you want to open the file in the program with which it was created, click the Open File for Editing button or choose File | Open for Editing.

Figure 3.3: To glimpse a file you found in Windows Explorer or My Computer, right-click it and choose Quick View from the shortcut menu.

Seeing How Much Space Is on the Hard Disk

Sooner or later, everyone has to answer the question, "How much disk space do you have?" You need to know before installing new software. Maybe your hard disk doesn't have enough room to install new software. Maybe the family next door has more disk space than you. To keep up with the Joneses, you might need a new hard disk. Figure 3.4

In Chapter 9, "Disk Cleanup: Uncluttering the Hard Disk" explains how to remove superfluous files from the hard disk and acquire more disk space.

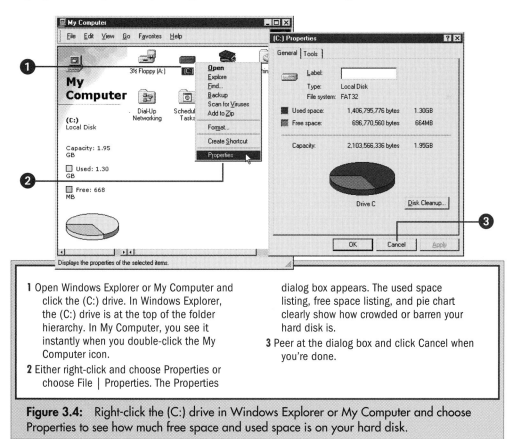

1 Open Windows Explorer or My Computer and click the (C:) drive. In Windows Explorer, the (C:) drive is at the top of the folder hierarchy. In My Computer, you see it instantly when you double-click the My Computer icon.

2 Either right-click and choose Properties or choose File | Properties. The Properties

dialog box appears. The used space listing, free space listing, and pie chart clearly show how crowded or barren your hard disk is.

3 Peer at the dialog box and click Cancel when you're done.

Figure 3.4: Right-click the (C:) drive in Windows Explorer or My Computer and choose Properties to see how much free space and used space is on your hard disk.

explains how, in Windows Explorer or My Computer, you can find out how much free and used disk space is on your hard disk.

When you view a folder as a Web page (choose View | As Web Page), you can tell how much used and free space is on the hard disk merely by opening My Computer or Windows Explorer and moving the pointer over the C drive icon, as shown in Figure 3.4. On the left side of the window, you see the disk's capacity, how much space is used, and how much space is free.

Looking for Files and Folders with the Find Command

So far, this chapter has explained how to look for folders and files with My Computer and Windows Explorer. But what if you try your hardest but simply can't find a folder or file. In that case, you have to abandon My Computer and Windows Explorer and ransack your computer with the Windows 98 Find command.

The next few pages explain this powerful command, how to review the results of a search, and how to save the parameters of a search so you can conduct it again. Meanwhile, ask yourself these questions. The answers will help aid the search.

TIP

If you deleted a file accidentally, you can still recover it. See "Recycle Bin: Recovering Deleted Files and Folders" later in this chapter.

- Where was I last working? In which folder, disk, network device?
- Was I using my desktop machine or my portable? Is the file on the machine I think it is on?
- Did I misspell the name of the file when I saved it?
- Could I have moved the file accidentally into the wrong folder?
- Did someone who also uses my machine rename or move my file?
- Did I incorrectly change the file's three-letter extension?
- When I tried to open the file with the Open dialog box, did I display the wrong file type in the dialog box?
- Did I delete the file?

Conducting the Search and Reading the Results

Before you learn the nitty-gritty of entering search criteria (described shortly), you should know how to conduct a search and read its results. Follow these steps:

SHORTCUT
Right-click a folder in Windows Explorer or My Computer and choose Find to conduct a search of a folder and its subfolders.

1. Click the Start button (or press CTRL-ESC).

2. Choose Find | Files or Folders. You see the Find window shown in Figure 3.5. In the figure, a search has already been conducted. The results appear in the bottom of the Find window.

3. Enter criteria for the search on the Name & Location, Date, or Advanced tabs. The next section explains how. You don't have to fill in all the boxes or all the tabs. If you conducted the same search previously and you saved the search results (step 6

Enter the search criteria on these tabs.　　　Choose where to search.　Click to start the search.

Find: Files named Chap*

File　Edit　View　Options　Help

Name & Location	Date	Advanced

Named: `Chap*`　　　　　　　　　　　　　Find Now

Containing text: `autoformat`　　　　　　　　　　Stop

Look in: `C:\Zudstuff`　　　　　　　　　　New Search

☑ Include subfolders　　　　　　　Browse...

Name	In Folder	Size	Type	Modified
Chap02	C:\Zudstuff\Comp Ref Word\Text	83KB	Microsoft Word Doc...	2/15/99 1:48 PM
Chap04	C:\Zudstuff\Comp Ref Word\Text	70KB	Microsoft Word Doc...	2/15/99 2:21 PM
Chap03	C:\Zudstuff\Comp Ref Word\Text	68KB	Microsoft Word Doc...	2/15/99 2:15 PM
Chap06	C:\Zudstuff\Comp Ref Word\Text	111KB	Microsoft Word Doc...	2/15/99 2:33 PM

Double-click a folder or file to open it.

52 file(s) found　　　　　Monitoring New Items

Figure 3.5: Results of the search appear in the bottom of the Find window. If nothing is found, "There are no items to show in this view" appears instead.

TIP

If the file you are looking for appears right away, or if the search drags on too long and you suspect that either nothing will come of it or it will yield too many files and folders, click the Stop button.

In Chapter 2, "Learn the Ways to View Folders and Files" explains how to arrange files in windows and thereby locate them more easily.

explains how), you can choose the name of the search from the Named drop-down menu and not bother entering criteria.

4. Click the Find Now button. The results of the search appear in the bottom of the dialog box. (If no files or folders turn up, you see the words "There are no items to show in this view.") The lower-left corner reports how many files were found.

5. To examine the search results, avail yourself of these opportunities:

   • **Open a Folder or File**   Double-click a folder to open it in My Computer; double-click a file to open it in the program in which it was created.

   • **Move Up and Down the List**   Use the scroll bar to see the different files. If necessary, move the pointer over the bottom of the dialog box and, when the pointer changes to double-arrows, click and drag the bottom of the dialog box southward to see more files or folders.

   • **Move Side to Side in the List**   Use the scroll bar along the bottom of the dialog box to move side to side and see all the columns. If necessary, click the Maximize button or drag a side of the dialog box toward the edge of the screen to see all five columns at once—Name, In Folder, Size, Type, and Modified.

   • **Sort the Files**   Rearrange the files in the dialog box by clicking the Name, In Folder, Size, Type, or Modified button. The Name, In Folder, and Type buttons arrange the files in alphabetical order in one of those respective categories; the Size button arranges the files by size; and the Modified button arranges the files by date of last modification.

   • **Make Columns Wider or Narrower**   Drag a border between two column buttons to make a column narrower or wider. For example, drag the border between In Folder and Size to see the complete path to each file and folder.

6. If you expect to conduct the same search again, save the results of the search so you don't have to re-enter the search criteria:

   - **On the Named Drop-Down List** Choose Options | Save Results to add the search to the Named drop-down list. Next time you conduct this search, click the down arrow to open the Named drop-down list and then select the name of the search—the name that is currently in the Named box.

   - **As a Shortcut Icon** Choose File | Save Search to place a Find shortcut icon on the desktop. Go this route if you expect to make the search often. Instead of choosing the Find command and wrestling with the Find window, all you have to do is double-click the Find shortcut icon on the desktop.

Files named
Chap@

7. End or prolong this little adventure:

   - **End All Searches** Click the Close button to close the Find window.

   - **Refine the Search** Enter new or different criteria on the Name & Location, Date, or Advanced tabs, and then click the Find Now button.

   - **Start a Different Search** Click the New Search button to erase the search criteria, enter new criteria, and embark on a different search.

   - **Open a File** Double-click a filename to open it as well as the program with which it was created.

   - **Open a Folder** Double-click a folder to open it in the My Computer window. To open the folder in which a file is kept, click the file and choose File | Open Containing Folder.

TIP

If you aren't sure whether your file is the right one, right-click it and choose Quick View.

Entering the Search Criteria

Searching with the Find command is a bit like searching the Internet. The more criteria you can enter to aid the search, the quicker and more accurate the search is. The Catch-22, however, is that entering many different criteria for a search increases the chances of making an error.

When you enter search criteria, you needn't fill in all three tabs—Name & Location, Date, and Advanced—in the Find window. And you don't have to fill in each box on each tab either. To pinpoint a folder or file, accurately enter the information that you know in any or all three tabs. And if at first you don't succeed, try, try, try again by changing the criteria and clicking the Find Now button.

Name & Location Tab

On the Name & Location tab, enter what you know about the file or folder's name and location, and, in the case of text files, the words inside the file:

- **Named**   Enter the name of the folder or file, or, if you vaguely remember the name, the part of the name that you can remember. For example, entering **chap** finds *Chap, chap01, Chapter 9, chaplain*, and *Schapstuckle*. To be specific about how capital letters are used in names, choose Options | Case Sensitive. With the Case Sensitive option selected, entering **chap** finds *chap01, chaplain*, and *Schapstuckle*, but not *Chap* or *Chapter 9*.

- **Containing Text**   If you know that somewhere inside the file itself is a specific word or name, enter it here. Be sure to pick an obscure word, not one that is found in most files. Entering a telephone number or fax number is a good way to find a file. These numbers fall in the "one of a kind" category and do not produce many files in search results.

- **Look In**   This is where you tell Windows 98 where to look. Click the Browse button to open the Browse for Folder dialog box. This dialog box works exactly like the left side of Windows Explorer. Click plus signs until you come to the folder in which to search, click the folder's name, and click OK. The path to the folder you chose appears in the Look In box.

- **Include Subfolders**   Leave the check mark here to look as well in the folders that are subordinate to the folder in the Look In box. To search exclusively in the Look In folder, uncheck this box.

EXPERT ADVICE

To keep searches from taking too long, enter a folder in the Look In box that is deep inside the folder hierarchy. Don't start searching on the C drive—the search takes too long. One way to burrow into a computer and find a good place to start searching is to use Windows Explorer. In Windows Explorer, examine folders until you find the right folder in which to start the search. Then right-click the folder and choose Find from the shortcut menu. The Find window opens with the folder you chose in the Look In box.

Date Tab

On the Date tab, describe when the file was last saved, when it was created, or, in the case of .html files, when it was last accessed:

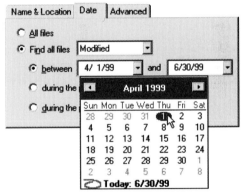

- **All Files**   Select this option to search all files, no matter the date they were created, last saved, or accessed.

- **Find All Files**   Click this option button to make time a search criterion. Then, from the drop-down menu, choose Modified to search by last saved date, Created to search by creation date, or Last Accessed to search by the date on which you last opened files with a browser.

- **Between**   Click this option button and enter the dates between which the file was created, modified, or accessed. You can click the down arrow and enter dates on the minicalendar. Click the arrows beside the month name to go forward or backward month by month. Click a date to select it.

- **During the Previous**   Click either of these option buttons and enter how many months or days previously the file was last saved, created, or accessed.

Advanced Tab

On the Advanced tab, declare what type of file you are looking for and how big or small it is:

- **Of Type**   Click the down arrow and choose a file type from the drop-down list. You will find many different file types on the list.

- **Size Is**   Choose At Least or At Most and enter a number in the KB box to describe in kilobytes the smallest or largest files to search for. One megabyte equals roughly 1,000 kilobytes (KB). To search for files larger or smaller than 1 megabyte, enter **1000** in the KB box.

Organizing and Managing Files and Folders

So far in this chapter, you have had a jolly good time learning how to locate files and folders with My Computer, Windows Explorer, and Windows' Find command. Having learned to locate files, you can start managing them. You can copy them, move them, and rename them. You can delete them, and, if you want, resuscitate them. These exciting tasks are explained in this part of the chapter, where you learn to organize and manage files and folders.

Creating a New Folder

Create a new folder when you start a new project or begin an undertaking that requires new files. You need a folder to store the new files so you always know where they are. Windows 98 offers two ways to create a new folder: in Windows Explorer and in My Computer.

See "Devise a Strategy for Storing Your Work on Disk" in Chapter 2 for advice about storing your work so you can find it easily.

Follow these steps to create a new folder for storing files or other folders:

1. In Windows Explorer or My Computer, locate and select the folder in which to put your new folder. In other words, find

the folder in the hierarchy to which the new folder will be subordinate. Earlier in this chapter, "Rummaging for Folders and Files with Windows Explorer and My Computer" explains how the programs work.

2. Choose File | New | Folder. A folder icon and the words "New Folder" appear.

3. Type a name for the folder. The name you type replaces the words "New Folder." Be sure to choose a descriptive name. The same rules that apply to filenames apply to folders—255 characters (but don't get carried away), spaces allowed, the following characters not allowed:

   / \ ? ; : " < > * |

4. Either press ENTER or click elsewhere on the desktop.

"Keeping Shortcut Icons in a Desktop Folder" in Chapter 2 explains how to create a folder on the desktop for shortcut icons. One or two desktop folders can help prevent crowding on the desktop.

Selecting Files and Folders

Learn the various and sundry ways to select files and folders and you will make the time pass quickly in Windows 98. In order to move, copy, delete, or rename a file or folder, you have to select it. And Windows 98 offers numerous ways to select several files or folders so you can move, copy, or delete several at once.

To select files or folders, display them in Windows Explorer or My Computer. Selecting one file or folder is easy enough—just click it. Instructions for selecting more than one are given in the following list. Don't be afraid to open the Views drop-down menu and experiment with different views as you select files and folders. Depending on how you select files and how many you want to select, some views are better than others.

- **To Select Various Items**   Hold down the CTRL key and click files and folders. As you click, the files are highlighted. After items have been selected, you can CTRL-click to unselect them.

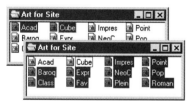

- **To Select Neighboring Items**   Click the first file or folder, then hold down the SHIFT key and click the last. Use this technique in List and Detail view when the items you want to select are next to one another. In Chapter 2, "Learn the Ways to View Folders and Files" explains how to change views of a folder.

- **To Select a Group of Items**   Click (but not on an icon or item name) and drag to form a box around the items you want to select. Use this technique in Large Icons or Small Icons view to select files that are found beside one another.

- **To Select All the Items**   Press CTRL-A or choose Edit | Select All. All the items in the folder are highlighted. CTRL-click if you want to unselect a few of them.

- **To Select All But One or Two Items**   Click the items you *don't* want and then choose Edit | Invert Selection when you want to select all but one or two items in a folder. Instead of laboriously CTRL-clicking a dozen items, using this technique saves a lot of time.

Copying and Moving Files and Folders

Except for the fact that Windows 98 offers so many different techniques for copying and moving files and folders, copying and moving is easy. The problem is finding the technique that suits you. Personally, I like the dragging method, but people who aren't adept with the mouse prefer cutting, copying, and pasting. In the spirit of democracy, all techniques are described here. By the way, when you

---

EXPERT ADVICE

You can't move or copy a file that is open. Try to do that and you see an "Error Moving File" message box. Click OK in the message box, close the file, and then move or copy it. After a file or folder is moved, all shortcut references to it are rendered invalid. Hyperlinks and OLE links to it are invalid as well. And you can't open it from the Documents menu or the bottom of the File menu in the Open dialog box. The moral: Think twice before moving important files and folders, or else plan carefully where to put them in the first place.

copy or move a folder, you copy or move all the folders and files inside
it as well.

Copying and Moving with the Copy, Cut, and Paste Commands

Figure 3.6 explains how to copy and move files and folders with the
Copy, Cut, and Paste commands. If you have copied or moved text or
data in a computer program with the Copy, Cut, and Paste

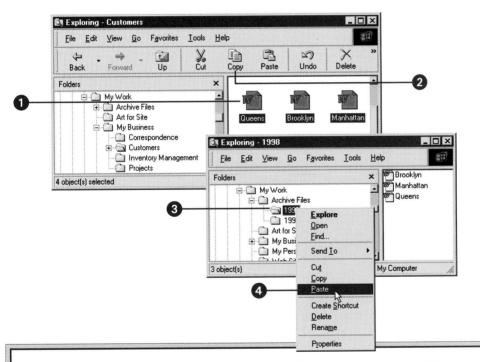

1 Open Windows Explorer or My Computer, locate the file(s) or folder(s) to copy or move, and then select the files or folders. Earlier in this chapter, "Selecting Files and Folders" explains how to do just that.

2 Choose a Copy or Move command. To copy, click the Copy button, choose Edit | Copy, press CTRL-C, or right-click and choose Copy. To move, click the Cut button, choose Edit | Cut, press CTRL-X, or right-click and choose Cut.

3 Display and click the folder that is to receive the files or folders. In Windows Explorer, you can simply display and click a folder on the left side of the screen without doing anything in the right side.

4 Click the Paste button, choose Edit | Paste, press CTRL-V, or right-click and choose Paste.

Figure 3.6: Moving and copying files and folders with the Cut, Copy, and Paste commands

commands, you will be delighted to know that copying and moving files and folders works exactly the same way.

Usually, but not always, Windows Explorer and My Computer present an accurate picture of what is in a folder. But suppose you minimize a folder window, fool with its contents, and then maximize the window later on. What you see will be inaccurate. A folder might have been moved. A file might have been deleted. The files might not be in alphabetical order. To see what's really in a folder, choose View | Refresh. Choose this command when you suspect that all is not what it seems in a Windows Explorer or My Computer window.

Dragging to Copy and Move Files and Folders

Dragging files and folders to copy or move them requires skill with the mouse. And you have to display both the folders and files you are copying or moving as well as the folder you will copy or move them to. And to complicate matters further, sometimes you have to press a key while you drag to copy or move files and folders. Oh well, it's not very hard when you get the hang of it.

Follow these steps to copy or move files and folders by dragging them:

1. In Windows Explorer or My Computer, find and display the folder that will receive the file(s) or folder(s) you want to move or copy. If necessary, see "Rummaging for Folders and Files with Windows Explorer and My Computer" earlier in this chapter

2. Locate and select the file(s) and folder(s) that you want to move or copy. Earlier in this chapter, "Selecting Files and Folders" explains how to do that.

3. Drag the files and folders to the destination folder, and then release the mouse button. As you drag, ghostly images of the files or folders appear onscreen so you know where to drop them.

   • **Copying** Hold down the CTRL key as you drag, unless you are copying files or folders to a different drive (3½ Floppy [A:], for example). You don't have to press CTRL when copying to a different drive because a copy is made automatically. A plus sign (+) appears below the pointer as you drag.

- **Moving**   Simply drag the files or folders. To move them to a different drive, hold down the SHIFT key as you drag. Without pressing SHIFT, the files are copied to the other drive, not moved there.

4. To be on the safe side, open the folder to which you copied or moved the files and folders to make sure that they landed in the right place.

EXPERT ADVICE

Folders get crowded when new files and folders are moved into them. You can prevent overcrowding in a folder by right-clicking an empty space inside its window and choosing Line Up Icons or Arrange Icons | Auto Arrange from the shortcut menu. These commands arrange icons in a strict military fashion so you can read and find them.

Making Backup Copies to a Floppy Disk

On the subject of copying files, Windows 98 offers a special command for backing up files and folders on the C drive to the A drive. You can do it in Windows Explorer or My Computer, of course. And, as Chapter 9 explains, Windows 98 offers a special program called Backup for backing up many, many files. Figure 3.7 explains how to make simple backup copies of important files or folders to a floppy disk.

By the way, if your computer has an A and B floppy-disk drive, you can very quickly copy all the files on one floppy disk to another floppy disk. To do so, put the disk whose contents you want to copy in one of the drives, put an empty disk in the other, open My Computer, right-click one of the drive icons, and choose Copy Disk from the shortcut menu. The Copy Disk dialog box appears. In the Copy To box, click the second drive's icon and then click the Start button. Be sure to use an empty disk. This command copies a disk's entire content, including blank space!

Renaming a File or Folder

Few things could be easier than renaming a file or folder. You can do it while you are opening a file in the Open dialog box, in Windows

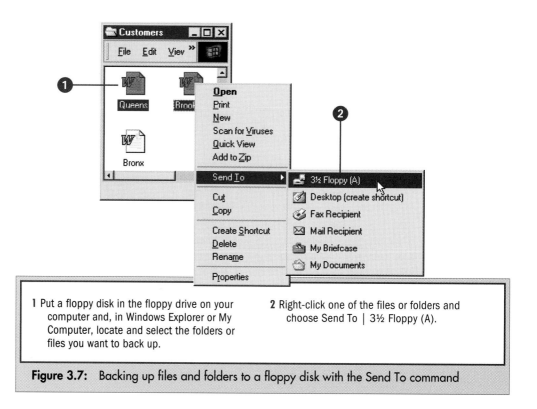

1 Put a floppy disk in the floppy drive on your computer and, in Windows Explorer or My Computer, locate and select the folders or files you want to back up.

2 Right-click one of the files or folders and choose Send To | 3½ Floppy (A).

Figure 3.7: Backing up files and folders to a floppy disk with the Send To command

SHORTCUT

If you're in a hurry to rename a file, click the file you want to rename, wait a second, and click the name again. Then type in the new name.

Explorer, or in My Computer. Follow these steps to give a file or folder a new name:

1. In Windows Explorer, My Computer, or the Open dialog box, find the file or folder you want to rename.

2. Click the file or folder.

3. Right-click and choose Rename from the shortcut menu, choose File | Rename, or press F2.

4. Type the new name. Be sure to keep the same file extension, if the file extension appears. You can click in the name that is already there and press BACKSPACE or DELETE to delete one or two letters before you start adding letters of your own.

5. Press ENTER or click elsewhere.

Deleting Files and Folders

Deleting files and folders is easy. And you can delete several at once. If only the same could be said for cockroaches and radio talk show hosts. Follow these steps to delete files and folders:

1. In Windows Explorer, My Computer, or the Open dialog box, find and select the folder(s) and file(s) you want to delete.

2. Press the DELETE key, choose File | Delete, or right-click an item you selected and choose Delete from the shortcut menu.

3. Click Yes (or No if you get cold feet) in the box that tells you how many files and folders will be deleted and asks if you want to go through with it.

For the mouse-inclined, the fastest way to delete a file or folder is to drag it from its present location in the Windows Explorer or My Computer window and drop it over the Recycle Bin icon on the desktop.

If you delete a file or folder accidentally, you can resuscitate it. The next section in this chapter explains how. In Chapter 9, "Disk Cleanup: Uncluttering the Hard Disk" explains how to remove unnecessary files from your computer.

CAUTION When you delete a folder, you also delete all the folders and files inside it.

TIP To delete a file without sending it to the Recycle Bin, press SHIFT-DELETE.

Recycle Bin: Recovering Deleted Files and Folders

Bottles, cans, and newspapers aren't the only items that can be recycled. You can also put the files, folders, and shortcut icons you deleted back in circulation with the Recycle Bin. This utility retains most files and folders that were deleted in case you regret deleting them. Files from DOS programs and a handful of other kinds of programs do not land in the Recycle Bin when you delete them. Read on to learn how to restore a file or folder from the Recycle Bin, purge files, and tell Windows 98 how many deleted files and folders to keep on hand.

Recycle Bin

Restoring a File You Deleted Accidentally

Figure 3.8 shows how to examine the files and folders in the Recycle Bin and maybe put one or two back in circulation. After you restore a file, it returns to the folder from which it was deleted. By the way, Details view is the best way to view files in the Recycle Bin window. In Details view, you can see the original location of each item and the date it was deleted. Choose View | Details to switch to Details view.

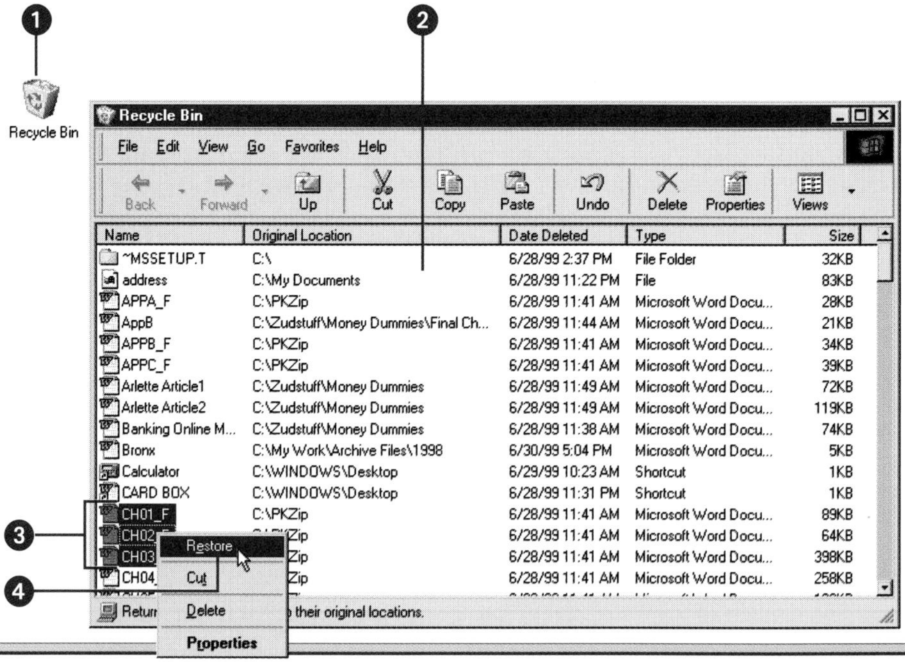

1 Double-click the Recycle Bin icon on the desktop to open the Recycle Bin window.

2 Examine the files and folders to find the ones you want to restore.

3 Select the files and folders you want to restore.

4 Choose File | Restore or right-click an item you selected and choose Restore from the shortcut menu. The items you restored are placed in the folder from whence they came.

Figure 3.8: You can restore files and folders you deleted accidentally with the Recycle Bin utility.

Purging Files from the Recycle Bin

If you are absolutely, positively, unmistakably certain that all files and folders in the Recycle Bin have no value, you can get rid of them all at once by right-clicking the Recycle Bin icon on the desktop and choosing Empty Recycle Bin from the shortcut menu. You can also choose File | Empty Recycle Bin in the Recycle Bin window. But do you really want to discard all the files? Maybe one or two are worth keeping.

A better strategy is to periodically open the Recycle Bin and remove only the files and folders that you know are useless. To do that, double-click Recycle Bin on the desktop, examine the files and folders in the Recycle Bin, select the ones that deserve deleting, press DELETE or choose File | Delete, and click Yes in the message box.

By the way, if you are no fan of the Recycle Bin and you want to delete files permanently when you give the Delete command, press SHIFT-DELETE to delete files. Or else right-click the Recycle Bin icon, choose Properties from the shortcut menu, and click the Do Not Move Files to the Recycle Bin check box, as shown in Figure 3.9.

EXPERT ADVICE

To begin with, 10 percent of the hard disk is devoted to storing deleted files in the Recycle Bin. When the 10-percent capacity is reached, the oldest files in the Bin are automatically erased. If you work with multimedia programs whose files can be very large, you might consider increasing the 10-percent capacity. And if you are running low on disk space, you might consider decreasing it to allow more room for files. To change the Recycle Bin's capacity, right-click the Recycle Bin icon and choose Properties. In the Recycle Bin Properties dialog box, shown in Figure 3.9, drag the Maximum Size slider and click OK.

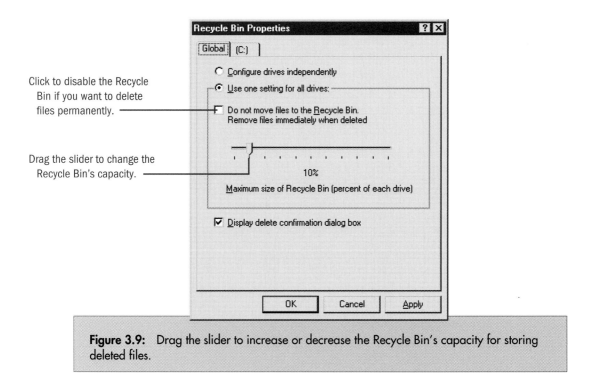

Click to disable the Recycle
  Bin if you want to delete
  files permanently.

Drag the slider to change the
  Recycle Bin's capacity.

Figure 3.9:   Drag the slider to increase or decrease the Recycle Bin's capacity for storing deleted files.

Sharing Data between Files

> **CAUTION**
>
> To successfully copy or move data, you almost always have to pass the data between files of the same type. Copying a graphics file into a word-processing file, for example, can be problematic. And you can make guacamole out of a perfectly good spreadsheet by copying it into a graphics program. Test and retest before you commit yourself to copying and especially moving data.

In my opinion, one of the best things going in Windows 98 is being able to copy and move data from one file to another. The thank-you letter to Aunt Ida, with a few small changes, can be used as a thank-you letter to Uncle Bert. The Address database table, with a bit of luck and a tweak here and there, can be used as a table in a word-processing file. You can even *link* two files so that changes made to part of one file are made automatically to a corresponding part in another file.

When you copy or move data, it is placed in an electronic holding tank called the *Clipboard.* The data stays there until you cut or copy new data and the new data takes the place of the old. These pages explain three methods for copying and moving data between files, how to create links between files, and how to open a handy device called the Clipboard Viewer for seeing what's on the Clipboard.

Moving and Copying Data from File to File

Copying data leaves the original stuff intact, but moving uproots the data for good. Following are three methods for shuttling data between programs—cut and paste, drag and drop, and scraps. You be the judge of which method works best.

Using the Cut, Copy, and Paste Commands

Follow these steps to copy or move data from place to place with the Cut, Copy, and Paste commands:

1. Select the data you want to copy or move. Different programs offer different techniques for selecting data, but you can almost always select it by clicking and dragging.

2. Move or copy the data to the Clipboard:

   - **Moving**   Choose Edit | Cut, click the Cut button, right-click and choose Cut, or press CTRL-X.

   - **Copying**   Choose Edit | Copy, click the Copy button, right-click and choose Copy, or press CTRL-C.

3. Click where you want the data to go.

4. Choose Edit | Paste, click the Paste button, or press CTRL-V.

TIP
Press the PRINT SCREEN key (sometimes labeled PRINT SCRN and located to the right of F12) to take a snapshot of your computer screen and copy it to the Clipboard. Press ALT-PRINT SCREEN to take a snapshot of the active window, not the entire screen.

Dragging and Dropping

Figure 3.10 explains a second, slightly speedier but more trying way to move or copy data. With the *drag-and-drop* method, you select data in one place and drag it to another (don't confuse the term with "drop and drag," which in deer-hunting circles means to kill the game and bring it to camp).

Copying Data with the "Scraps" Technique

Yet another drag-and-drop technique is to create *scraps* on the desktop. Use this technique to copy data from many different files and then assemble the data in a single file. With this method, you open files one at a time or several at once, select data in each file, and drag it onto the Windows desktop to form a scrap. Then, with the scraps

Word Documi..

WordPad Document S...

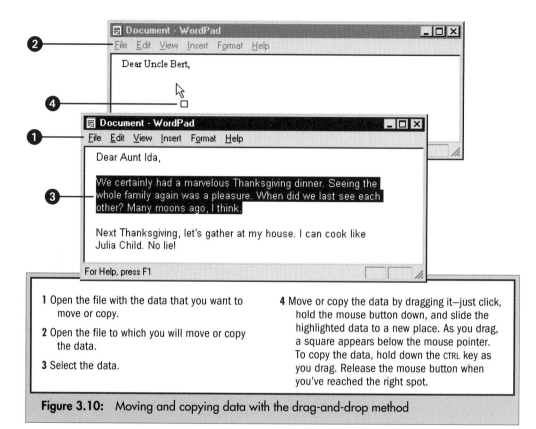

Figure 3.10: Moving and copying data with the drag-and-drop method

1 Open the file with the data that you want to move or copy.

2 Open the file to which you will move or copy the data.

3 Select the data.

4 Move or copy the data by dragging it—just click, hold the mouse button down, and slide the highlighted data to a new place. As you drag, a square appears below the mouse pointer. To copy the data, hold down the CTRL key as you drag. Release the mouse button when you've reached the right spot.

arranged neatly on the desktop, you drag them one at a time into a single file. Follow these steps to copy data by creating scraps:

1. One by one or several at once, open the files from which you want to copy data.

2. Select data in one file.

3. Drag it out of the window and onto the desktop to make a scrap—an icon with a picture of a torn page or picture along with cryptic words that describe where the scrap came from and what it is.

4. Repeat steps 1 through 3 until you've assembled all the scraps on the desktop.

5. Open the file to which you will copy the data scraps.

6. One by one, drag the scraps into the file.

SHORTCUT

To get rid of the scraps that litter the desktop, hold down the CTRL key and click each one. Then press DELETE.

Clipboard Viewer: Seeing or Saving What's on the Clipboard

If you doubt what's on the Clipboard, want to get a better look at what's there, or want to save what's on the Clipboard to a file, open the Clipboard Viewer by following these steps:

1. Click the Start button and choose Programs | Accessories | System Tools | Clipboard Viewer. You see whatever is on the Clipboard in the Clipboard Viewer window.

2. To save what's on the Clipboard, choose File | Save As and fill in the Save As dialog box.

3. Click the Close button to close the Clipboard Viewer.

Linking Data Between Files with OLE

Besides conventional ways of copying text, you can link two files so that changes made in the original are made to its copy automatically. Windows calls this ability *object linking and embedding* (OLE). If a list in a file you are working on happens to be useful in the annual report, you can link the files so that updates made to the list are made immediately in the annual report as well.

In linking and embedding, the original file from which the copy is made is called the *source file*. Its cousin, which gets updated when the source file changes, is called the *destination file*. Follow these steps to create a dynamic link between files so that changes made to the source file are made automatically in the destination file:

1. Open the source file, or master copy, whose changes will affect the other file.

2. Select the part of the source file that you will copy to the destination file.

3. Choose Edit | Copy, click the Copy button, or press CTRL-C.

4. Open or switch to the destination file and place the cursor where you want the copy to go.

CAUTION

OLE links are broken when files are renamed or moved. If you are disciplined and know how to plan ahead, go ahead and make OLE links between files. But if you often move and rename files, object linking and embedding is more trouble than it's worth. Very carefully create or choose folders for storing OLE files. For practical purposes, you can't move these files after you create them.

5. Choose Edit | Paste Special. You see the Paste Special dialog box.

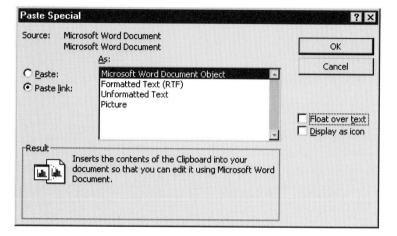

6. Choose Options in the Paste Special dialog box:

- **As**   Windows 98 should already have made a correct choice here. The As box describes the type of information you are copying—a document or picture, for example.

- **Paste** *or* **Paste Link**   Click Paste Link to create a link between the files and be able to update the destination file automatically. If you choose Paste, a copy is placed in the destination file, but it isn't updated automatically. However, you can open the program with which the copied data was created and edit the copied data merely by double-clicking the copied material in the destination file.

7. Click OK to close the Paste Special dialog box.

In the destination file, you can tell where the link is because it turns gray when you click it. Changes made to the source file are made automatically to the destination file if both files are open or as soon as the destination file is reopened.

Suppose you want to break a link, you suspect that a link isn't up to date, you moved the source file, or you want to open the source file and make changes there. Better follow these steps:

1. In the destination file, click the link and then choose Edit | Links. You see the Links dialog box.

2. Click a button in the dialog box:
   - **Update Now**   Click this button to update the link.
   - **Open Source**   Click this button to open the source file so you can make editorial changes there.
   - **Change Source**   Click this button if you moved the source document to a new folder. In the Change Source dialog box, find the source file, click it, and click Open to reestablish the link.
   - **Break Link**   Click this button to break the link between the source file and the destination file.

3. Click OK.

CHAPTER 4

Doing the Setup Work

INCLUDES

- Installing and removing software programs
- Installing a new hardware device
- Installing a new printer on your system
- Loading fonts and viewing fonts
- Resetting the clock, date, and time zone
- Connecting your computer to the Internet

FAST FORWARD

Install New Software ➥ pp. 91–93

1. Click the Start button and choose Settings | Control Panel.
2. In the Control Panel, double-click the Add/Remove Programs icon.
3. Click the Install button.
4. Insert the CD or floppy disk with the program you want to install, click the Next button, and follow the setup program's instructions for installing the new software.

Enlist Windows' Help to Remove a Program ➥ p. 95

1. Click the Start button and choose Settings | Control Panel.
2. Double-click the Add/Remove Programs icon.
3. On the list of programs at the bottom of the dialog box, find and click the name of the program you want to remove.
4. Click the Add/Remove button and click Yes in the "Are you sure?" message box.

Install a New Hardware Device on Your System ➥ pp. 96–100

- To install a plug-and-play device, turn off the computer and install the hardware. When you turn on the computer, Windows notices the new hardware device and installs a driver to make it run successfully.
- To install a device that isn't plug and play, click the Start button, choose Settings | Control Panel, and double-click the Add New Hardware icon. In the Add New Hardware Wizard dialog boxes, keep making choices and clicking the Next button.

Install a New Printer ➡ pp. 100–103

Add Printer

1. Click the Start button, choose Settings | Printers, and double-click the Add Printer icon.
2. If the next dialog box asks whether to install a local or network printer, choose one or the other and click Next. Otherwise, click Next right away, and, in the second Add Printer Wizard dialog box, click on the name of the company that made your printer and the model name of your printer. Then click Next.
3. Choose the port for your printer, probably LPT1, click Next, and click the Yes option button if you want your new printer to be the default printer.

Find Out Which Fonts Are Available on Your System ➡ pp. 103–104

Fonts

1. Click the Start button, choose Settings | Control Panel, and double-click the Fonts shortcut icon.
2. In the Fonts folder, double-click the font that you want to examine.

Reset the Clock, Date, and Time Zone ➡ pp. 107–108

1. Double-click the clock in the lower-right corner of the screen.
2. On the Date & Time tab, enter the correct date and time, and click OK.

Time

5:38:35 PM

Set Up an Internet Connection to Your ISP ➡ pp. 109–115

Internet Options

1. Click the Start button and choose Settings | Control Panel, and double-click the Internet Options icon.
2. In the Internet Properties dialog box, click the Connections tab, and then click the Setup button to start the Connection Wizard.
3. Answer the questions in the Connection Wizard dialog boxes.

In the bad old days, a chapter like this about installing software and hardware on a computer might require dozens and dozens of pages. But times have changed for the better. Instead of skirmishing, software and hardware manufacturers realized that the mere mortals who operate computers would be happier if standard procedures for installing software and hardware were developed. This chapter explains what those standard procedures are and also how to uninstall a program that you don't want anymore.

You also find advice for installing software or hardware for which there isn't a standard setup program that Windows 98 can read. Installing and uninstalling software and hardware like that can be tricky. Equally tricky— in fact, harder than ever—is making a connection between your computer and the Internet. This chapter tackles that difficult subject, too.

You also discover how to load and unload *fonts*, the typeface designs that come with Windows 98, and how to tell Windows 98 the correct date and time. You want the clock in the lower-right corner of the screen to tell the right time, don't you? For cosmopolitan globetrotters, this chapter also explains how to change regional settings.

Installing and Uninstalling Software Programs

Appendix A explains how to install and reinstall Windows 98 or its various components.

These days, software that's worth anything comes with an installation program. All you have to do is tell the installation program to go to work, click a few buttons, and make a cup of tea while the software loads itself. When the time comes to uninstall the software because you no longer require it, all you have to do is run the software's uninstall program.

Old programs and programs from second-rate developers, however, do not come with uninstall programs. The only way to remove an old program is to practice a scorched-earth policy of deleting the folders in which it is stored. Installing a program for which there isn't an installation program is also a clumsy and rough undertaking. Read on to find out how to install software programs, uninstall them, and upgrade to a newer version of software that is already loaded on your computer.

Installing New Software

Before you try to install a new software program, find out whether the software comes with an installation program. If it does, you can rely on the installation program to do most of the work. Do the following to see if an installation program is on the CD or floppy disk that the software comes on:

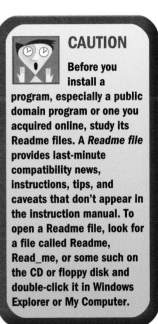

CAUTION

Before you install a program, especially a public domain program or one you acquired online, study its Readme files. A *Readme file* provides last-minute compatibility news, instructions, tips, and caveats that don't appear in the instruction manual. To open a Readme file, look for a file called Readme, Read_me, or some such on the CD or floppy disk and double-click it in Windows Explorer or My Computer.

- **CD**   In some computers, the installation program starts automatically as soon as you slide the CD in the CD-ROM drive. If the installation program doesn't start, open My Computer or Windows Explorer, click the CD-ROM drive icon (probably [D:]), and look for a file called setup.exe or install.exe. (If you don't see file extensions such as .exe, choose View | Folder Options, click the View tab in the Folder Options dialog box, uncheck the Hide File Extensions for Known File Types check box, and click OK.)
- **Floppy Disk**   Put Disk #1 in the floppy drive, open My Computer or Windows Explorer, click the floppy-drive icon (probably [A:]), and look for a setup.exe or install.exe file.

If you don't see a setup.exe or install.exe file, you're on your own. You have to install the file yourself. Following are instructions for installing software with the help of a program and installing software yourself. Be sure to quit running all programs before you install new software.

Installing Software with an Installation Program

If you just finished investigating whether the CD or floppy disk has an installation program and you are staring at a setup.exe or install.exe file in My Computer or Windows Explorer, double-click the .exe file to start the installation program. You can skip the following steps, which explain how to get Windows' help to locate and start installation programs. To begin at the beginning, follow these steps:

Add/Remove
Programs

1. Close all the files and computer programs that are open.

2. Click the Start button and choose Settings | Control Panel. You see the Control Panel window.

3. Double-click the Add/Remove Programs icon. The Add/Remove Programs Properties dialog box shown on the left side of Figure 4.1 appears.

4. Click the Install button. You see the Install Program From Floppy Disk or CD-ROM dialog box.

5. Insert the CD in the CD-ROM drive or, if you are installing the program from a floppy disk, insert the first disk in the floppy drive.

6. Click the Next button. If all goes correctly, the dialog box changes names to Run Installation Program, as shown on the right side of Figure 4.1, and SETUP.EXE or INSTALL.EXE appears in the Command line box. If for some reason a filename doesn't appear, click the Browse button, and, in the

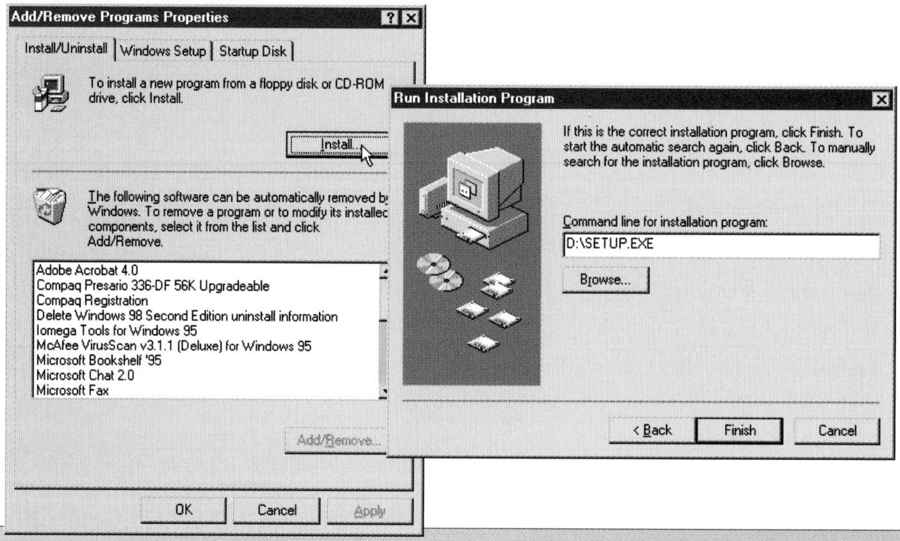

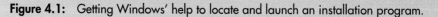

Figure 4.1: Getting Windows' help to locate and launch an installation program.

Browse dialog box, locate the installation file, click it, and click the Open button to make it appear.

7. Click the Finish button.

What happens next depends on the program you want to install, how big it is, and how many settings it requires you to make. Usually, a bunch of dialog boxes appear, you make choices in each dialog box, and then the ordeal ends. When you are done, a new program name is added to the Programs menu, and, in some cases, a new shortcut icon lands on the desktop.

Most installation programs do the following as part of the installation procedure:

- Ask you for a code number to prove you really purchased the software
- Check for sufficient space on the hard disk
- Check the computer for compatibility problems
- Create new folders for the new software
- Prompt you, if you are installing the program from floppy disks, to insert new disks
- Make changes to your computer's system files
- Add new fonts and drivers
- Tell you when the installation is over and whether it was successful

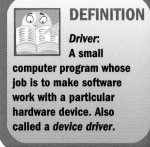

DEFINITION

Driver: A small computer program whose job is to make software work with a particular hardware device. Also called a *device driver*.

Installing Software on Your Own

The program you want to install doesn't come with its own installation program? Don't fret—worse things have happened. To install the program, create a new folder for it on your computer and copy the program's folders and files into the folder you created. The trick is to copy all the folders and files, including the hidden files. To make sure you copy the hidden files, follow these steps before you start copying:

At the end of Chapter 2, "Decide How to List Files in Folders and Dialog Boxes" explains the vagaries of listing three-letter file extensions and hidden files in dialog boxes, Windows Explorer, and My Computer.

1. Click the Start button and choose Settings | Folder Options.

2. Click the View tab in the Folder Options dialog box.

3. Under Hidden Files, check the Show All Files option button if a check mark isn't already there.

4. Click OK.

When you install a program on your own, its name isn't entered on the Programs menu. To put it there, see "Adding a Program Name to a Menu" in Chapter 5. "Create the Shortcut Icons You Need" in Chapter 2 explains how to create a shortcut icon for a program.

Upgrading to a Newer Version of a Program

 ppendix A explains how to install Windows 98 and what happens when you upgrade from Windows 95.

Upgrading to a newer version of a program is simply a matter of installing the newer version. Everything is done in the background, as the installation program notices the older version of the software on your computer and installs the newer version over the older one. If the software is worth anything, the personal settings you made in the last version of the software—such as screen colors and the default font you like so well—are retained when the new version is installed.

EXPERT ADVICE

Before you upgrade, find out if files created in the new version of the program can be read by the old version. Co-workers and friends who have the old version of the program might not be able to read the files you create with the new one. Fortunately, almost all programs provide a means of saving a file so that it can be read by older versions. If the old version of the program can't read files created in the new version, be sure to save files in a format that the old version can read before you pass the files to co-workers and friends who are stuck with the old version.

Removing Unwanted Software Programs

When you no longer need a program, you might as well remove it, especially if you are running low on disk space. Programs that you or someone else installed with an installation program can be removed cleanly and safely by Windows 98. But if you can't get Windows' help to remove a program, you have to remove it yourself by deleting its files. Read on to learn how to remove programs with Windows' help and remove them on your own.

Using Windows to Uninstall a Program

Figure 4.2 explains how to find out if Windows can uninstall a program and then proceed to uninstall it. When you are finished uninstalling, the Remove Programs From Your Computer dialog box appears and tells you what was uninstalled. Click the Details button in the dialog box and you see a list of the files that were not removed from your computer. You can open Windows Explorer or My Computer and delete the files on your own.

CAUTION

As you remove a program, the Remove Shared File? message box appears if you try to delete a shared file. A *shared file* is a file that several programs rely on, not just the program whose files you are deleting. Leaving shared files intact does no harm. I suggest clicking the No or No to All button in the Remove Shared File? message box.

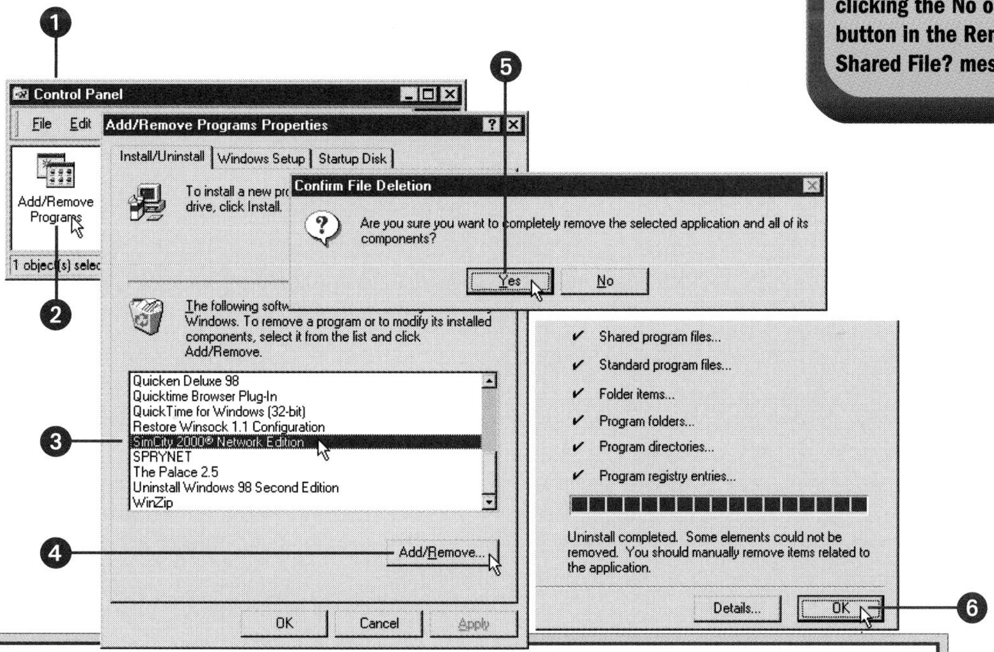

1 Close all programs that are running, and then click the Start button and choose Settings | Control Panel.

2 In the Control Panel, double-click the Add/Remove Programs icon.

3 In the list in the bottom of the Add/Remove Programs dialog box, scroll to the name of the program you want to remove and click its name. Windows can remove all programs on the list.

4 Click the Add/Remove button.

5 In the message box that asks if you have the guts to go through with it, click Yes. Items are checked off the list as they are removed.

6 Click OK in the Remove Programs From Your Computer dialog box when the deed is done.

Figure 4.2: Getting Windows' help to remove unwanted software programs.

Scorched-Earth Policy: Removing a Program on Your Own

If the program you want to remove can't be found in the Add/Remove Programs dialog box (see Figure 4.2), you have to remove it yourself. Be sure to consult the manual before doing so. If the program is a big or important one, your system might suffer when you uproot its files and remove it. You might leave behind accessory files. You might delete files that other programs need.

After you decide to take the plunge, identify the folders and files that belong to the program and delete them. Go ahead—strike them dead and hope for the best. Removing small programs this way has never done any harm to my computer, but I might be lucky.

Installing a New Piece of Hardware

See "Installing a New Printer" later in this chapter if the hardware device you want to install happens to be a printer.

For the purposes of this book, "hardware" does not refer to screws, winches, hammers, or nails. In computer terminology, *hardware* is anything having to do with computers that has a hard surface—a monitor, mouse, or keyboard, for example. Software, if you could touch it, would crumble to dust.

The following few pages explain how to install a new piece of hardware and what to do if the installation doesn't work. If the hardware you want to install falls in the *plug-and-play* category, you've got it made. Plug-and-play devices can be installed in a matter of minutes (well, usually) because you don't have to dive into the Windows 98 operating system and describe the device after you have plugged it into your system. To install a device that is not plug and play, you have to run the Hardware Wizard. Keep reading.

EXPERT ADVICE

My advice for shopping for computer hardware is to shop in local stores. That way, you can take items back if they don't work or don't work the way they are supposed to. Returning a hardware device you bought over the Internet or by mail is much, much harder. Furthermore, before you carry your purchase out the door, open the box it comes in. See if the box contains, for example, the speakers, not to mention the rebate certificate, that the salesperson told you about. And one more thing: Don't buy expensive service contracts for hardware devices. If the thing doesn't work, take it back. The manufacturer is responsible for making a product that works, not a product that works only if it is sold with a service contract.

Installing a Plug-and-Play Hardware Device

To install a plug-and-play device, turn off your computer, carefully follow the instructions in the box to see how to plug the device into the computer, and turn the computer on. You're done. When you turn on the computer, Windows notices the new hardware device and installs a driver to make it run. If the device doesn't run, try installing it with the directions in the section that follows, and see "If the Hardware Device Doesn't Work…" later in this chapter.

Installing a Hardware Device That Isn't Plug and Play

To install a device that is not the plug-and-play variety, you have to attach it to your computer and then tell Windows what it is. Windows can search for the device on your system for you. If it finds the device, all is well. Windows installs the correct drivers to run the device and that's the end of it. However, if Windows can't find the device, you state what it is, who manufactured it, and its model name yourself so that Windows knows which drivers to install. Follow these steps to run the Hardware Wizard and tell Windows about a new hardware device that isn't plug and play:

1. Close all programs, if any are running.

2. Click the Start button and choose Settings | Control Panel.

3. Double-click the Add New Hardware icon in the Control Panel.

Add New
Hardware

4. Click Next in the first Add New Hardware Wizard dialog box.

5. Click Next again. Then wait as Windows searches for new plug-and-play devices on your system and fails to find any.

6. In the next dialog box, click Yes (Recommended) and click Next to have Windows search your system for new hardware devices that aren't plug and play.

7. The next dialog box warns you that the search can take several minutes (how true!). Click Next and be patient.

8. When the search is complete, either click the Finish button because it was successful, or click Next in the message box that tells you that Windows couldn't find any new devices (and keep reading). If you click Next, you see the Add New Hardware Wizard box shown on the top of Figure 4.3.

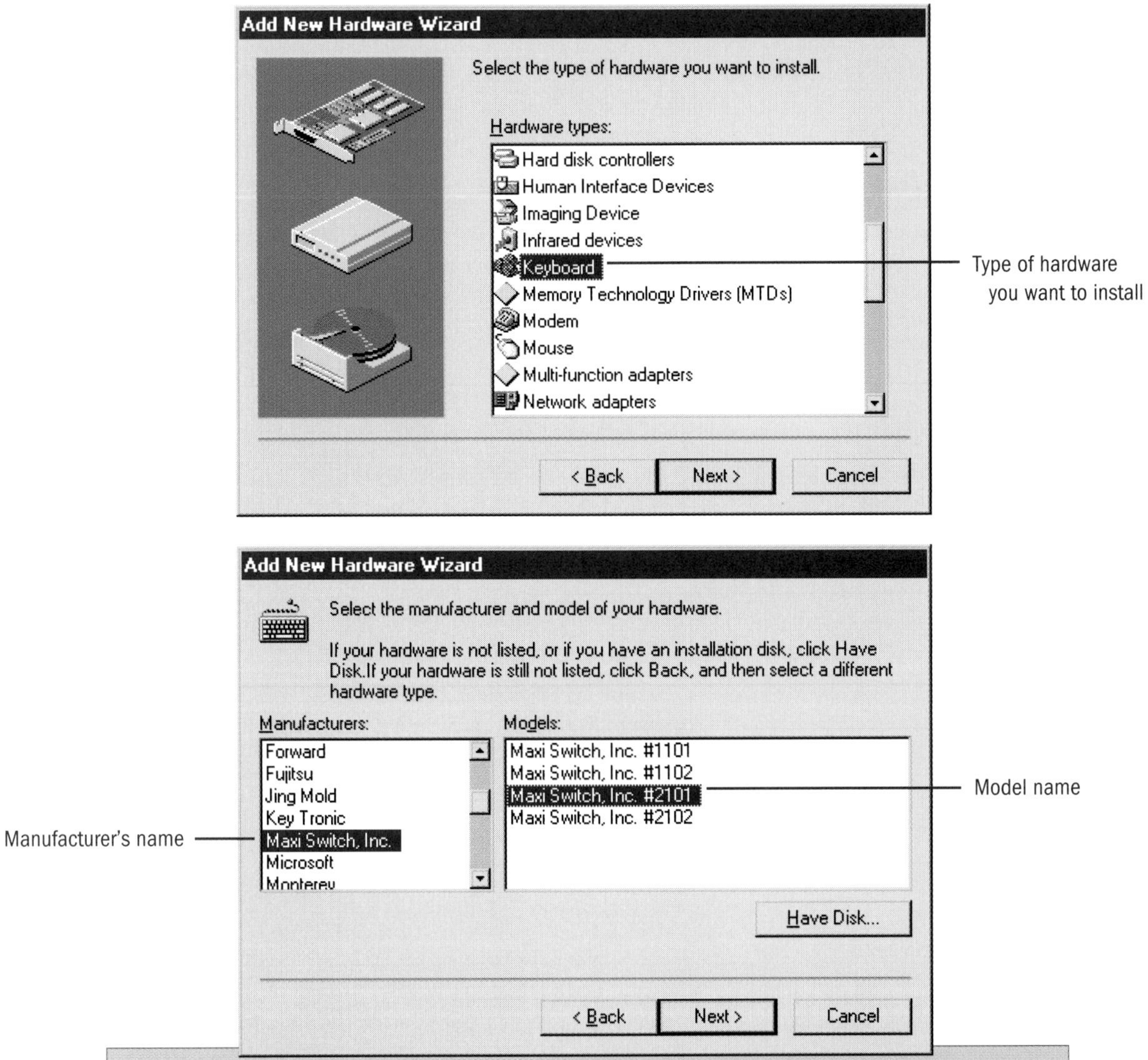

Figure 4.3:   If Windows can't tell what kind of hardware you installed, you have to tell it what's what.

9. Click the kind of hardware you installed and click Next. The second wizard dialog box in Figure 4.3 appears.

10. Select the name of the manufacturer on the left side of the dialog box, the model name on the right side and click Next.

11. Click the Next button when Windows tells you that it will install new drivers to support the new hardware device. If the right drivers are not available, you are asked to insert either a disk from the manufacturer, the Windows CD, or a Windows installation disk.

12. Click the Finish button when the ordeal is over.

13. Shut down and restart the computer.

If the Hardware Device Doesn't Work...

Nothing is more infuriating than installing a new piece of hardware and finding out that it doesn't work. You almost got electrocuted when you plugged in the power cord. You scraped your knee while snaking wires and cables around desk legs. And now the thing doesn't work!

Before you angrily take your new purchase back to the shop, try these tactics:

- See if the cables are fitted properly.
- Find out if the device is turned on and plugged in a wall socket.
- Reread the manufacturer's installation instructions to see if you followed them correctly.
- Run the Hardware Wizard again. Dunno why, but sometimes the second or third time is the charm.
- Turn to "Getting Information About Your System" in Chapter 9 and follow the instructions for going to the Device Manager tab of the System Properties dialog box. On this tab, you can find out whether a device is really working. Look on the bottom of the Resources tab to see if the device conflicts with another device. If your new device doesn't appear in the System

Properties dialog box, Windows doesn't know it's there. Probably it's not plugged in correctly.

- Write down error messages if you see any. Usually, a technician can interpret them for you, if speaking to a technician proves necessary.
- Try the hardware conflict troubleshooter.

A *hardware conflict* occurs when two hardware devices attempt to use the same resources. When that happens, one device wins and one loses, and the losing device doesn't function correctly. The hardware conflict troubleshooter can help find out if a hardware conflict has occurred. To use it, follow these steps:

1. Click the Start button and choose Help.
2. Click the Index tab in the Help program, type **hardware conflict** in the box, and click the Display button.
3. On the right side of the Help window, click the hyperlink (it says "Click here") to start the hardware conflict troubleshooter.
4. Keep answering questions, clicking Next, and hoping for the best.

Installing a New Printer

"All about Printing" in Chapter 7 explains how to print a file and change a printer's default settings.

Before you can print anything, you have to tell Windows 98 what kind of printer you use. All printers are not created equal. Some can print on envelopes and on paper of various sizes. Some can print in color. In order to print anything, Windows needs to know precisely which printer will do the work. Windows needs to know that so it can send the correct instructions to the printer.

If your printer is plug and play, all you likely have to do to install it is turn off the computer, plug in the printer, and turn the computer on. Maybe you don't have to fool with printer settings, but if you purchase a new printer, you have to alert Windows 98.

By the way, installing a printer simply means to tell Windows 98 about a printer you intend to use. More than one printer can be installed on a computer. Before you install a new printer, you don't have to uninstall another. Follow these steps to introduce Windows 98 to a new printer:

1. Following the manufacturer's instructions, plug the printer into your computer.

2. Click the Start button and choose Settings | Printers. The Printers folder opens. In the folder are icons for each printer that has been installed and an icon called Add Printer:

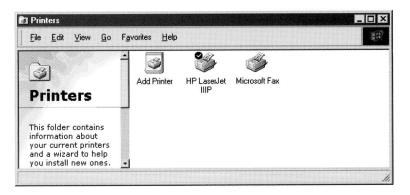

Add Printer

3. Double-click the Add Printer icon to see the Add Printer Wizard dialog box.

4. Click Next (or, if your computer is connected to a network, choose whether to install a local or network printer and then click Next). As shown in Figure 4.4, the Add Printer Wizard dialog box asks who manufactured your printer and which model it is. Windows has drivers for all printers listed in this dialog box.

5. From the Manufacturers list, find and click on the name of the company that made your computer.

6. From the Printers list, find and click the model name of your printer. You can find this name on the printer itself. (If your printer isn't on the manufacturer's list, perhaps you can put it there by updating your copy of Windows 98. See Chapter 9.)

7. Click the Next button.

TIP

If you can't find your printer on the Manufacturer's list, insert the disk that came with your printer into the floppy drive, click the Have Disk button, and click the Browse button in the Install From Disk dialog box. Consult the manual to find out which file to install, then select the file on the disk and click OK to return to the Add Printer Wizard dialog box.

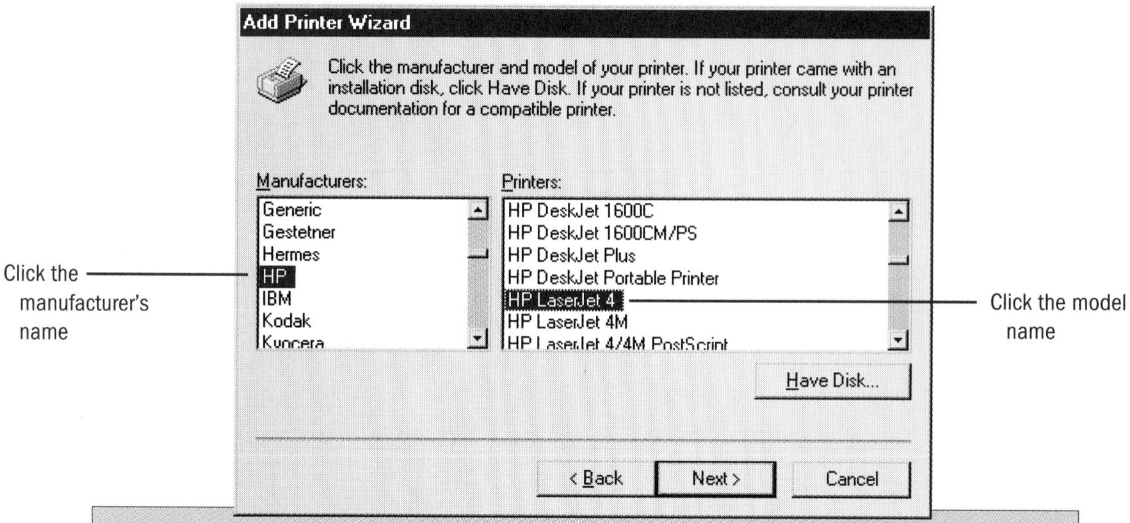

Add Printer Wizard

Click the manufacturer and model of your printer. If your printer came with an installation disk, click Have Disk. If your printer is not listed, consult your printer documentation for a compatible printer.

Manufacturers:

Generic
Gestetner
Hermes
HP
IBM
Kodak
Kyocera

Printers:

HP DeskJet 1600C
HP DeskJet 1600CM/PS
HP DeskJet Plus
HP DeskJet Portable Printer
HP LaserJet 4
HP LaserJet 4M
HP LaserJet 4/4M PostScript

Click the manufacturer's name

Click the model name

Have Disk...

< Back   Next >   Cancel

Figure 4.4:   Choosing the new printer's manufacturer and model.

TIP

If you change your mind about which printer is the default printer, click the Start button and choose Settings | Printers to open the Printers folder. Then right-click the printer that should be the default and choose Set as Default from the shortcut menu.

8. Choose the port through which you connected the printer to your computer (probably LPT1) and click Next. If you intend to hook two printers to your computer, consult the printer manual to find out which port to plug the second computer into.

9. In the next dialog box, click the Yes option button if you want your new printer to be the default printer. The *default printer* is the one that appears automatically in the Print dialog box when you give the command to print. You can still print with your new printer if it is not the default, but you have to select it first in the Print dialog box.

10. Click Next.

11. Click Yes (recommended) to test-drive the new printer.

12. Click the Finish button. If all the driver files for your new printer are already on the computer's hard disk, you are done, but Windows probably needs to copy the files from the Windows 98 CD or a Windows 98 floppy disk.

13. Insert the CD or the floppy disk (be sure to insert the right floppy) and click OK.

An icon for your new printer lands in the Printers folder. If your new printer is the default printer, a black check mark appears beside the icon.

All About Fonts

People who create fancy documents, signs, or certificates owe it to themselves to load many different fonts on their computers. That way, you get to choose among different fonts in your work. If it helps you understand what fonts are, "font" is a synonym for "typeface." Fonts have lovely names—Garamond, Mistral, Verdana. As a connoisseur of Windows 98, you have the opportunity to use many fonts. Don't be shy about experimenting with fonts to find one that sets the right tone or calls attention to the right part of a page. But don't go overboard, either. A page with too many fonts looks like a ransom note.

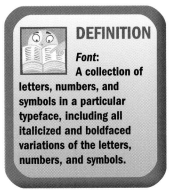

DEFINITION

Font:
A collection of letters, numbers, and symbols in a particular typeface, including all italicized and boldfaced variations of the letters, numbers, and symbols.

Besides the fonts that come with Windows 98, other programs load fonts on your computer, so you likely can choose from a number of fonts. Generally speaking, fonts fall in two categories:

- **TrueType Fonts** These fonts look the same onscreen as they do when printed on paper. When in doubt, choose a TrueType font because you can be sure what it will look like on the printed page. The letters "TT" precede TrueType font names in dialog boxes and the Fonts folder.
- **Printer Fonts** These fonts are less reliable than TrueType fonts. They are designed for use by printers and sometimes look different onscreen and on the printed page. Next to the names of printer fonts in dialog boxes is a tiny image of a printer.

The next few pages explain how to find out which fonts are on your system and print samples of your fonts, load more fonts or remove fonts, and insert symbols and special characters in files.

Viewing Fonts and Printing Font Samples

So you want to get a clear look at the fonts you have, perhaps to find out which ones to use in a desktop-publishing file or to find out which are expendable and can be deleted. Figure 4.5 shows how to examine the fonts on your system. By the way, do you know why, in Figure 4.5 and in typing class, "the quick brown fox jumps over the lazy dog"? Because that sentence requires every letter of the alphabet, including x and z.

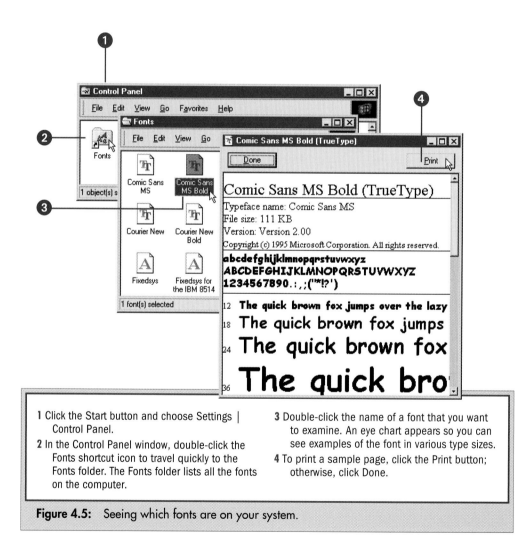

1 Click the Start button and choose Settings | Control Panel.

2 In the Control Panel window, double-click the Fonts shortcut icon to travel quickly to the Fonts folder. The Fonts folder lists all the fonts on the computer.

3 Double-click the name of a font that you want to examine. An eye chart appears so you can see examples of the font in various type sizes.

4 To print a sample page, click the Print button; otherwise, click Done.

Figure 4.5: Seeing which fonts are on your system.

Loading More Fonts on Your System

Follow these steps to load more fonts on your computer:

1. Click the Start button, choose Settings | Control Panel, and double-click the Fonts shortcut icon to open the Fonts folder (see Figure 4.5).

2. In the Fonts folder window, choose File | Install New Font.

3. In the Add Fonts dialog box, show Windows the way to the fonts you want to load by clicking choices in the Drives and possibly in the Folders list.

SHORTCUT

The fastest way to load a new font on your system is to copy its font file to the C:/Windows/Fonts folder.

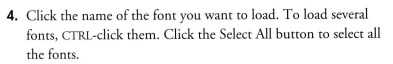

4. Click the name of the font you want to load. To load several fonts, CTRL-click them. Click the Select All button to select all the fonts.

5. Click OK. The new font is placed in the C:\Windows\Fonts folder. When you select a font in a Fonts dialog box, the name of your new font will appear on the list beside the other fonts.

Fonts can eat up valuable disk space. To remove a font, open the Fonts folder, click the name of the font or CTRL-click to select several names, and choose File | Delete. Don't delete Windows 98 fonts because Windows needs them for its menus. Only delete fonts that you installed yourself.

Character Map: Inserting Symbols and Special Characters

Character Map

On the subject of fonts and characters, you can enter a foreign character or strange symbol in sophisticated programs like WordPerfect and Word merely by choosing a menu command. That isn't so in most programs. In most programs you can't enter an unusual character directly, so you have to seek the help of the Character Map by following these steps:

1. Click the Start button and choose Programs | Accessories | System Tools | Character Map. You see the Character Map shown in Figure 4.6. The symbol or character you select here will be copied to the Clipboard. From the Clipboard, you will paste the symbol or character into a file.

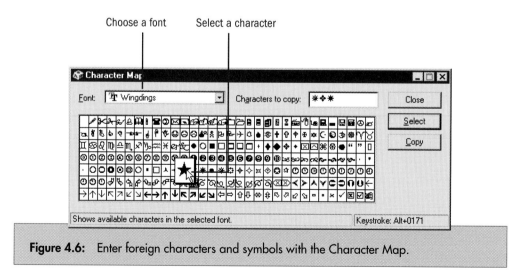

Figure 4.6: Enter foreign characters and symbols with the Character Map.

2. Choose a font from the Font menu.

3. Click to select a symbol or character. To get a good look, click and hold down the mouse button.

4. Click the Select button. The symbol or character you selected lands in the Characters to Copy box. You can select more than one character.

5. Click the Close button.

6. Back in your file, place the cursor where you want the symbol or character to go and press CTRL-V, choose Edit | Paste, or click the Paste button.

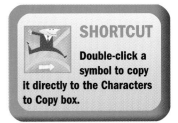

SHORTCUT
Double-click a symbol to copy it directly to the Characters to Copy box.

Resetting the Clock, Calendar Date, and Time Zone

On the right side of the Taskbar, the clock tells the time. And if you gently slide the mouse pointer over the clock, you can learn today's date and the day of the week. Now and then, make sure the clock is accurate and reset the clock, if necessary. And if you cart your computer or laptop to a new time zone, reset the clock and tell Windows 98 which time zone you crossed into. Windows uses the clock to time-stamp and date-stamp files when you save them. Unless the clock is accurate, you can't tell precisely when files were saved and which files are most up to date.

Figure 4.7 explains how to reset the time and date in the Date/Time Properties dialog box. As for the Automatically Adjust Clock for Daylight Savings Changes check box, Windows automatically sets the clock forward or backward at the appropriate hour if the check box is selected. Unless you live in one of those enlightened Midwestern towns where daylight savings time is not honored, leave the check mark in the check box.

TIP
If you don't care to see the clock on the Taskbar, click the Start button and choose Settings | Taskbar & Start Menu. On the Taskbar Options tab of the Taskbar Properties dialog box, uncheck the Show Clock check box.

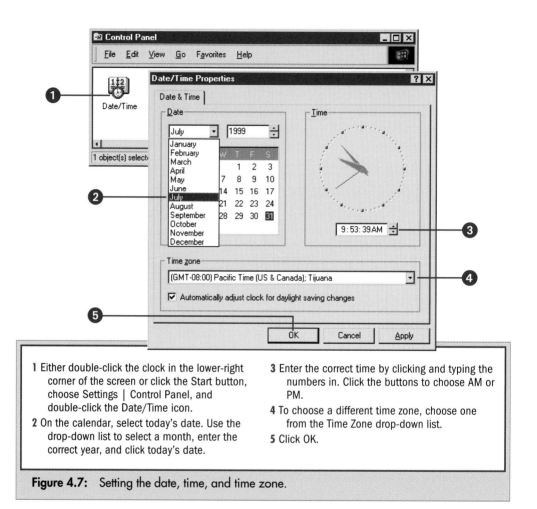

1 Either double-click the clock in the lower-right corner of the screen or click the Start button, choose Settings | Control Panel, and double-click the Date/Time icon.
2 On the calendar, select today's date. Use the drop-down list to select a month, enter the correct year, and click today's date.

3 Enter the correct time by clicking and typing the numbers in. Click the buttons to choose AM or PM.
4 To choose a different time zone, choose one from the Time Zone drop-down list.
5 Click OK.

Figure 4.7: Setting the date, time, and time zone.

Deciding How Numbers, Times, Dates, and Currency Are Displayed

When you installed Windows 98, you declared which language you speak and which region you live in. On the basis of that choice, Windows 98 displays numbers, times, and dates in a certain way. Windows 98 also chose a currency symbol for you. For example, if you chose English (United States) as your language and region, numbers are displayed to two decimal points, the dollar symbol ($) is the currency symbol, and time is displayed in AM/PM format. Many programs get their display formats from the choices you make in Windows.

Suppose you move to a different region of the world or you want to change number, time, date, or currency formats. In that case, visit the Regional Settings Properties dialog box by following these steps:

1. Click the Start button and choose Settings | Control Panel.
2. In the Control Panel, double-click the Regional Settings icon. You see the Regional Settings Properties dialog box.
3. Either go to the Regional Settings Properties tab and choose a new region from the drop-down menu, or visit the Number, Currency, Time, and Date tabs and change the settings there.
4. Click OK.
5. Click Yes when Windows informs you that you have to restart the computer to make the settings take effect.
6. Twiddle your thumbs while the computer restarts.

Regional Settings

Did you know that writers don't have to pay income tax in Ireland? I should emigrate to that most civilized of countries.

Connecting Your Computer to the Internet

The last part of this chapter takes on a thorny subject—how to set up your computer so it can connect smoothly with the Internet. Unfortunately, software standards haven't been devised to make setting up the connection easy. If you access the Internet through an Internet service provider (ISP), the setup procedure is a monumental chore. People who use the big-time online services—America Online, AT&T WorldNet, CompuServe, Prodigy, and Microsoft Network—have an easier time establishing the connection because online services usually provide a setup disk that you can use to make the connection.

Read on to find out how to connect your computer to an ISP and how to change the connection settings if that proves necessary. By the way, if your computer is connected to a network, it is probably

DEFINITION
Internet service provider (ISP): A telecommunications service that provides Internet access to subscribers for a fee.

EXPERT ADVICE

These days, many ISPs provide an on-disk setup program that you can use to establish a connection between a computer and the Internet. The following instructions are for doing the setup work yourself, but if your ISP provides a program for doing it, by all means see if the setup program can do the job before you attempt to establish the connection on your own.

connected to the Internet already. See your network administrator if the connection between your computer and the network isn't working correctly or you can't get on the Internet.

Making the Connection to an ISP

Every Internet service provider is different, so you have to choose a bunch of different options and make a number of different settings to establish the connection between your computer and your ISP. Before you try to make the connection, collect all the information you need (I explain the information you need shortly).

By the way, how to shop for an ISP is not a topic for this book, but when you choose an ISP (if you haven't chosen one already), be sure to find a local ISP. Users of the Internet are billed by their ISPs and the phone company when they cruise the Internet. If your ISP is not in the same area code as your computer, you will be billed for a long distance call each time you surf the Net.

Getting Information from Your ISP

Call your Internet service provider on the phone and read the following little speech: "Hello, I'm setting up my computer and modem to connect to your ISP and I need some information. To connect to you, Windows 98 says I need all or some of this information." Then read the questions in Table 4.1 and scribble the answers in the margin of this book. The italicized step numbers in Table 4.1 refer to numbered steps in "Internet Connection Wizard: Setting Up Your ISP Connection," the next section in this chapter. Of course, you can get all this information from a manual instead of

Topic	What to Ask Your ISP
ISP Phone Number	
1. Phone Number	What's the dial-in phone number of the Internet service provider (ISP)? (*step 5*)
Dial-Up Connection: Advanced Connection Settings*	
2. Connection Type	Do you use a PPP (Point-to-Point Protocol) or SLIP (Serial Line Internet Protocol) connection? (*step 5*)
3. Logon Procedure	Do I need to type commands when I log on? If I do need to type commands in a terminal window, what commands do I type? Can I use a logon script? If I can use a script, tell me exactly how to type the commands in the script. (A *script* is a series of commands that are always the same.) (*step 5*)
4. IP Address	What Internet Protocol (IP) address do I use? Do you automatically assign one to me? If not, what is the IP address I should always use when I dial in? (*step 5*)
5. DNS Server Address	When I sign in, do you automatically assign me a DNS (Domain Name Server) address? If not, what is the address of the DNS server? Can you give me an alternate DNS server address in case the main DNS is not available? (*step 5*)
Internet Mail Account: E-Mail Server Types and Addresses	
6. Incoming Mail Server (POP3 or IMAP)	What type of server, POP3 or IMAP, do you use to process incoming mail? (*step 10*)
7. Incoming Mail Server Address	What is the address of the incoming mail server? (*step 10*)
8. Outgoing Mail (SMTP) Server	What is the address of the outgoing mail server? Is it the same as the address of the incoming mail server? (*step 10*)
9. Secure Password Authentication (SPA)	Do you provide Secure Password Authentication (SPA), or do I have to enter my e-mail account name and a password each time I log on? (*step 10*)

* In most instances, you don't need to know the advanced connection settings. If your ISP says you needn't concern yourself with this stuff, your ISP is probably right.

Table 4.1:   ISP Information That the Internet Connection Wizard Needs

calling your ISP if you feel like slogging through the pages of a manual. Or maybe your ISP is ahead of the game and can send you all this information on a printout called "Setting Up Your ISP for Windows 98."

Internet Connection Wizard: Setting Up Your ISP Connection

With the answers to the questions in Table 4.1 in hand, and knowing what your password and user name are, follow these steps to start the Internet Connection Wizard and tell Windows how to make the connection between your computer and your Internet service provider:

Internet
Options

1. Click the Start button and choose Settings | Control Panel, then double-click the Internet Options icon.

2. In the Internet Properties dialog box, click the Connections tab, and then click the Setup button to start the Connection Wizard.

3. In the first wizard dialog box, click the last option button, "I Want to Set Up My Internet Connection Manually, or I Want to Connect Through a Local Area Network (LAN)." Then click Next.

4. In the Setting Up Your Internet Connection dialog box, make sure "I Connect Using My Phone Line and a Modem" is chosen, and click Next. (If you are on a network, by all means let the network administrator do the work of connecting your computer to the Internet. That's what he or she is being paid for.)

Area code:	Telephone number:
415	– 555-4321

Country/region name and code:

United States of America (1)

5. In the Internet Account Connection Information dialog box, enter the phone number of your ISP, the answer to question 1 in Table 4.1. Make sure the area code and country code are correct. If the call to your ISP is not a long-distance call, uncheck the "Dial Using the Area Code and Country Code" check box. Click Next to go to the next dialog box.

Look at the answers you scribbled next to questions 2 through 5 in Table 4.1. If you made no marks next to questions 2 through 5 because your ISP doesn't require this information, you can click Next. However, click the Advanced button and fill in the Advanced Connection Properties dialog box if that is necessary. You can fill in the dialog box by referring to the answers you scribbled next to Table 4.1.

6. In the Internet Account Logon Information dialog box, enter your user name and password. Be sure to type upper- and lowercase letters correctly if that is necessary. Asterisks appear when you enter your password. The ISP should have provided you a password when you signed on. The user name is the part of your e-mail address that appears before the at symbol (@). For example, if your e-mail address is John_Doe@remain.com, John_Doe is your user name. Click Next.

User name: PeterW
Password: ********

7. In the Configuring Your Computer dialog box, enter a descriptive name for the connection settings you just entered; and then click Next.
You can enter your ISP's name if you want. If you need to go back and change these connection settings at a later date, you will refer to them by the name you enter here. For example, if you name your dial-up connection settings "Peter's Direct Connection" and you need to change the settings later on, perhaps to change the phone number, you will select Peter's Direct Connection in a dialog box and then revisit the Dial-Up Connection dialog boxes to change the settings.

Connection name:
Peter's Direct Connection

8. In the Set Up Your Internet Mail Account dialog box, click Yes if you intend to send and receive e-mail messages with this account. In the unlikely event that you don't want to send or receive e-mail, click No and then click the Finished button. (If you already have one Internet account, you see the Internet Mail Account dialog box after you click Next. Click the "Create a New Internet Mail Account" option button and then click Next if you maintain accounts with two ISPs and you want to configure your computer to connect to the second one.)

9. In the Your Name dialog box, type your name as you want it to appear in the From line of outgoing messages. When others get messages from you, this is the name they will see along with the message. Then click Next.

Display name: Peter Weverka
For example: John Smith

10. In the Internet E-mail Address dialog box, type the e-mail address that others need in order to send you e-mail messages. Be sure to enter your e-mail address correctly. Then click Next.

E-mail address: peter_weverka@email.msn.com
For example: someone@microsoft.com

11. In the E-mail Server Names dialog box, refer to the answers you scribbled next to questions 6 through 8 in Table 4.1 and fill in the boxes. Then click Next.

12. In the Internet Mail Logon dialog box, click the second option button if your ISP uses Secure Password Authentication. (Refer to question 9 in Table 4.1 for the answer.) Otherwise, enter your password again, as I have done in the following illustration. Click Next.

Internet Connection Wizard	☒

Internet Mail Logon

Type the account name and password your Internet service provider has given you.

Account name: PeterW

Password: ✗✗✗✗✗✗✗✗

☑ Remember password

If your Internet service provider requires you to use Secure Password Authentication (SPA) to access your mail account, select the 'Log On Using Secure Password Authentication (SPA)' check box.

☐ Log on using Secure Password Authentication (SPA)

     < Back   Next >   Cancel

13. In the last dialog box, click Finish to see if your connection to the Internet works. If it doesn't work, keep reading.

Changing the ISP Connection Settings

Internet
Options

Suppose your ISP changes phone numbers. Or you change your password. Or you did something wrong in the setup procedure and you have to change a connection setting. To fix the problem, click the Start button, choose Settings | Control Panel, and double-click the Internet Options icon. In the Internet Properties dialog box, click the Connections tab, as shown in Figure 4.8. The Dial-Up Settings box lists the connection between your computer and your ISP (or ISPs).

Follow these instructions to fine-tune your Internet connection:

- **Change the Connection Settings**   Click a connection, if necessary, and then click the Settings button. You see the

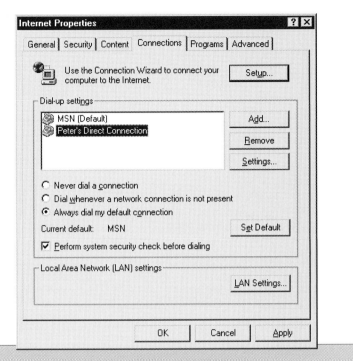

Figure 4.8:   Go to the Connections tab of the Internet Properties dialog box to fine-tune an Internet Connection.

Settings dialog box. From here, you can change the settings you entered when you set up the connection. Click the Properties button to change phone numbers.

- **Choose a Default Connection**   If your computer is connected to more than one ISP, select the ISP you want to connect to automatically when you start Internet Explorer. To do so, select a connection name and then click the Set Default button.

- **Remove a Connection**   If you end your relationship with an ISP, sever the connection between your computer and the ISP as well. To do so, click a connection name and then click the Remove button.

CHAPTER 5

Working Faster in Windows 98

INCLUDES

- Creating and switching to different user profiles
- Changing the speed of the mouse and the look of the mouse pointers
- Making the keyboard work better
- Launching a program automatically when the computer starts
- Telling Windows which program is to open a file
- Moving names in, adding names to, and removing names from the Windows 98 menus
- Changing the appearance of the screen
- Ten ways to reduce eyestrain

Switch to Another User Profile
or Use the Communal Settings ➥ pp. 123–124

1. Click the Start button, choose Log Off, and click Yes in the confirmation box.
2. In the Enter Password dialog box, click Cancel to use the communal settings or else select a user name and enter a password, if necessary, to work under a user profile.

Change the Speed of the Mouse
and the Size of Mouse Pointers ➥ pp. 125–127

1. Click the Start button, choose Settings | Control Panel, and double-click the Mouse icon.
2. On the Buttons tab of the Mouse Properties dialog box, adjust the double-click speed.
3. On the Pointers tab, change the look of the mouse pointers.
4. On the Motion tab, change the speed at which the pointer moves.

Type the location and name of the item you want to create a shortcut to. Or, search for the item by clicking Browse.

Command line:

"C:\Program Files\Microsoft Office\Microsoft Excel.lnk"

Browse...

Start a Computer Program
Automatically When Windows Starts ➥ pp. 129–131

- Create a shortcut icon for the program and place it in the C:\Windows\Start Menu\Programs\StartUp folder.
- Right-click the Taskbar and choose Properties. In the dialog box, click the Start Menu Programs tab, click the Add button, and click Browse. Locate and select the .exe file of the program, click the Open button, click Next, and select the StartUp folder. Click Next again, enter a name for the shortcut icon, click Finish, and click OK.

Registered file types:

- Internet Document Set
- Internet Location Service
- Internet Shortcut
- IomegaBackupFile
- JPEG Image
- JScript Script File
- M3U file
- Macromedia Director Movie
- Macromedia Director Protected Mo...

Tell Windows Which Program
Opens a Certain Kind of File ➥ pp. 131–134

1. Click the Start button, choose Settings | Folder Options, and click the File Types tab.
2. In the Folder Options dialog box, select the type of file you want to reassign and click the Edit button.
3. In Edit File Type dialog box, click the word "open" and then the Edit button.
4. In the Editing Action for Type dialog box, click Browse, find the .exe file of the program, and click the Open button.

Remove a Program Name
from a Windows Menu ➥ p. 136

1. Right-click the Taskbar, choose Properties, and click the Start Menu Programs tab.
2. Click the Remove button, locate and select the name of the program whose name you want to remove, click the Remove button, and click Close.

Move a Program Name
Up or Down a Menu ➥ p. 139

1. Move the pointer over the program name, click, and drag the mouse pointer up or down on the menu. A black line shows where the menu name will appear when you release the mouse button.
2. Release the mouse button.

Make the Screen Easier to
Read and Understand ➥ pp. 140–141

1. Right-click on the desktop and choose Properties.
2. Click the Appearance tab in the Display Properties dialog box.
3. From the Scheme drop-down menu, choose a design for the screen and click OK.

Choose a Wallpaper
Design for the Desktop ➥ p. 141

1. Right-click a photo or image you like and choose Set As Wallpaper.
2. Right-click on the desktop, choose Properties, and go to the Background tab of the Display Properties dialog box.
3. On the Display menu, choose Center, Tile, or Stretch.

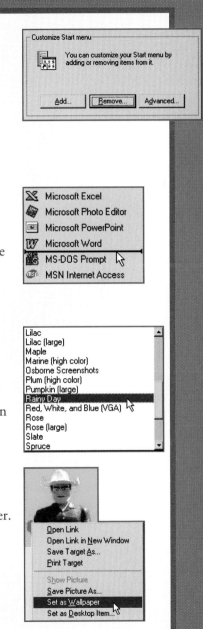

This chapter picks up where Chapter 2 left off. Chapter 2 explains the handful of things you can do to make working with Windows 98 easier. In this chapter, you learn the handful of things you can do to work faster. Study this chapter carefully and you will spend less time in front of your computer. Not that you'll become a member of the leisure class, but you will get the time for those tap dancing lessons you've always wanted.

This chapter shows how to make the mouse and keyboard function better. You learn how to make your favorite program appear instantly each time you start the computer and how to put the names of your favorite programs on the Start and Programs menus where you can find them in a hurry. You also learn how to tell Windows 98 to always open a particular kind of file with a particular computer program. Oh, and this chapter also describes how to make the screen easier to look at and offers ten ways to reduce eyestrain.

By the way, if you share a computer with others and you start tinkering with the computer settings, they might get mad at you. To keep that from happening, you can save your supercharged settings as a "user profile." When others sit at the computer, they see and use their own settings or the communal settings, but you get your own personalized settings. How to keep settings to yourself is the subject of the first part of this chapter.

When People Share a Computer: Using User Profiles

Suppose you want to redecorate your computer screen with a tie-dyed background and remove the names of programs you never use from the Programs menu. If you share your computer with others, you owe it to them to save your modifications as a "user profile." That way, others who use your computer do not have to be unpleasantly surprised by the strange settings you made.

Keeping your settings to yourself requires doing two things:

- Creating a *user profile*—a user name and perhaps a password—for the new settings you want to make. After you create the user profile, changes you make to settings are made to your profile. They do not affect what others see when they use the computer.
- Teaching others who use your computer how to log on so that they see the settings they want to see, not the settings that are part of your user profile or a third party's user profile.

The next few pages explain how to create, erase, and change a profile. You also learn how to log on to the computer in order to work with the communal settings or work with the settings that belong to a particular user profile.

CAUTION

Be sure to tell the others who use your computer that you intend to create a user profile. After you create one, users see the Enter Password dialog box each time they start the computer. Tell others that they can simply click Cancel or press ESC in this dialog box to start the computer in the normal way.

Creating a New User Profile

When you work under a user profile, all customized settings are kept in that profile. They have no effect whatsoever on other profiles or the communal settings that all users of your computer share. Do the following to create a new user profile under which to keep the new settings you or others make to a computer:

1. Click the Start button and choose Settings | Control Panel.
2. In the Control Panel, double-click the Users icon. If this is the first time you've created a user profile, you see the Enable Multi-User Settings dialog box. Otherwise, you see the User Settings dialog box.
3. Either click the Next button or, if you've already created a user profile, click the New User button and then click Next.
4. In the Add User dialog box, enter a descriptive name for the user profile. Type your name, the name of another person who uses your computer, or the name of a certain kind of task you want to do. Then click Next. You don't have to enter a password. Leave the Enter a New Password dialog box empty

Users

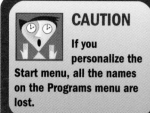

CAUTION

If you personalize the Start menu, all the names on the Programs menu are lost.

and simply click Next if you think a password for protecting computer settings is unnecessary.

5. In the Enter New Password dialog box, enter the same password in the Password and Confirm Password text boxes. Passwords are not case-sensitive.

6. Click the Next button.

7. In the Personalized Items Settings dialog box, check each part of Windows 98 that you want to customize. In the list, "Desktop folder" refers to everything on the desktop—its background, shortcut icons, and so on. Items that you do not check cannot be customized. They retain all the settings that are also found in the communal settings.

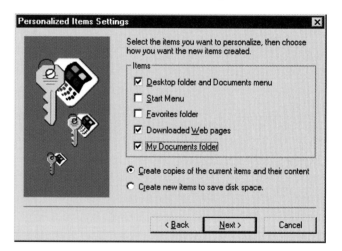

TIP

You can create as many user profiles as you want. If you use your computer for very different tasks—working on spreadsheets, desktop publishing, creating Web pages—create a user profile for each type of work you do. You'll save time that way. As this chapter demonstrates, Windows 98 offers many different settings. Some are more suitable than others for working in different types of programs.

8. On the bottom of the dialog box, choose how you want to start changing the computer's settings:

   • **Create Copies of the Current Items and Their Content**
   Choose this option to use the settings that are in place and onscreen as the starting point for your new settings.

   • **Create New Items to Save Disk Space**   Choose this option to start from scratch with bare-bones settings for the items you chose in step 7. For example, if you checked Start menu and Desktop folder in step 7, almost all items are removed from the Programs menu and only a few icons remain on the desktop.

9. Click the Next button.

10. Click the Finish button and wait while Windows takes note of your personal settings.

You go back to the User Settings dialog box if you've created user profiles already. Click Close in the dialog box. If this is the first user profile you've created, take these additional steps:

1. Click Yes to restart Windows 98. When Windows restarts, you see the Enter Password dialog box.

2. Enter your password and click OK (or simply click OK if you didn't enter a password for your user profile).

Start changing the settings. All changes you make become a part of your new user profile.

Switching to the Communal Settings or Another User Profile

When you work under the auspices of a user profile, all changes you make to settings are made to that profile, not to other profiles or the communal settings. Suppose you want to switch to a different profile or use the communal settings that all users of your computer share. Windows 98 offers a special Log Off command for switching profiles. Where is the Log Off command? It's right under your nose, on the Start menu.

Follow these steps to switch to a new user profile or the standard settings that all users share:

1. Click the Start button and choose Log Off. If you are working under a user profile, the name of the profile appears after the words "Log Off."

2. Click Yes when Windows asks if you are sure about logging off.

3. From the Enter Password dialog box, either switch user profiles or use the communal settings:

   • **Different User Profile**   Click the profile's name, enter its correct password (or don't bother with the password if you never assigned one), and click OK.

   • **Communal Settings**   Click the Cancel button or press ESC.

Users also see the Enter Password dialog box when they start the computer. Be sure that everyone who uses your computer knows exactly what to do when they confront this forbidding dialog box.

Deleting and Altering User Profiles

The following steps explain how to delete a profile, alter a profile, or change its password. You can't delete a profile if you are logged on the computer under the name of the profile you want to delete.

Users

1. Click the Start button and choose Settings | Control Panel.

2. In the Control Panel, double-click the Users icon. You see the User Settings dialog box shown in Figure 5.1.

3. Under Users, click the name of the profile that needs changing.

4. Click a button to delete the profile, change its password, or change its settings:

   • **Delete**   Click the Delete button to erase a profile. Then click Yes when Windows asks if you really want to do it.

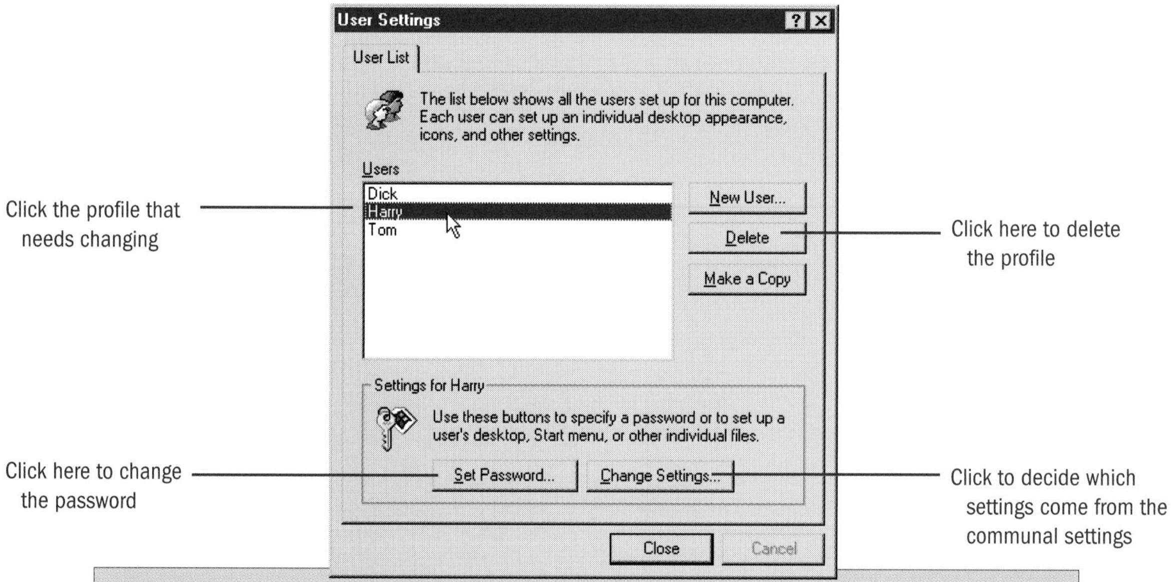

Click the profile that needs changing

Click here to delete the profile

Click here to change the password

Click to decide which settings come from the communal settings

Figure 5.1:   Deleting and altering a user profile.

- **Set Password** To change or remove a password, click the Set Password button. In the Change Windows Password dialog box, enter the old password and the new password twice to assign a new password to a profile. To remove a password, simply enter the old password in the Old Password text box. Then click OK and click OK again in the message box.

- **Change Settings** Click this button to change which settings the profile has in common with the communal settings. When you click the Change Settings button, you see the Personalized Items Settings dialog box that you saw when you created the profile in the first place. Check items that you want to customize and uncheck items whose settings are to come from the communal settings. Then click OK.

5. Click Close in the User Settings dialog box.

A Sleeker, Faster Mouse

Speed demons who prefer pointing and clicking with the mouse to giving commands with the keyboard can fine-tune the mouse and make it work just right. Windows 98 offers many ways to adjust the mouse. You can change the double-click speed and pointer speed, change the look of mouse pointers, and even swap the left mouse button and right mouse button, a courtesy to left-handers. Read on.

Changing the Double-Click Speed and Pointer Speed

No matter what you want to do to the mouse, start by opening the Mouse Properties dialog box. Follow these steps to open it and change the double-click speed and the speed at which the pointer travels across the screen when you roll the mouse across the mousepad on your desk:

1. Click the Start button and choose Settings | Control Panel.

Mouse

2. In the Control Panel, double-click the Mouse icon. You see the Buttons tab of the Mouse Properties dialog box.

3. Under Double-click speed, drag the slider toward Slow or Fast, and then try double-clicking the Jack-in-the-Box in the Test area.

   If Jack doesn't spring out of or go back in his box right away, you didn't double-click fast enough. Instead of double-clicking, you clicked twice in a row. The Fast setting on the extreme right is so fast, you might need to change your medication to accomplish a successful double-click.

4. Experiment with double-click speeds until you find one that is comfortable.

5. Click the Motion tab in the Mouse Properties dialog box. On this tab you can adjust the speed at which the mouse pointer moves onscreen and see if pointer trails are for you.

DEFINITION

Pointer trail:
A series of ghostly pointer images that describe in which direction the pointer is traveling onscreen. Pointer trails are a big help to laptop users because finding the pointer on a laptop screen can be difficult.

6. To experiment with pointer speeds, drag the Pointer Speed slider toward Slow or Fast, click the Apply button, and roll the mouse gingerly across the top of your desk. Repeat this experiment until you find the right pointer speed.

7. To see whether pointer trails are for you and how thick a trail the pointer should leave, click the Show Pointer Trails check box, drag the slider toward Short or Long, and roll the mouse across the top of your desk. What do you think? Keep experimenting.

8. Click OK to close the Mouse Properties dialog box.

Changing the Pointer's Size and Shape

As you must have noticed by now, Windows 98 throws different pointers on the screen, depending on what you want to do or the computer says you must wait to do. When the computer is busy, you see an hourglass. When you move the pointer over text in a word processing file, you see the text select pointer, a vertical stripe that looks like a large letter "I." You can change the size and look of pointers by following these steps:

1. Click the Start button and choose Settings | Control Panel.
2. Double-click the Mouse icon in the Control Panel.
3. In the Mouse Properties dialog box, click the Pointers tab.
4. Open the Scheme drop-down menu and choose an option. The pointer to the right of the Scheme menu and the other pointers in the Pointers tab change shape so you can see what your choice means in real terms.
5. Experiment until you find a suitable pointer scheme and then click OK or Cancel.

Mouse

For Lefties: Swapping the Mouse Buttons

In our democratic society, dedicated to total equality, where every man and woman is the same before the law, not being able to swap the functions of the left and right mouse buttons would be criminal. Lefties, like their right-handed brethren, must be able to click and drag with the index finger and display a shortcut menu by clicking with the middle finger. To strengthen our democracy, the Buttons tab of the Mouse Properties dialog box offers an option button called Left-Handed that left-handers may click to achieve equality with their right-handed confrères. To afford yourself of this democratic luxury, visit the Buttons tab of the Mouse Properties dialog box and click the Left-Handed option button.

Supercharging the Keyboard

DEFINITION

Cursor:
The vertical line that marks the place onscreen where text appears when you start typing.

Fast typists and people with sensitive fingertips can supercharge their keyboards. Well, "supercharge" is an exaggeration, but you can decide for yourself how sticky to make the keys and even tell Windows 98 how fast to make the cursor blink. Figure 5.2 shows how to tell your keyboard exactly how to behave and the cursor how often to blink.

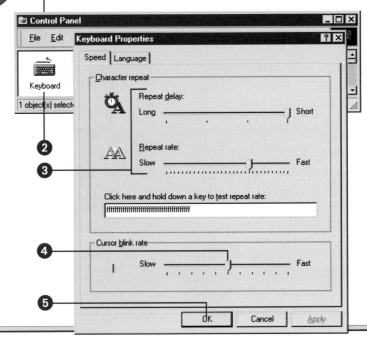

1 Click the Start button and choose Settings | Control Panel.

2 Double-click the Keyboard icon in the Control Panel. You see the Keyboard Properties dialog box.

3 Play with the Repeat Delay and Repeat Rate settings until you find a character repeat rate that is comfortable. You can test your settings by typing in the text box.

4 Under Cursor Blink Rate, watch the sample cursor and drag the slider between Slow and Fast until you find a comfortable rate. Eight out of ten doctors recommend a cursor blink rate that matches your heartbeat.

5 Click OK to close the dialog box.

Figure 5.2: Telling Windows how sticky to make the keys and how often to make the cursor blink.

Starting Your Favorite Program When You Start Windows

Everybody has a favorite program that they use time and time again. Instead of going to the trouble of starting your favorite program, you can kill two birds with one stone and make your favorite program start automatically when you turn on the computer. To accomplish this little magic trick, you have to know where on your computer the program file (the .exe file) of the program you want to start automatically is located. (Most .exe files are located in the C:\Program Files folder and its subfolders.)

SHORTCUT The fastest way to tell Windows to start a program automatically is to simply create a shortcut icon for the program and place it in the C:\Windows\Start Menu\Programs\StartUp folder.

Follow these steps to put a shortcut to your favorite program in the C:\Windows\Start Menu\Programs\StartUp folder so that Windows opens your favorite program when you start the computer:

1. Either click the Start button and choose Settings | Taskbar & Start Menu or right-click the Taskbar and choose Properties.

2. Click the Start Menu Programs tab in the Taskbar Properties dialog box.

3. Click the Add button. You see the Create Shortcut dialog box. In this dialog box, you create a shortcut to the .exe file of the program you want to start automatically.

4. Click the Browse button and, in the Browse dialog box, find and select the .exe file. To find the file, double-click folder icons, use the Look In drop-down menu, and click the Up One Level button as necessary. "Decide How to List Files in Folders and Dialog Boxes" in Chapter 2 explains what file extensions such as .exe are and how to list them in dialog boxes, Windows Explorer, and My Computer. Click the Details button in the Browse dialog box and look in the Type column for the word "Application" to locate .exe files.

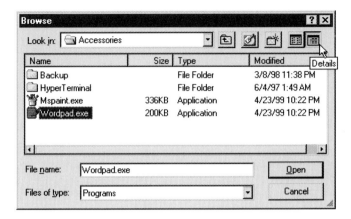

5. Click the Open button after you have selected the .exe file. Back in the Create Shortcut dialog box, the path to the .exe file appears in the Command line box.

6. Click the Next button.

7. In the Select Program Folder dialog box, scroll to the bottom of the folder list and select StartUp. In this step, you are putting the shortcut you created in the StartUp folder.

8. Click the Next button. You see the misnamed Select a Title for the Program dialog box.

9. Enter a name for your shortcut icon—probably the program's name. If you decide later on to remove this shortcut icon from the StartUp folder so the program doesn't open automatically, you will do so by deleting the shortcut icon you name in this step.

10. Click the Finish button.

11. Click OK in the Taskbar Properties dialog box.

Suppose you change your mind and decide not to start the program automatically. To keep that from happening, do either of the following:

• Open the C:\Windows\Start Menu\Programs\StartUp folder in Windows Explorer or My Computer and delete the shortcut icon you created (right-click the icon and choose Delete from the shortcut menu).

- Revisit the Start Menu Programs tab in the Taskbar Properties dialog box, click the Remove button, open the StartUp folder in the dialog box that appears, select the shortcut icon you created, and click the Remove button.

EXPERT ADVICE

To tell Windows 98 not to start programs automatically when you start your computer, hold down the SHIFT key while Windows starts. With too many program shortcuts in the StartUp folder, a computer can take a long time to get going, but holding down the SHIFT key is a good way to get going in a hurry.

Telling Windows Which Program Opens a File

Suppose, in Windows Explorer or My Computer, you double-click a file to open it but it opens the wrong program. Perhaps the wrong graphics program appears when you try to open a file and you want the file to open in a better, newer graphics program. You can tell Windows 98 which program you want a certain kind of file to open in by default.

Windows keeps track of which file types work with which programs in a thing called the *Registry.* When you install a new program, information about the file types that the program works with is added to the Registry. The Registry tells Windows 98 which program opens which file type automatically. In the instructions that follow, you alter the Registry by giving new program-file assignments, but that doesn't mean you can't try to open any file whatsoever with the program of your choice. All you are dealing with here is the default mechanism for opening files.

Follow these steps to tell Windows 98 which program to use to automatically open files of a certain type:

1. Click the Start button and choose Settings | Folder Options.

2. In the Folder Options dialog box, click the File Types tab. You see a list of Registered File Types, as shown in Figure 5.3. Windows recognizes all the files on the list. Windows has preconceived ideas about which program to automatically open these files in.

DEFINITION

Registry: An all-important file in which Windows keeps information about computer programs and their settings, including which programs open which files automatically.

4. Scroll down the list and select the type of file you want to reassign. In the bottom half of the dialog box, next to the words "Opens With," you can see which program automatically opens the file you chose. When you have finished reassigning the file, a new program name will appear beside the words "Opens With."

5. Click the Edit button. You see the Edit File Type dialog box shown on the left side of Figure 5.4.

6. In the Actions box, click the word "open," and then click the Edit button (you will find it below the Actions box, next to the New button). You see the Editing Action for Type dialog box shown in the middle of Figure 5.4.

7. Click the Browse button. You see the Open With dialog box shown on the right side of Figure 5.4.

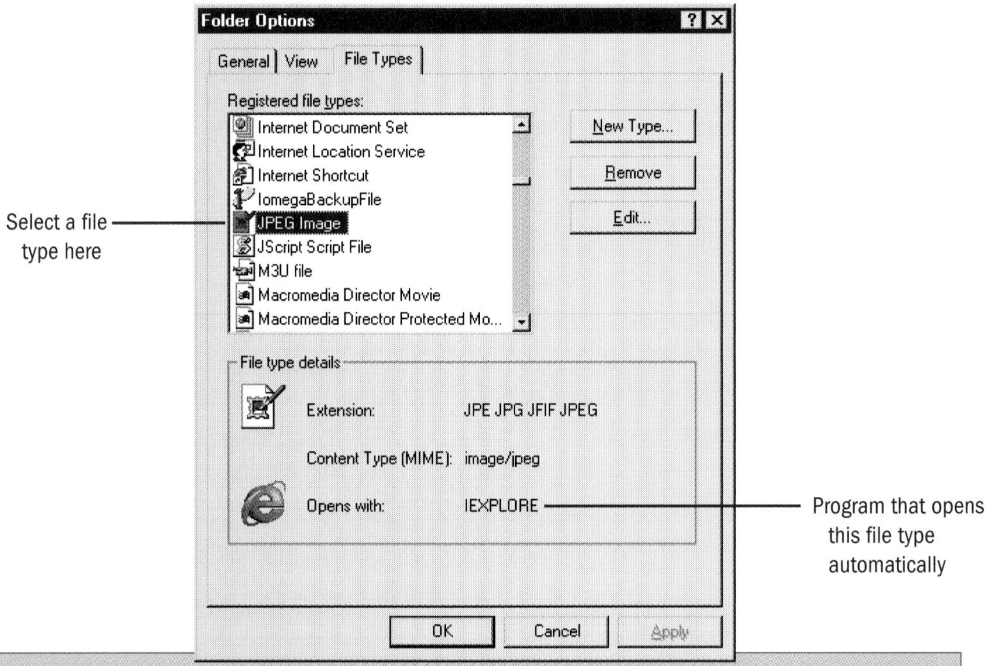

Select a file type here

Program that opens this file type automatically

Figure 5.3: On the File Types tab, you can see the file types that Windows 98 recognizes and the program that opens files of each type by default.

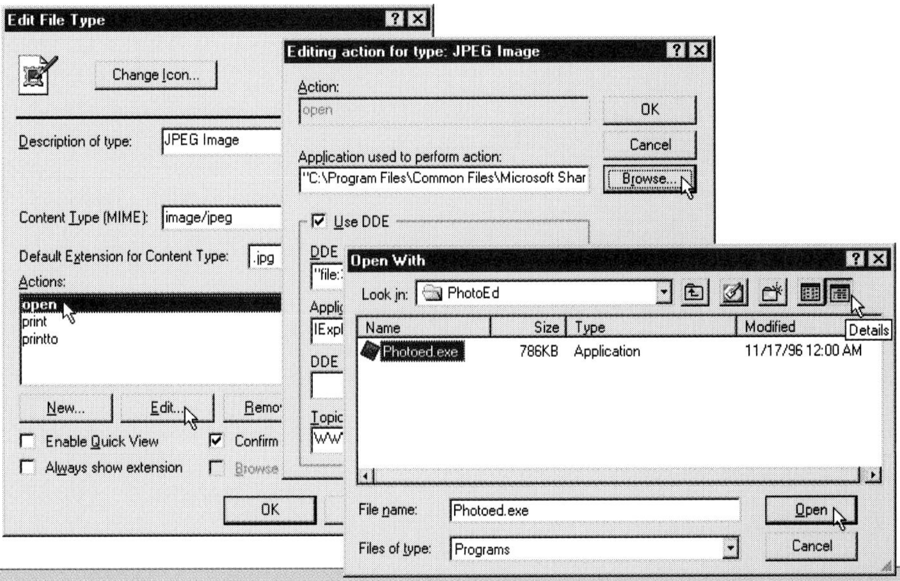

Figure 5.4: Assigning a file type to a different program.

Your next step is to find and select the program file (the .exe file) of the program with which you want to open files of the type in question. Try clicking the Details button and looking for the word "Application" in the Type column as you look for the .exe file.

8. Find and click the .exe file, and then click the Open button. You return to the Editing Action for Type dialog box, where the path to the .exe file you chose appears in the Application Used to Perform Action box.

9. Click OK to return to the Edit File Type dialog box. (While you're there, you might as well click the Enable Quick View check box so you can preview files of this type with Quick View.)

10. Click Close to return to the Folder Options dialog box (see Figure 5.3). The program you chose in step 8 appears beside the words "Open With" in the bottom of the dialog box.

11. Click the Close button.

TIP

Finding .exe files in the tiny Open With dialog box can be a chore. To make it a little easier, open Windows Explorer and see if you can locate the .exe file there. Most program files are located in the C:\Program Files folder and its subfolders. To help the search, switch to Details view and look for the word "Application" in the Type column.

If I were you, I would open My Computer or Windows Explorer, find a file of the type you expect to open automatically with your new program, and double-click it to make sure Windows 98 opens the file with the right program.

Customizing the Windows 98 Menu System

The Windows menus—the Start menu, Programs menu, and the submenus on the Programs menu—can get awfully crowded. Sometimes finding the name of a program you want to open is difficult. And sometimes the name of a program you want to open doesn't appear on any menu.

To make it easier for you to select programs on the Windows menus, this section explains how to remove a program name from a menu, add a program name to a menu, create your own submenu, and move a program name or submenu from one menu to another. Windows offers special commands for doing these chores, and you can also move and remove program names in Windows Explorer if you are adept with that program. Read on.

The Fast Way to Move and Remove Program Names and Submenus

In Chapter 2 "Create the Shortcut Icons You Need" explains how shortcuts work.

Most names on the Windows menus are really shortcuts icons. When you click a program name on a menu, you activate a shortcut to the program that you want to open. Windows maintains the shortcuts in special folders in the C:\Windows\Start Menu folder and its subfolders. By moving a program's shortcut icon to a different folder or subfolder, you can also move its name to a different menu. By deleting a program's shortcut icon in a folder, you can remove its name from a menu.

Figure 5.5 shows the Programs menu and the contents of the C:\Windows\Start Menu\Programs folder (in My Computer). Do you notice the similarities between the names on the Programs menu and the names of the shortcut icons in the Programs folder? If you look closely at the figure, you can see that Programs menu selections are identical to the shortcut icons in the folder.

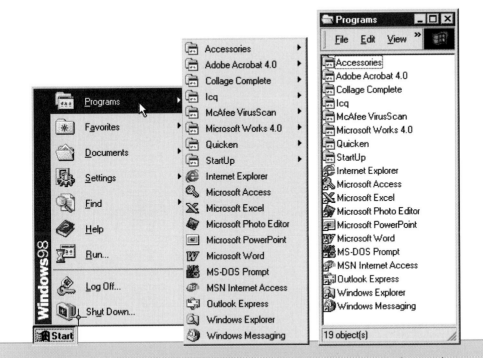

Figure 5.5: You can decide where or whether program names appear on the Windows menus (left) by moving and removing program shortcut icons in C:\Windows\Start Menu and its subfolders (right).

As long as you know your way around the C:\Windows\Start Menu subfolders and you are comfortable moving and deleting shortcut icons in Windows Explorer or My Computer, you've got it made. You can simply open Windows Explorer or My Computer to C:\Windows\Start Menu or one of its subfolders and do the following:

- **Move or Copy a Program's Name to a Different Menu**   Drag the program's shortcut icon to a different folder. For example, to move the CD Player from the Programs | Accessories | Entertainment menu to the Programs menu, move the CD Player shortcut icon from the C:\Windows\Start Menu\Programs\Accessories\Entertainment folder to the C:\Windows\Start Menu\Programs folder.

- **Move a Submenu to a New Location**   Drag a folder into another folder. For example, to move the Accessories submenu

TIP

As you fool with the menus and program names, leave Windows Explorer open on the right side of the screen. After you move a program's name, click the Start button and see if you can find it on the menus. If you can't find it or you moved it to the wrong location, choose Edit | Undo Move in Windows Explorer and start all over.

from the Programs menu to the Start menu, drag the Accessories folder into the Start Menu folder.

• **Remove a Program's Name from a Menu**   Right-click the program's shortcut icon and choose Delete.

Removing a Program Name from a Menu

Removing a program name from a menu in no way removes the program from your computer. The program is removed in name only. Figure 5.6 shows how to remove a program name from a menu, either because you removed the program itself or you intend to open the program with a shortcut icon.

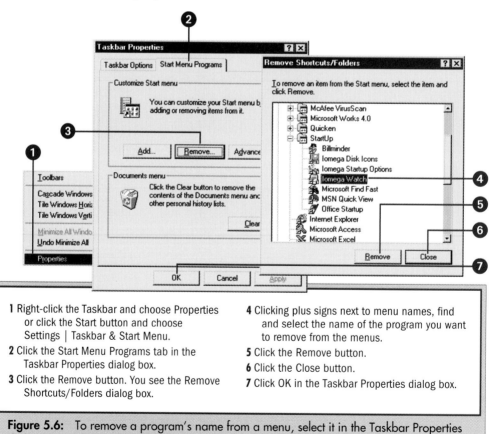

1 Right-click the Taskbar and choose Properties or click the Start button and choose Settings | Taskbar & Start Menu.

2 Click the Start Menu Programs tab in the Taskbar Properties dialog box.

3 Click the Remove button. You see the Remove Shortcuts/Folders dialog box.

4 Clicking plus signs next to menu names, find and select the name of the program you want to remove from the menus.

5 Click the Remove button.

6 Click the Close button.

7 Click OK in the Taskbar Properties dialog box.

Figure 5.6:   To remove a program's name from a menu, select it in the Taskbar Properties dialog box and click Remove.

Moving a Program Name or Submenu to a Different Menu

When you attempt to move a program name or submenu to a different menu, Windows 98 opens Windows Explorer to help you along. Guess what? Moving a program name or submenu requires the techniques described earlier in "The Fast Way to Move and Remove Program Names and Submenus." Follow these steps:

1. Click the Start button and choose Settings | Taskbar & Start Menu or right-click the Taskbar and choose Properties.

2. Click the Start Menu Programs tab in the Taskbar Properties dialog box.

3. Click the Advanced button. There it is—Windows Explorer open to the Start Menu folder.

Turn back a few pages to learn how to move program names and submenus in Windows Explorer. Be sure to click the Start button and make sure that you moved the program name or submenu to the right place. If you didn't, choose Edit | Undo Move in Windows Explorer and try again.

Adding a Program Name to a Menu

Sometimes you install a new program and shortly find out that the program's name isn't on a menu. You can fix that problem as long as you know where on the hard disk to find the program file (the .exe file) of the program whose name you want to add to a menu. Follow these steps to add a program name to one of the Windows 98 menus:

1. Right-click the Taskbar and choose Properties from the shortcut menu.

2. Click the Start Menu Programs tab in the Taskbar Properties dialog box.

3. Click the Add button. You see the Create Shortcut dialog box. In this dialog box, you will create a shortcut to the program whose name you want to put on a menu.

TIP

To quickly put a program name at the top of the Start menu, find the program's .exe file in Windows Explorer and drag the file onto the Start menu.

4. Click the Browse button.

5. In the Browse dialog box, find and select the .exe file of the program whose name you want to add, and then click the Open button. You return to the Create Shortcut dialog box. The path to the program appears in the Command Line text box.

Browse			? X
Look in: 🗁 Accessories			
Name	Size	Type	Modified
🗀 Backup		File Folder	3/8/98 11:38 PM
🗀 HyperTerminal		File Folder	6/4/97 1:49 AM
🖼 Mspaint.exe	336KB	Application	4/23/99 10:22 PM
📝 Wordpad.exe	200KB	Application	4/23/99 10:22 PM
File name:	Mspaint.exe		Open
Files of type:	Programs		Cancel

6. Click the Next button. You see the Select Program Folder dialog box. This is where you tell Windows 98 which menu or submenu to put the program name on. Each folder represents a menu or submenu.

7. Click the folder whose name corresponds to the menu or submenu that you want to put the program name on, and then click Next.

8. Enter a program name. The name you enter will appear on the menu or submenu you chose in step 6.

9. Click the Finish button and click OK in the Taskbar Properties dialog box.

In Chapter 2 "Create the Shortcut Icons You Need" explains shortcut icons. In Chapter 3, "Making Backup Copies to a Floppy Disk" explains how to use the File | Send To menu to quickly back up files.

Adding a Folder Name to the File | Send To Menu

Windows Explorer and My Computer offer the File | Send To command for quickly sending files to different folders on your computer, to a floppy disk, or to different places on the network that your computer is connected to. To begin with, only a few folder names appear on the File | Send To menu, but you can add a folder or two by following these steps:

1. Create a shortcut to the folder in question and give it a descriptive name.

2. In My Computer or Windows Explorer, open the SendTo folder located at C:\Windows\SendTo.

3. Copy or move the shortcut icon into the SendTo folder.

Rearranging Names on Menus

New program names land at the bottom of menus. Suppose you want to move a program name to the top, middle, or bottom of a menu. To move a name up or down the ladder, click and drag it upward or downward. When the black line is where you want the program name to be, release the mouse button. You can't rearrange menu names on the Start menu, by the way.

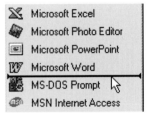

Creating Your Own Submenu

So you want to create a new submenu and put all your favorite programs on it. To do that, follow these steps:

1. Open Windows Explorer and go to the C:\Windows\Start Menu\Programs folder.

2. On the left side of the window, select the Start Menu folder to put your new submenu on the Start menu, or select Programs to put your new submenu on the Programs menu.

3. Choose File | New Folder, enter a name for your new submenu, and press ENTER.

Now all you have to do is put program names on your new submenu. Happy hunting!

Making the Screen Easier to Look At

In Chapter 2 "Make the Desktop Look Just-So" presents other ways to make the screen easier to look at.

Eyes were not meant to stare at computer screens all day, which makes being able to change the screen appearance all the more valuable. Experiment with different screen designs freely and often to find one that suits you. These pages explain how to choose one of the prefabricated Windows schemes for the desktop, choose a wallpaper image for the desktop, and prevent eyestrain.

Choosing a Screen Design

Figure 5.7 explains how to change the look of the Windows desktop. Since this book is for busy people®, I neglect to explain the Item and

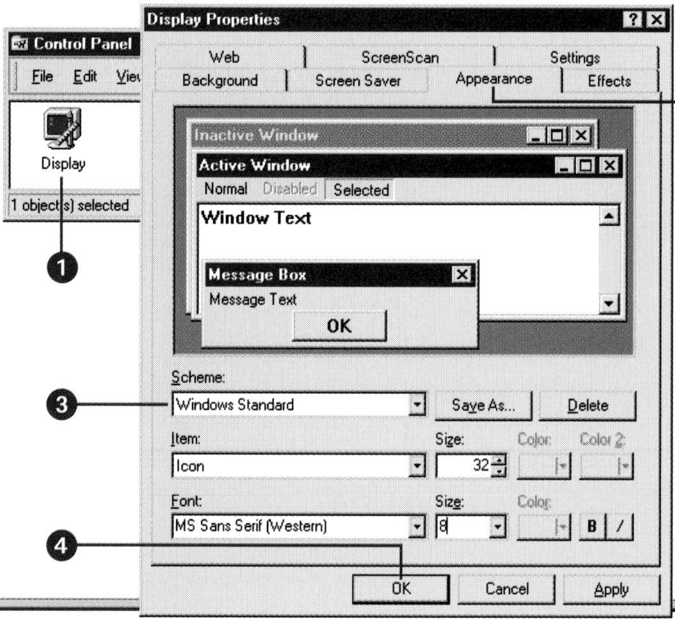

1 Either right-click the desktop and choose Properties or click the Start button, choose Settings | Control Panel, and double-click the Display icon.

2 Click the Appearance tab in the Display Properties dialog box.

3 From the Scheme drop-down menu, choose a screen design that tickles your fancy or is easy on your eyes. At the bottom of the menu are schemes that make text larger and easier to read.

4 Click OK to close the Display Properties dialog box.

Figure 5.7:   For a design scheme that is easy on the eyes, visit the Appearance tab.

Font choices on the Appearance tab (refer to Figure 5.7). One of these days, if you're not busy, if you're desperate for anything to do, revisit the Appearance tab and choose a part of the screen from the Item menu, then choose a size and color for the part of the screen you chose. If the part of the screen is a title bar, menu, or other component with writing on it, you can choose a font size and color for the letters from the Font menu. In the end you will click Cancel to destroy the monster you created or else choose Windows Standard from the Scheme drop-down menu.

Choosing Wallpaper for the Desktop

Another way to decorate the desktop is to right-click an image or photo you like and choose Set As Wallpaper from the shortcut menu. The image appears in the center of your desktop or repeatedly on your desktop, depending on which option you choose on the Background tab of the Display Properties dialog box.

To get to the Background tab, right-click a blank space on the Windows desktop, choose Properties, and click the Background tab. Then open the Display menu and choose Center, Tile, or Stretch. The sample screen in the dialog box shows you what your choice looks like in real terms. To remove the so-called wallpaper from the desktop, choose None from the Wallpaper menu on the Background tab.

Ten Ways to Prevent Eyestrain

People who spend many working hours in front of a computer screen owe it to themselves to look after their health. Computers are dangerous to the lower back, the wrists, and the eyes. In Window 98, you can do a number of things to reduce eyestrain. You can do ten things, in fact. Several of the techniques for reducing eyestrain listed here are described elsewhere in this book, but all are mentioned here so you can pick and choose the techniques that help you.

As nature made you, you were not meant to stare at a computer screen all day. Nature wants you to scour the horizon for edible plants, high-protein animals, and ferocious predators. Fortunately, Windows offers many techniques for reducing eyestrain. Herewith are some of them.

1. Keep the Monitor in the Proper Light.

Glare on a monitor screen causes eyestrain. Keep the monitor out of direct light to reduce glare and use an adjustable light to illuminate whatever it is you are working with besides your computer and monitor. If you are using a laptop, put the monitor in direct light. Laptops are sidelit or backlit, and they work better in full lighting.

2. Play with the Knobs on the Monitor.

Those funny knobs on the monitor can be useful indeed. Twist them, turn them, and experiment until you find a look that is comfortable for your eyes.

3. Opt for a Smaller Screen Resolution.

With a smaller screen resolution, or area, everything looks bigger, although things can get cramped, too. To get a smaller resolution, right-click on the desktop and choose Properties. In the Display Properties dialog box, click the Settings tab. Then drag the Screen area slider to the left, so the setting reads 640 by 480 pixels, and click OK. Try this setting on for size.

4. Put Large Icons on the Desktop and in Folders.

To make the icons on the desktop and in folders larger, right-click on the desktop and choose Properties. In the Display Properties dialog box, click the Effects tab, check the Use Large Icons check box, and click OK.

5. Make the Icons on the Start Menu Larger.

To make the icons on the Start menu larger, right-click the Taskbar and choose Properties. Then, in the Taskbar Properties dialog box, uncheck the Show Small Icons in Start menu check box, and click OK.

6. Use Large Display Fonts.

Large display fonts make menu choices and icon names easier to read. To see if you like them, right-click the desktop and choose Properties to open the Display Properties dialog box, and click the Settings tab. Then click the Advanced button. On the Font Size drop-down menu, choose Large Fonts. Windows says that the large fonts can only take effect after you restart the computer. Restart the computer and see how you like large fonts.

7. Make the Mouse Pointers Larger.

Another way to make your eyes last longer is to make the mouse pointers larger. Click the Start button and choose Settings | Control Panel. Then double-click the Mouse icon, click the Pointers tab in the Mouse Properties dialog box, and choose Windows Standard (extra large) or Windows Standard (large) from the Scheme drop-down menu.

8. For Laptop Users: Use Mouse Pointer Trails.

Pointer trails can help laptop users find the mouse pointer onscreen. To tell Windows to display pointer trails, click the Start button and choose Settings | Control Panel. Then double-click the Mouse icon, click the Motion tab, and check the Show Pointer Trails check box in the Mouse Properties dialog box.

9. Choose a High-Contrast Screen Appearance.

As a drastic measure, choose a high-contrast screen appearance. Right-click the desktop and choose Properties. In the Display Properties dialog box, click the Appearance tab, click the Scheme drop-down menu, and choose one of the High Contrast options.

10. Gaze at the Horizon.

Every so often, leave your desk, step to the window, part the curtains, and stare. Stare at the most faraway point you can see. Stare and dream. Then blink a few times and marvel at how good the world looks when you're not staring at a computer screen.

CHAPTER 6

Traveling the Internet with Internet Explorer

INCLUDES

- Connecting to and disconnecting from the Internet
- Surfing the Internet quickly and productively
- Finding people's phone numbers and addresses on the Internet
- Subscribing to Web sites
- Choosing which Web site you go to first when you connect to the Internet
- Copying photos, pictures, and text from the Web

Internet
Explorer

Start Internet Explorer in a Bunch of Different Ways ➥ pp. 148–149

- Double-click the Internet Explorer icon on the desktop or Quick Launch toolbar.
- Click the Start button, choose Favorites | Links, and choose the name of a Web site.
- Enter or choose a Web address on the Address toolbar and press ENTER.

Status
Disconnect

Disconnect from the Internet ➥ p. 150

- Double-click the Internet icon and choose Disconnect in the Connected To dialog box.
- Right-click the Internet icon and choose Disconnect.

Search

Search for Data on the Internet ➥ pp. 152–157

1. Click the Search button.
2. Enter keywords for the search in the text box in the Search bar, and then click the Search button.

People | Advanced
Name: | Rasheed Wallace
E-mail:

Bigfoot

Find Someone's Address or Phone Number on the Internet ➥ pp. 154–155

1. Click the Start button and choose Find | People.
2. Choose a search service from the Look In list, enter a name, and click the Find Now button.
3. You can also click the Web Site button and search for addresses at a service's Web site.

Go Back to Web Pages You Visited
Before ➥ pp. 154–157

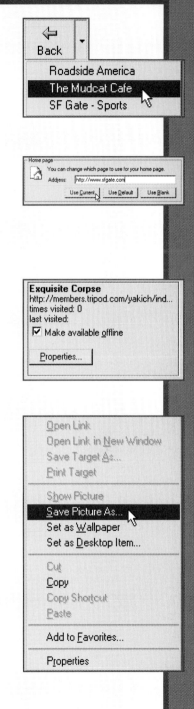

- Click the Back or Forward button—or open the drop-down Back or Forward menu and choose a Web page.
- Click the History button, click a day or week on the Explorer bar, click a Web site name, and then click a page to display it onscreen.

Choose a Home Page—the Page You
Go to First ➥ p. 162

1. Go to the page you want to be your home page and choose Tools | Internet Options.
2. Click the Use Current button.

Download Web Pages Automatically So You Can
View Them Offline ➥ pp. 162–164

1. Choose Favorites | Organize Favorites and double-click the Links folder icon.
2. Click the Web page you want to download automatically and then click the Make Available Offline check box.

Copy a Picture, Web Page, or Text from a
Web Site ➥ pp. 164–165

- **Pictures and Photos**   Right-click the picture and choose Save Picture As. Then locate the folder in which to save the picture and click the Save button in the Save Picture dialog box.
- **Text**   Drag over the text and choose Edit | Copy or press CTRL-C.
- **Web Pages**   Choose File | Save As, find a folder for storing the page in the Save Web Page dialog box, and click the Save button.

Windows 98 comes with a *browser* called Internet Explorer for traveling the Internet. In this chapter, you learn how to explore cyberspace with Internet Explorer. Here you will find instructions for searching the Internet, finding the addresses and phone numbers of people on the Internet, subscribing to Web sites, and scavenging pictures and text from the Web. You also learn how to choose which Web site you visit first when you go on the Internet.

DEFINITION

Browser: A computer program that connects to Web sites and displays Web pages.

The Basics: Connecting and Disconnecting

Near the end of Chapter 4 "Connecting Your Computer to the Internet" explains how to set up a connection between your computer and the ISP or online service that you use.

After you have established the connection between your computer and an Internet service provider (ISP), you are ready to blast off. The next few pages explain how to start Internet Explorer, what to do if the connection doesn't work, and how to shut down Internet Explorer. Better fasten your safety belts.

The Nine Ways to Start Internet Explorer

Figure 6.1 demonstrates the nine different ways to start Internet Explorer and begin traveling the Internet. Don't worry, you won't be quizzed about the nine ways. Some are better than others. It's hard to beat double-clicking the Internet Explorer icon on the desktop, but typing an address into the Address bar is convenient as well if you are a good typist and you know exactly where you want to go. Cruise the Internet a few times and you quickly discover your favorite techniques.

As soon as you attempt a connection, Internet Explorer appears onscreen and you see a password dialog box. Fill it in, if necessary, and click OK. Some chirping sounds come from your telephone and then Internet Explorer opens your home page (refer to "Eight Ways to

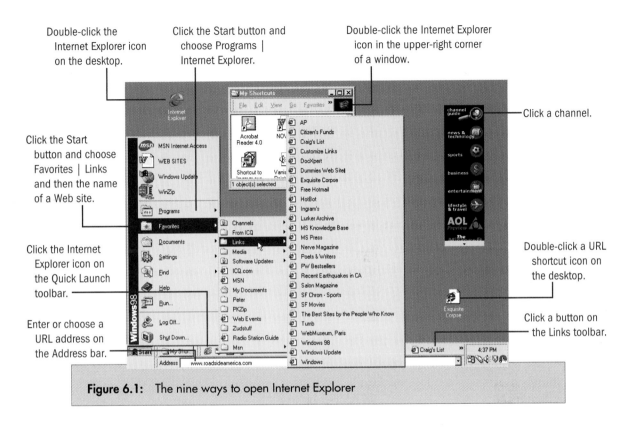

Figure 6.1:   The nine ways to open Internet Explorer

Search the Internet Faster" later in this chapter if you don't like the home page you see). You can tell when you are truly online because the Internet icon—a pair of blinking computer monitors—appears in the lower-right corner of the screen next to the clock.

If You Can't Connect to the Internet...

A failed connection can occur for many reasons. The fault might lie not with you, but elsewhere. There might be too much static on the phone line or a busy signal at the other end. To fix a missed connection from your side, try these techniques:

- See if the modem is connected correctly. Is the phone line plugged into the right place on both the computer and the modem?

- Make sure the address of your home page was entered correctly. Internet Explorer goes straight to the home page when you go online, but if the address is wrong it can't do that. If worse comes to worse, choose Tools | Internet Options and click the Use Default button on the General tab in the Internet Properties dialog box. Your default home page (probably **http://www.msn.com**) is sure to work.

- While the Internet Properties dialog box is open, click the Connections tab and make sure the Always Dial My Default Connection button is selected (if you aren't working on a network).

- I hate to say it, and it would certainly be tragic to have to do the setup work again, but see if you set up the connection between your computer and your Internet service provider or online service incorrectly. (See "Connecting Your Computer to the Internet" in Chapter 4.) If necessary, re-establish the connection.

Disconnecting from the Internet

Disconnecting from the Internet is certainly easier than getting on it. Follow these instructions to disconnect from the Internet:

- Double-click the Internet icon and click the Disconnect button in the Connected To dialog box. Notice that the dialog box also shows how long you've been online and how fast your modem is.

- Right-click the Internet icon in the lower-right corner of the screen and choose Disconnect.

- Choose File | Work Offline.

Surfing the Internet

Surfing the Internet is a skill and entire books have been written on the subject. To keep you from having to slog through one of those long, tedious, boring computer books, the following pages tell it in a hurry. These pages explain how to visit a Web site whose address you know, search the Internet, revisit sites you've been to, and bookmark a site so you can return to it. Also in this section are eight tried-and-true techniques for surfing the Internet quickly.

Visiting a Web Site Whose Address You Know

Every Web site and Web page has an address, also known as a URL, or *uniform resource locator*. While you are online, you can read the addresses of Web pages by glancing at the Address bar in Internet Explorer (if you don't see the Address bar, right-click a toolbar or the menu bar and choose Address Bar). To go to a Web site whose address you know, carefully type the address in the Address bar and press ENTER.

Later in this chapter, "Bookmarking a Site So You Can Go to It Quickly" explains how to bookmark sites so you can visit them later merely by making a menu selection.

Type an address...

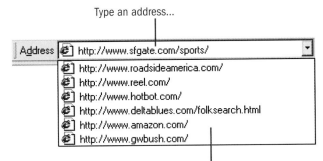

...or choose one from the drop-down menu.

If you've entered the address before, you're in luck. You don't have to enter it again. Click the down arrow on the Address bar and, on the menu of addresses that appears, click the address of the Web page you want to visit, and press ENTER.

Clicking Hyperlinks to Go Here and There

After you arrive at a Web site, you are sure to find many hyperlinks. Hyperlinks come in the form of text, pictures, and images. You can tell when your pointer is over a hyperlink because the pointer turns

Muffler Men Home Page.

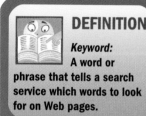

DEFINITION

Hyperlink:
An electronic shortcut between two Web pages or Web sites. By clicking a hyperlink, you can go directly to another location on the Web.

into a gloved hand. What's more, a brief description of where the link will take you appears onscreen as well.

Probably the most adventurous way to surf the Internet is to click hyperlinks and see where your search takes you. Fans of the World Wide Web are fond of saying that the Web is a three-dimensional world that brings together like-minded people from different places and different times. Click a few hyperlinks, see where your search leads, and decide for yourself whether the Web is a three-dimensional world or a mishmash of infomercials and unsound opinions. You can always backtrack by clicking the Back button, as "Revisiting Web Sites You've Been to Before" explains later in this chapter.

Searching for Information on the Internet

To look for information on the Internet, you choose a search service, enter criteria for the search, click the Search button, note how many Web pages your search yielded, look through the list of Web pages, click a page that you want to visit, and see the page onscreen. Sounds simple enough, but searching the Internet can be frustrating because the Internet is crowded with all sorts of junk. Follow these steps to search the Web with Internet Explorer's search commands:

1. Click the Search button. The Explorer bar appears on the left side of the screen, as shown in Figure 6.2. At the top of the Explorer bar are four option buttons for telling Internet Explorer what to search for. Make sure Find a Web Page is selected. You can click and drag the border between the Explorer bar and the Internet Explorer window to make the Explorer bar wider or narrower.

2. In the Find a Page Containing box, enter a keyword or keywords for the search.

3. Click the Search button (or the Find It button or whatever its called) on the Explorer bar. In a moment or two, a list of Web site names appears below the button. The order in which sites are listed depends on "keyword density," the number of times a keyword appears on the site and the keywords' proximity to the start of the page.

DEFINITION

Keyword:
A word or phrase that tells a search service which words to look for on Web pages.

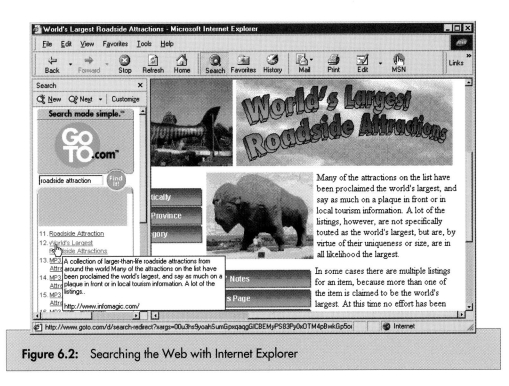

Figure 6.2:   Searching the Web with Internet Explorer

4. Scroll down the list and click on a Web page that interests you (at the bottom of the list is a button you can click to see the next set of Web pages). By placing the pointer over a Web site name, you can read a brief description of the Web site. In a moment, the page you clicked appears on the right side of the screen if indeed it is there and Internet Explorer can find and display it.

EXPERT ADVICE

The secret to finding what you are looking for on the Internet is to enter the right keyword or combination of keywords for the search. The more carefully you choose keywords, the more fruitful your search will be. Choose keywords that pinpoint what you are looking for. For example, entering *giants* finds all Web pages with that word on it—a lot of Web pages, no doubt. But entering *giants san francisco baseball schedule* yields only Web pages with all five of those keywords—considerably fewer Web pages than a search for *giants* yields.

TIP

To find what you are looking for on a long Web page, choose Edit | Find or press CTRL-F, enter a word or two in the Find dialog box, and click Find Next. The page scrolls to the word or words you entered.

5. Click the Search button to hide the Explorer bar and be able to read the Web page better. To see the Explorer bar again, click the Search button one more time.

6. To visit a different Web page, click its name on the list in the Explorer bar.

You can go back to the Explorer bar and click another Web page to visit it. For that matter, you can click the down arrow beside the Next button and choose a different search service. Here's another bit of advice: Try pressing F11 to shrink the Internet Explorer buttons and get a better look at the Web page. Press F11 a second time to get the buttons back.

Finding People's E-Mail Addresses and Phone Numbers on the Internet

Data isn't the only thing you can search for on the Internet. You can also look for lost loves, long-lost friends, schoolyard bullies from days gone by, and bass players and drummers from obscure rock and roll bands. Figure 6.3 shows how to search for others' e-mail addresses, street addresses, and phone numbers.

Revisiting Web Sites You've Been to Before

Surfing the Internet is an adventure and many a Web surfer ventures too far and wishes to return to a page that he or she visited before. Fortunately, backtracking is pretty easy. By clicking the Back button

EXPERT ADVICE

You can search with your favorite search service from the Explorer bar. To do so, click the Customize button in the Explorer bar, and, in the Customize Search Settings dialog box, select your favorite service and click the Use One Search Service for All Searches option button. The service you choose will appear automatically in the Explorer bar next time you click the Search button.

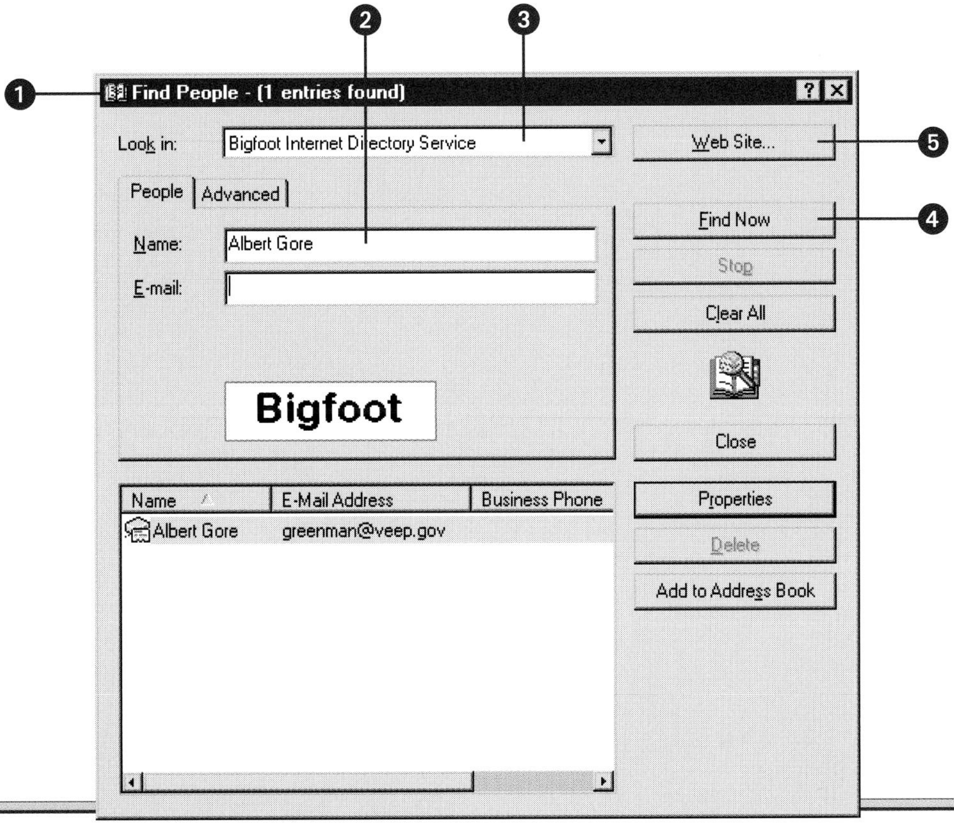

1 While you are connected to the Internet, click the Start button and choose Find | People.
2 Enter a person's name.
3 Choose a search service.

4 Click the Find Now button. A list of e-mail addresses (and sometimes phone numbers as well) appears at the bottom of the dialog box.
5 Click the Web Site button to search for street addresses and phone numbers. You arrive at the search service's Web site.

Figure 6.3: Searching for people's e-mail addresses, phone numbers, and street addresses on the Internet

or its drop-down menu, you can visit the pages you viewed since you started Internet Explorer. You can even view a Web page you visited in the past 20 days by clicking the History button. Following are the numerous ways to revisit sites with Internet Explorer.

BACK AND FORWARD BUTTONS   Click the Back button (or press BACKSPACE) to see the page you last saw; click the Forward button to move ahead to the page from which you just retreated. Next to the Back and Forward buttons are drop-down menus that you can click to leap backward or forward by several Web pages. Don't be shy about using these drop-down menus. All you have to do to leap forward or backward is click the down-arrow and click a Web page name.

HISTORY BUTTON   Internet Explorer is watching you! The program keeps a record of the Web sites and Web pages you visited in the past 20 days. To return to one of those Web pages, you can click the History button and take it from there. Figure 6.4 demonstrates how to backtrack by clicking the History button.

FAVORITES BUTTON   The fastest way to revisit a site is to bookmark it (the subject of the next part of this chapter). To visit a site you bookmarked, do either of the following:

- Click the Favorites button. The Explorer bar opens and you see the contents of the C:\Windows\Favorites folder. Click the Links folder to see sites you bookmarked and then click a name.
- Choose Favorites | Links and click the name of the site you want to visit.

EXPERT ADVICE

Don't want your supervisor to know which Web sites you've been visiting? To remove a Web site from the History list in the Explorer bar, right-click the site and choose Delete. To remove all of the Web sites on the list, choose Tools | Internet Options and click the Clear History button on the General tab of the Internet Options dialog box. You can also tell Internet Explorer how many days' worth of Web sites to stockpile by entering a number in the Days to Keep Pages in History text box.

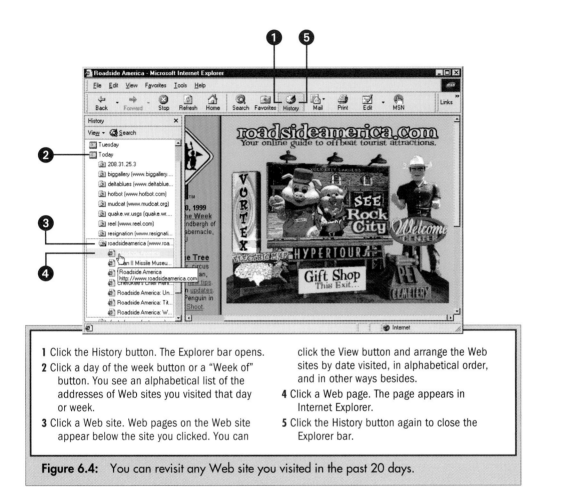

1 Click the History button. The Explorer bar opens.

2 Click a day of the week button or a "Week of" button. You see an alphabetical list of the addresses of Web sites you visited that day or week.

3 Click a Web site. Web pages on the Web site appear below the site you clicked. You can click the View button and arrange the Web sites by date visited, in alphabetical order, and in other ways besides.

4 Click a Web page. The page appears in Internet Explorer.

5 Click the History button again to close the Explorer bar.

Figure 6.4: You can revisit any Web site you visited in the past 20 days.

Bookmarking a Site So You Can Go to It Quickly

When you bookmark a site in Internet Explorer, you put a shortcut to it in the Favorites\Links folder. From there, opening it is easy (as the last paragraph in this chapter makes plain). Don't be shy about bookmarking a site—you can always "unbookmark" it, as I explain shortly. These pages describe how to bookmark sites and manage your bookmarks.

DEFINITION

Bookmark:
To mark a Web site so that you can revisit it quickly later on.

Bookmarking Your Favorite Web Sites

Figure 6.5 shows how to bookmark a site and make visiting it very, very easy. You are hereby encouraged to bookmark a site if you feel the least bit desire to return to it later. Unless you bookmark a site, finding it again can be like finding the proverbial needle in a haystack.

EXPERT ADVICE

Be sure to click the Links folder and place the shortcut to your Web site there. If you forget to do so and put the shortcut in the Favorites folder, your Favorites folder will soon fill up with shortcuts to Web sites. As "Speedy Ways to Open Files" in Chapter 1 explains, the fastest way to get to files you use most often is to place shortcuts to those files in the Favorites folder. But if you crowd the Favorites folder with Web site shortcuts, you'll have trouble finding anything—a Web site or file— in the Favorites folder.

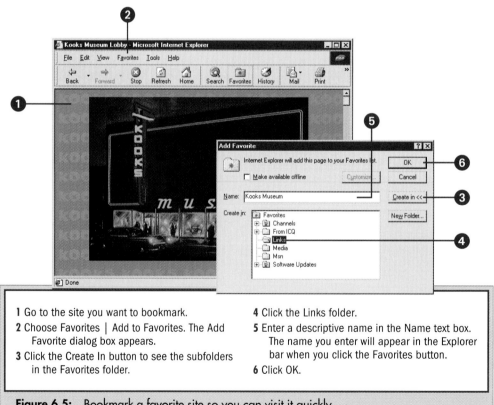

1 Go to the site you want to bookmark.

2 Choose Favorites | Add to Favorites. The Add Favorite dialog box appears.

3 Click the Create In button to see the subfolders in the Favorites folder.

4 Click the Links folder.

5 Enter a descriptive name in the Name text box. The name you enter will appear in the Explorer bar when you click the Favorites button.

6 Click OK.

Figure 6.5: Bookmark a favorite site so you can visit it quickly.

Renaming, Deleting, and Managing Bookmarks

Follow these steps to rename a bookmarked site, "unbookmark" it, or change its position on the menu:

1. Choose Favorites | Organize Favorites. You see the Organize Favorites dialog box.

2. Click the Links folder to see the names of Web sites you have bookmarked.

3. Click a Web site name.

4. Delete, rename, or move the bookmark:

    *   **Delete**   Click the Delete button and then click Yes when you are asked if you really want to delete it.
    *   **Rename**   Click the Rename button and type a new name.
    *   **Move to a Different Folder**   Click the Move to Folder button and select another folder in the Browse for Folder dialog box.
    *   **Move Up or Down in the List**   Drag a Web site name up or down the dialog box to move it up or down on the Explorer bar and Favorites | Links menu.

SHORTCUT

The fast way to delete a bookmark is to right-click it on the Explorer bar and choose Delete.

EXPERT ADVICE

It would be a sad day if your computer crashed and you lost the shortcuts to all the sites you bookmarked. To make a backup copy of your bookmarks, open the C:\Windows\Favorites\Links folder and copy all of the shortcuts in the folder to a floppy disk. If your computer fails, copy the backup shortcuts on the floppy disk to the C:\Windows\Favorites\Links folder.

Eight Ways to Surf the Internet Faster

In some circles, the World Wide Web is known as the "World Wide Wait." If you get impatient when you surf the Internet, try one of these eight techniques for surfing the Internet faster. Some of the techniques are described elsewhere in the book, but all are gathered here because waiting for the Web is most frustrating indeed, and, busy person that you are, I want you to be able to pick and choose quickly among speed techniques.

1. Start the Search from a Service's Home Page.

The easiest way to search the Internet is to take the time to go to the home page of a search service and use the search options that the service provides. Table 6.1 lists the Web addresses of different search services, or search engines as they are sometimes called. The services in the table each provide special commands for searching the Internet. After you have experimented with a few services, you will find one you like—and you will learn to use its search commands well.

2. Learn to Use the Back Button and Forward Button Drop-Down Menus.

Most people know that there is a Back button in Internet Explorer for revisiting pages and a Forward button for returning to pages you retreated from. But many people don't realize that you can click the down arrow beside the Back or Forward button and see a menu with all the pages you visited. Instead of going backward or forward one page at a time, use the Back or Forward drop-down menus to leap several pages ahead or behind.

Search Service	Address
Ask Jeeves	www.askjeeves.com
Excite	www.excite.com
HotBot	www.hotbot.com
Infoseek	www.infoseek.com
Lycos	www.lycos.com
Magellan	www.mckinley.com
Snap!	www.snap.com
WebCrawler	www.webcrawler.com
Yahoo	www.yahoo.com

Table 6.1: Search Services and Their Home Page Addresses

3. Bookmark Pages You Intend to Revisit.

By bookmarking pages and putting them in the Links folder in the Favorites folder, you can get to them quickly. All you have to do is click the Favorites button, click the Links folder icon, and click the page. You can also choose Favorites | Links and click the name of a page. See "Bookmarking a Site So You Can Go to It Quickly " earlier in this chapter.

4. Change Your Home Page.

When you start Internet Explorer and connect to the Internet, you go by default to what Microsoft calls your "home page." You also go there when you click the Home button. And, unless you tinker with the default settings, the home page you go to is none other than Microsoft's. You go to **http://www.msn.com**. Do you really want to go there every time you visit the Internet? Do you want to go to a glittery corporate Web site that takes a long time to load? Aren't you getting enough Microsoft propaganda already?

Instead of Microsoft's home page, choose a home page that you are genuinely interested in and visit often. For that matter, choose a page that loads quickly so you don't have to wait before leaping onto the Internet. To choose a home page of your own, go to the page you want to make your home and choose View | Internet Options. You see the General tab of the Internet Options dialog box. Click the Use Current button. The address of the page you like appears in the Address box. Click OK.

5. Open a Second Window for Surfing.

Here's a little trick that makes surfing the Internet a little faster: Open a second Internet Explorer window. With two windows open, you can surf the Internet in one window and leave the other open to a page you want to stick with. And if you get stuck on a Web page that is taking too long to download, you can simply click the Close button to close the window without closing Internet Explorer altogether.

To open a second window, press CTRL-N or choose File | New | Window.

6. Make Use of the Edit | Find Command on Long Web Pages.

On a Web page with lots of text, finding what you are looking for can be difficult. Rather than strain your eyes, use the Find command. All you have to do is enter the text you're looking for and click the Find Next button. The page scrolls to the text you entered. Choose Edit | Find to activate the Find command.

7. Click the Stop Button Early and Often.

Don't be afraid to click the Stop button. If you click a hyperlink and nothing happens for a moment or two, chances are nothing will happen. Click the Stop button to stop the search and turn it in another direction.

8. Don't Display Fancy Stuff on Web Pages.

A lot of time on the Web is wasted waiting for fancy pictures and animations to arrive on your computer. To spare yourself the wait, you can tell Internet Explorer not to download fancy stuff but instead only download it if you say so. Follow these steps:

1. Choose Tools | Internet Options.
2. Click the Advanced tab in the Internet Options dialog box.
3. Scroll to Multimedia in the list and uncheck Show Pictures, Play Animations, Play Videos, and/or Play Sounds.

You can still see pictures or play animations on Web pages after you have elected not to show them. To do so, right-click the picture or animation icon on the Web page and choose Show Picture on the shortcut menu.

Making Web Pages Available for Offline Viewing

To save a bit of time and keep the telephone lines from being tied up, you can download Web pages from the Internet and view them offline. Despite appearances, a Web page is nothing more than a computer file. After the Web page files have been downloaded to your computer, you can view them at your leisure. You can view them as though you were viewing them on the Internet. Viewing pages offline is a fast way to surf the Internet because you don't have to wait for the pages to download from the Internet—the pages are already downloaded and on your computer. However, downloading the pages can take time, depending on how many graphics, animations, and other fancy gizmos they contain.

In order to download a Web page automatically, you must have bookmarked it. Figure 6.6 shows how to tell Internet Explorer which Web pages you want to download automatically and read while you are not connected to the Internet.

Earlier in this chapter, "Bookmarking Your Favorite Web Sites" explains how to bookmark Web pages.

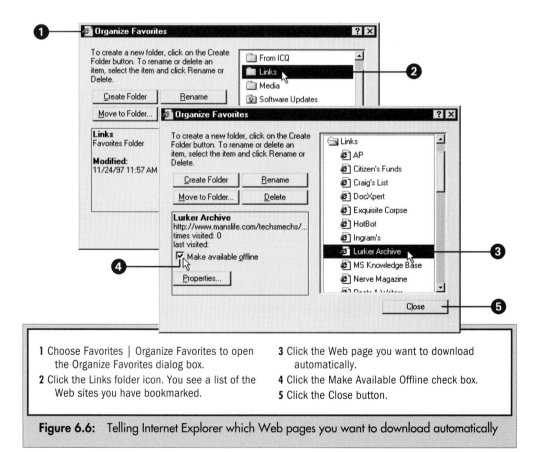

1 Choose Favorites | Organize Favorites to open the Organize Favorites dialog box.
2 Click the Links folder icon. You see a list of the Web sites you have bookmarked.
3 Click the Web page you want to download automatically.
4 Click the Make Available Offline check box.
5 Click the Close button.

Figure 6.6: Telling Internet Explorer which Web pages you want to download automatically

To download the pages you have earmarked for downloading, go online and choose Tools | Synchronize. You see the Items to Synchronize dialog box. Make sure a check mark appears beside each page you want to download, and then click the Synchronize button. The Synchronizing dialog box appears as Web pages are copied to your computer.

After you disconnect from the Internet, choose Favorites | Links and then choose the name of the Web page you downloaded to your computer to view the Web page. Of course, you can also click the Favorites button, click the Links folder in the Explorer bar, and click the name of the Web page.

EXPERT ADVICE

If you prefer to view Web pages while you are offline, you likely need more room for storing download pages. To get more room, choose Tools | Internet Options and then click the Settings button on the General tab of the Internet Options dialog box. In the Settings dialog box, drag the Amount of Disk Space to Use slider to the right to get more space for Web pages.

Copying Pictures, Photos, and Text from the Internet

To the delight of copyright lawyers and the displeasure of photographers and artists, you can copy any picture on the Internet.

You can also copy text and entire Web pages. Follow these steps to copy an image, photograph, or picture:

1. Wait until the image, picture, or photograph has downloaded to your computer.

2. Right-click the image and choose Save Picture As.

3. Use the tools in the Save Picture dialog box—the drop-down Save In menu and Up One Level button—to locate the folder in which you want to save the image.

4. Double-click the folder so its name appears in the Save In box.

5. Enter a descriptive name for the image in the File Name text box if you want to.

6. Click the Save button.

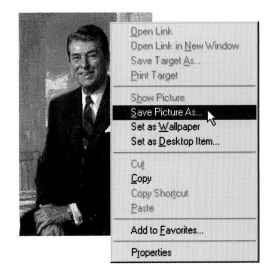

CAUTION

Copying text or art that you didn't write or create yourself is okay, but using the material in your own work without obtaining the permission of the creator or owner is considered a violation of the copyright laws.

To copy text from a Web page, simply drag the mouse pointer over it (or press CTRL-A to copy the entire page). When the text is highlighted, right-click it and choose Copy from the shortcut menu. The text is copied to the Clipboard. Click where you want to paste it, and choose File | Paste or click the Paste button.

To copy an entire Web page, choose File | Save As. In the Save Web Page dialog box, locate the folder where you want to save the Web page, and click the Save button.

To print an entire Web page, click the Print button. That's all there is to it. If you want to be choosy about how the page is printed, choose File | Print and choose from the options in the Print dialog box. Go this route, for example, if you want to print more than one copy or print the pages that are linked to the page you want to print.

Print

CHAPTER 7

Communicating with the Outside World

INCLUDES

- Storing the addresses of clients and friends in the Address Book
- Sending and receiving e-mail messages and files
- Visiting, posting messages to, and subscribing to newsgroups
- Printing files and canceling print jobs

Look Up a Name and Address in the Address Book ➡ pp. 172–173

1. In Outlook Express, click the Addresses button.
2. Scroll to find a name on the list, and click the name to see a box with addressee information.

Send an E-Mail Message ➡ pp. 174–176

1. Click the New Mail button.
2. Fill in the New Message window and click the Send button.

Send a File with an E-Mail Message ➡ p. 176

1. Click the Attach button.
2. In the Insert Attachment dialog box, locate and select the file or files you want to send. To select more than one file, hold down the CTRL key and click.

Read E-Mail Messages That Were Sent to You ➡ pp. 177–179

1. Click the Inbox folder to open the Inbox window.
2. Click the message you want to read in the top of the window. The message text appears in the bottom of the Inbox window.

Explore the Newsgroups to Find One of Interest ➡ pp. 181–183

1. Click the folder icon of the news server you want to explore.
2. Click the Newsgroups button.
3. Type a search word in the Display Newsgroups Which Contain text box.
4. Click a newsgroup name and click the Go To button.

Subscribe to a Newsgroup ➡ pp. 183–184

- Click a newsgroup in the Newsgroup Subscriptions dialog box and then click the Subscribe button.
- Right-click a newsgroup's name in the Outlook bar and choose Subscribe on the shortcut menu.

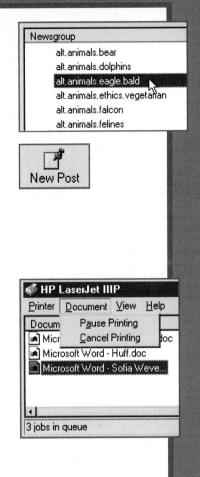

Post a Message on a Newsgroup ➡ pp. 184–186

- Click the message that needs a reply, if you want to reply to a message.
- Click the New Post button to submit a message on a new topic, the Reply Group button to reply to someone else's message, or the Reply button to reply directly to the author of a message.

Keep a File from Being Printed ➡ pp. 188–189

1. Double-click the Printer icon in the lower-right corner of the screen.
2. In the Printer window, either choose Printer | Purge Print Documents to keep all files from printing, or click a file on the list and choose Document | Cancel Printing to keep a single file from printing.

This chapter explains how to communicate with the rest of the world from your computer. You've been hibernating too long. Everyone is asking about you. The world wants to know where you've been, what your opinions are, and how long you propose to stay in hiding. In this chapter you learn how to bust out of your cyber-cocoon and tell the world what's what.

Windows 98 includes a program called Outlook Express for sending e-mail and for visiting newsgroups and posting messages to newsgroups on the Internet. This chapter explains Outlook Express. It also spells out how to print files. You also learn how to keep the addresses of friends, co-workers, and clients in the Windows Address Book where you can get to them in a hurry.

Outlook Express: Sending and Receiving E-Mail

In Chapter 4, "Connecting Your Computer to the Internet" explains how to establish a connection between your computer and the Internet.

As long as you have a modem and an Internet connection, you can send and receive e-mail messages. *E-mail*, or *electronic mail*, is the computer equivalent of letters sent through the post. It goes without saying, but e-mail messages reach their recipients faster than letters and postcards (people who prefer e-mail to conventional mail sometimes call conventional mail services "snail mail"). You can even attach files to e-mail messages, as the following pages demonstrate. Sorry, you can't send chocolate by e-mail. Nor can you put a drop of perfume on an e-mail message or enclose a lock of hair.

Read on to find out how to send and receive e-mail, send and receive computer files, and keep addresses in the Address Book. Oh, I almost forgot: To start Outlook Express, double-click the Outlook Express icon on the desktop or the Quick Launch toolbar, or else click the Start button and choose Programs | Outlook Express.

Outlook
Express

Entering Addresses in the Address Book

Rather than enter the e-mail addresses of clients and friends over and over again when you send them e-mail, you can keep addresses in the Address Book. After an address is in the book, all you have to do to address an e-mail message is select a name from a list. Besides e-mail addresses, you can keep street addresses, phone numbers, fax numbers, and other stuff in the Address Book. The Address Book is a good place to store information about clients, co-workers, and friends. Following are instructions for entering a name in the Address Book, looking up a name, and changing the particulars about a person whose name you entered.

SHORTCUT

To very quickly enter the e-mail address of someone who has sent you e-mail, right-click the sender's message in the Inbox and choose Add Sender to Address Book on the shortcut menu.

Entering a Name and Address in the Address Book

Figure 7.1 demonstrates how to enter a person's name, e-mail address, and other pertinent information in the Address Book. Entering a name is pretty simple, except where these tabs in the Properties dialog box are concerned:

- **Choosing How to Display the Entry in the Address Book**   On the Name tab, open the Display drop-down menu and choose how you want the name or business to appear in the Address Book. Names appear last name first, unless you choose a different option from the Display drop-down menu.

- **Recording E-mail Addresses**   Enter the e-mail address in the E-Mail Addresses text box on the Name tab and click the Add button.

- **Noting Why You Entered the Person**   On the Other tab, describe the person and say why you entered him or her in the Address Book. Later, when you remove names from the book, you can go to the Other tab, and find out who the person is and whether he or she needs removing.

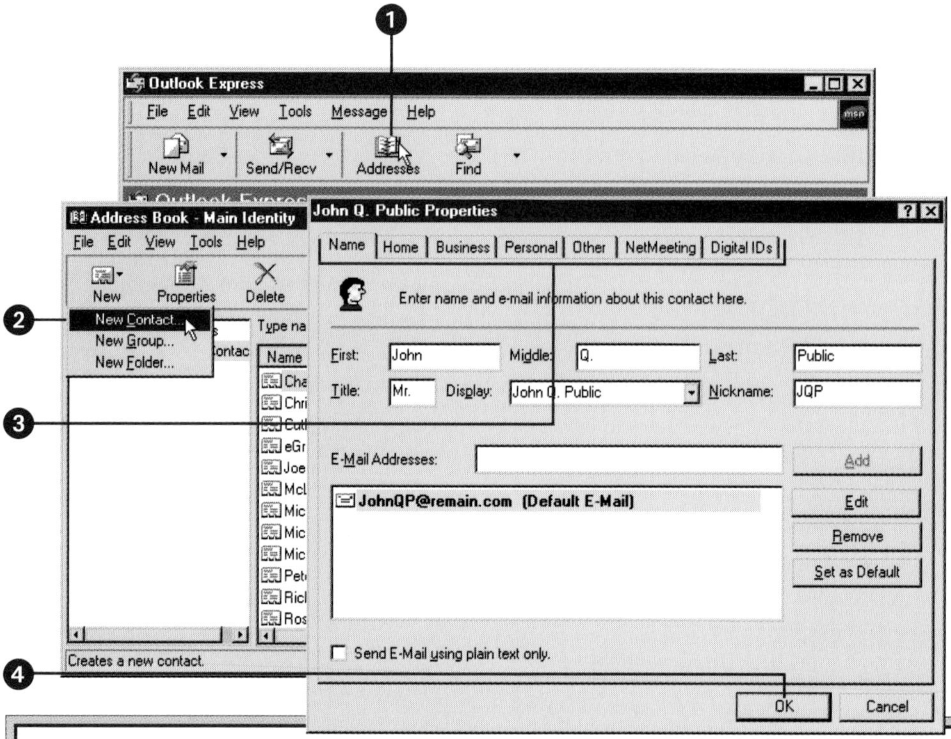

Figure 7.1: Entering a person in the Address Book.

1 Click the Addresses button (if you don't see it, click the Outlook Express folder, the topmost folder on the left side of the screen).

2 In the Address Book window, click the New button and then the New Contact command on the drop-down window.

3 Fill out the different tabs in the Properties dialog box.

4 Click the OK button.

Looking Up Names and Perhaps Changing Addressee Information

Figure 7.2 shows how to look up a client or friend in the Address Book and perhaps change the particulars concerning his or her address, phone number, and whatnot. In an Address Book with many names, try these techniques for finding a name if scrolling doesn't do the job:

- Enter the first couple of letters in the Type Name or Select from List text box. The list scrolls to the name you entered.
- Click the Name button (it's located at the top of the Name column—choose View | Details if you don't see it). Click once to arrange names in alphabetical order from Z to A, again to arrange names by first name, and again to arrange names by first name from Z to A.
- If worse comes to worse, click the Find People button, enter a name, and click the Find Now button in the Find People dialog box.

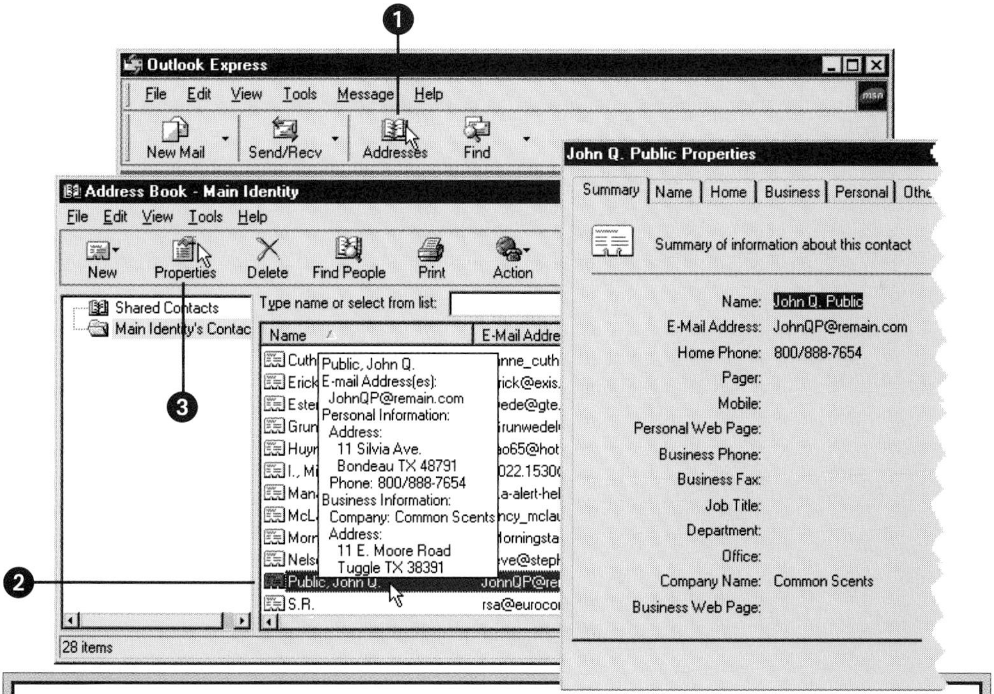

1 Click the Addresses button (click the Outlook Express folder, the topmost folder on the left side of the screen, if you don't see the Address button).

2 Find and click the name you are looking for. A box appears with the addressee's particulars.

3 Click the Properties button or double-click to see the particulars better and perhaps change addressee information.

Figure 7.2: Looking up a name in the Address Book.

EXPERT ADVICE

Losing an Address Book with many important names and addresses would be tragic. To back up the Address Book, go to the C:\Windows\Application Data\Microsoft\Address Book folder and copy the .wab file to a floppy disk. While you're visiting the Address Book folder, create a desktop shortcut for the Address Book if you often look up names there. "Create the Shortcut Icons You Need" in Chapter 2 explains how to create a shortcut.

Composing and Addressing an E-Mail Message

As long as the address of the person to whom you want to send an e-mail message is on file in the Address Book, composing an e-mail message is pretty simple. Follow these steps to do so:

New Mail

1. Click the New Mail button. You see the New Message window.

🗐 AMC Pacer										_ □ ×
File Edit View Insert Format Tools Message Help										

Send | Cut | Copy | Paste | Undo | Check | Spelling | Attach | Priority | Sign | Encrypt

From: | Peter_Weverka@msn.com   (My E-Mailer)
To: | Cuthbertson, Joanne
Cc: | Thomas, Stephane
Subject: | AMC Pacer

Joanne--

Want to buy my AMC Pacer? It's a good car and an American classic.

--Peter

2. On the Subject line, briefly describe your message. When others receive the message, they will see what you type on the Subject line first. Notice how the New Message window changes names after you enter a subject.

3. Type your message in the bottom half of the New Message window. You can use the buttons in the New Message window

to format the message in various ways. For example, you can boldface or italicize parts of the message. And don't forget to press F7 or choose Tools | Spelling to spell-check your message.

4. To tell Outlook Express who gets the message, click the tiny envelope next to the word "To." You see the Select Recipients dialog box with the names of people in the Address Book who have e-mail addresses.

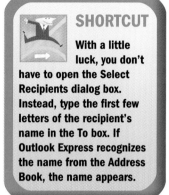

SHORTCUT

With a little luck, you don't have to open the Select Recipients dialog box. Instead, type the first few letters of the recipient's name in the To box. If Outlook Express recognizes the name from the Address Book, the name appears.

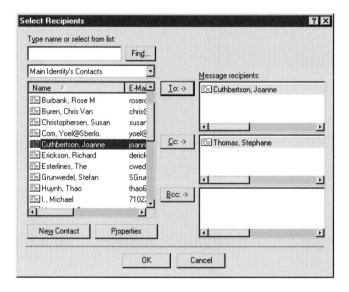

5. Click a name on the list and then click the To button. The name you chose appears in the Message recipients box. You can also send copies and blind copies of messages:

- **Copy (Cc)**   When you send a copy of the message, the person who receives it is told that a copy has been sent and is given the name of the people who received copies. To send a copy, click a Name on the list and then click the Cc button.

- **Blind Copy (Bcc)**   When you send a blind copy, the person who receives the message is *not* told that a copy was sent to a third party. To send a blind copy, click the name and then click the Bcc button.

6. Click OK to close the Select Recipients dialog box. The names of people who will receive the message now appear in the New Message window.

7. Click the Send button (or choose File | Send Later).

 Outbox

The message is sent right away if you happen to be connected to the Internet, but if you are not connected, the Connect To dialog box appears. Click Cancel if you want to hold off sending the message. Until you send a message, it is kept in the Outbox. To edit or perhaps delete a message that you haven't sent yet, click the Outbox folder in the Outlook bar on the left side of the screen, select the message, and click Delete to delete it or double-click to read and change it.

Sending a File Along with Your E-Mail Message

Yes, it can be done. You can send files along with e-mail messages. Follow these steps to send a file and an e-mail message at the same time:

1. While the New Message window is open and you are composing a message, either click the Attach button or choose Insert | File Attachment. You see the Insert Attachment dialog box.

2. Locate and select the file or files you want to send. To select more than one file, hold down the CTRL key and click.

3. Click the Attach button. A new text box called Attach appears in the New Message window and you see the names of the file or files you want to send:

Attach: Fig7-02.pcx (74.1 KB)   Fig7-01.pcx (57.8 KB)

TIP

To merely send or receive your mail, click the down arrow beside the Send/Recv button and choose Receive All or Send All.

Sending and Receiving Your E-Mail

Sending and collecting e-mail is kind of confusing, since how the mail is sent and received depends on whether your computer is connected to the Internet and how you give the command to send and receive e-mail:

- **Connected to the Internet**   When you are connected to the
  Internet and you click the Send button to send an e-mail
  message or the Send/Recv button to receive and collect your
  mail, outgoing messages are sent from the Outbox and
  incoming messages arrive in the Inbox.
- **Not Connected to the Internet**   When you are not connected
  to the Internet and you click the Send or Send/Recv button,
  you see the Connect To dialog box so you can connect to the
  Internet and send your messages.

After you are connected, you see a message box like the one shown
here. It shows how many messages are being received. You can click
the Details button to see, on the Tasks tab at the bottom of the
message box, whether e-mail is being successfully sent and received.

If you've received mail, the word "Inbox" next to the Inbox folder
appears in boldface, the number of messages you've received appears in
parentheses beside the Inbox folder, and a tiny image of an envelope
appears in the lower-right corner of the screen next to the clock.

Reading E-Mail Messages and Files

Messages arrive in the Inbox folder. To see the Inbox and read
messages there, click the Inbox folder icon in the Outlook bar. As
shown in Figure 7.3, you can see senders' names, message subjects,
and the date on which messages were received in the top half of the
Inbox window. In the bottom half is the text of the message that has
been selected.

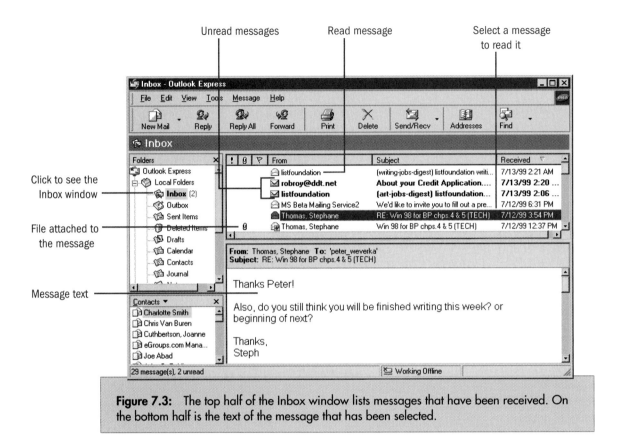

Figure 7.3: The top half of the Inbox window lists messages that have been received. On the bottom half is the text of the message that has been selected.

To get a quick read of what is in the Inbox window, observe the following:

- An open envelope appears next to messages that have been read. Next to unread messages is a closed envelope.
- A paperclip appears next to a message if a file was sent along with it.
- Click the From button or the Received button (located at the top of the From and Received columns) to arrange messages by name or by date.
- Drag the border between the top and bottom half of the window to see more messages or to get more room for displaying the text of a message.

EXPERT ADVICE

To make text easier to read in the Outlook window, try this technique: Choose Tools | Options and click the Read tab in the Options dialog box. Then click the Fonts button, and, in the Fonts dialog box, choose a font you find easy to read. You can also choose a Font Size option to make text larger or smaller.

Reading an E-Mail Message

To read an e-mail message, click it in the top half of the Inbox window (see Figure 7.3) and read it in the bottom half. Use the scroll bar to read a message in its entirety, or, if the message is especially large, double-click the sender's name in the top half of the window. The message appears in a window of its own. Click the Maximize button to make the window fill the screen and so that you can read the message more comfortably.

Opening and Saving Files That Were Sent to You

When a file has been sent along with an e-mail message, a paperclip appears next to the message in the Inbox window. And if you click the message, a somewhat larger paperclip appears on the stripe between the top and bottom half of the Inbox window. Click the large paperclip and you can read the name of the files that were sent to you.

Follow these instructions to open or save files that were sent to you:

- **Opening a File** Click the paperclip and then click the name of the file. The file opens onscreen. Choose File | Save As to save the file in a folder of your choice.

- **Saving a File** Click the paperclip and then click the File Attachments command. You see the Save Attachments dialog box. Click the Browse button, find and select the folder where you want to save the file, and click OK. Then click the Save button in the Save Attachments dialog box.

SHORTCUT

To find out what is in a file without having to open it, double-click the message in the top of the Inbox window. In the message window, right-click the filename and choose Quick View.

Replying to and Forwarding E-Mail Messages

Suppose you receive a message that deserves a reply. Rather than go to the trouble of addressing a reply, you can click the Reply button and simply enter your message. Outlook Express also offers a Reply All button for addressing messages to all parties who received copies of the original message and a Forward button for forwarding a message to a third party.

Follow these steps to reply to or forward a message:

1. Starting in the Inbox window, select the message you want to reply to or forward. The message appears in its own window.

2. Click the Reply, Reply All, or Forward button:

- **Reply** Opens the New Message window with the sender's name already entered in the To box and the original message in the text box below. Write a reply and click the Send button.

- **Reply All** Opens the New Message window with the names of all parties who received the message in the To and Cc boxes. Type your reply and click the Send button.

- **Forward** Opens the New Message window with the text of the original message. Click the small envelope next to the To button to open the Select Recipients dialog box and choose the names of the parties to whom the message will be forwarded. Click OK, and then add a word or two to the original message and click the Send button.

Storing and Managing E-Mail Messages

When you click the Delete button to delete a message in the Inbox folder, the message doesn't disappear forever. It lands in the Deleted Items folder. Likewise, copies of the messages you send are placed in the Sent Items folder. Being able to reread a message you sent or recover a message you deleted is nice, of course. To review a sent or deleted message, click the Sent Items or Deleted Items folder in the Outlook bar, and then find and select the message.

However, the Deleted Items and Sent Items folders soon get crowded with useless e-mail messages. To get rid of these messages, open the Sent Items or Deleted Items folder, and hold down the CTRL key as you click the messages you want to delete. Then click the Delete button and click Yes when Outlook Express asks if you really want to delete the messages.

SHORTCUT

To erase all the messages in the Deleted Items folder, right-click the folder and choose Empty 'Deleted Items' Folder on the shortcut menu.

Outlook Express: Exploring Newsgroups

Besides being an e-mail program, Outlook Express doubles as a *newsreader,* a computer program for reading e-mail messages on and submitting e-mail messages to newsgroups. Newsgroups come and go, but they number in the tens of thousands. In theory, each newsgroup concerns one topic, but newsgroups are not regulated. No rules pertain. A crackpot can drop a message about any topic whatsoever in a newsgroup and no one can stop him.

DEFINITION

Newsgroup: A collection of messages, or postings, about a certain topic.

CAUTION

A lot objectionable material is found on newsgroups. Newsgroups are not monitored or regulated. Cranks and crackpots like nothing better than posting their messages on newsgroups. If you are easily offended or have a low opinion of others' ability to argue intelligently, be careful which newsgroups you visit.

   To visit a newsgroup, you connect to Usenet, a news server that tracks the names of all newsgroups. Then you visit a newsgroup that interests you and read a few messages. If the newsgroup is one that piques your interest, you can subscribe to it. Subscribing makes it easy to revisit a newsgroup later on. Of course, you can also add your two-cent's worth and post a message of your own on a newsgroup. Better read on.

Finding a Newsgroup that Interests You

Before you can start exploring newsgroups, you have to connect to a news server. The most common news server is netnews, the one provided by Usenet, the primary source for newsgroups. Online services such as America Online offer their own news server as well. You can tell which news servers are available on your computer by scrolling to the bottom of the Outlook bar and glancing at the news server folder names. You will find one folder for each news server that is accessible from your computer.

msnnews.msn.com
netnews.msn.com
news server

   Follow these steps to connect to a news server and find newsgroups that interest you:

1. On the left side of the Outlook Express screen, click the folder icon of the news server whose newsgroups you want to explore.

2. What you do next depends on whether you have subscribed to any newsgroups on the server:

   Newsgroups

   • **Subscriber**   The names of newsgroups you subscribe to appear in the window. Click the Newsgroups button to see the Newsgroup Subscriptions dialog box shown in Figure 7.4.

Enter the name of a
topic of interest

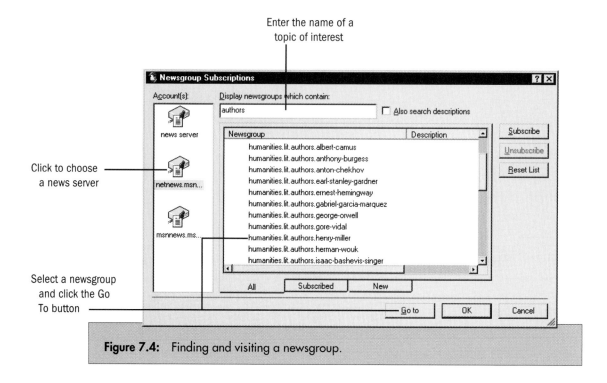

Click to choose
a news server

Select a newsgroup
and click the Go
To button

Figure 7.4: Finding and visiting a newsgroup.

- **Nonsubscriber** If you have not subscribed to any newsgroups or this is the first time you have attempted to connect to the news server, a dialog box asks if you would like to see a list of newsgroups. Click Yes. You see the Newsgroup Subscriptions dialog box shown in Figure 7.4. However, if you have never connected to the server before, you are invited to download the names of newsgroups to your computer. Downloading the names takes a while, but when the names have downloaded you see the Newsgroup Subscriptions dialog box shown in Figure 7.4.

3. In the Display Newsgroups Which Contain text box, type a word that describes a topic that interests you. Newsgroup names with the word you entered appear in the dialog box.

4. Scroll through the list and click a name that seems promising.

5. Click the Go To button. The name of the newsgroup appears in the Outlook bar on the left side of the Outlook Express window.

6. Do one of the following, depending on whether you are currently online:

   - **Not Online**   If you are not online, click the Connect button and, in the Connect To dialog box, click the Connect button there to visit the newsgroup.

   - **Online**   You go straight to the newsgroup. A list of the last 300 messages posted to the newsgroup—messages on the list are called "headers"—is sent to your computer.

7. Click a message to read it (later in this chapter, "Reading and Posting Messages on Newsgroups" explains the details of reading messages).

Visiting, Subscribing to, and Unsubscribing from Newsgroups

Subscribe to a newsgroup if there is even the slightest chance that you want to visit it again. Newsgroups are so numerous, and their names are so cryptic, finding one you've been to before is nearly impossible unless you subscribe. Besides, unsubscribing is easy. To unsubscribe, right-click the newsgroup's name in the Outlook bar and choose Unsubscribe from the shortcut menu.

Follow these instructions to subscribe to a newsgroup after you have found it:

- **In the Newsgroup Subscriptions Dialog Box**   (See Figure 7.4) Click a newsgroup and then click the Subscribe button.

- **In the Outlook Express Window**   Right-click the newsgroup's name in the Outlook bar and choose Subscribe on the shortcut menu.

After you subscribe to a newsgroup, you can download messages that have been posted to the group to your computer. Then you can read the messages at your leisure. Figure 7.5 explains how to download messages from a newsgroup.

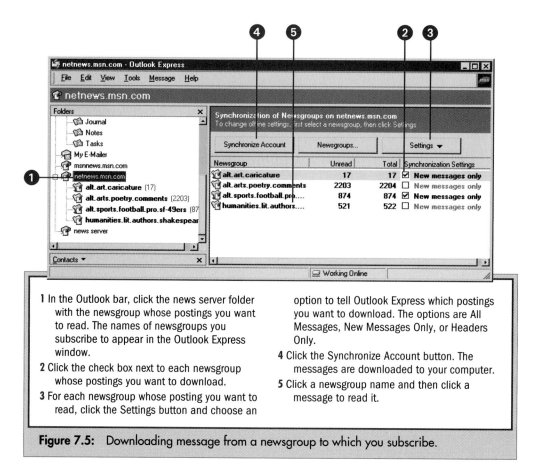

Figure 7.5:   Downloading message from a newsgroup to which you subscribe.

1 In the Outlook bar, click the news server folder with the newsgroup whose postings you want to read. The names of newsgroups you subscribe to appear in the Outlook Express window.

2 Click the check box next to each newsgroup whose postings you want to download.

3 For each newsgroup whose posting you want to read, click the Settings button and choose an option to tell Outlook Express which postings you want to download. The options are All Messages, New Messages Only, or Headers Only.

4 Click the Synchronize Account button. The messages are downloaded to your computer.

5 Click a newsgroup name and then click a message to read it.

Reading and Posting Messages on Newsgroups

After you arrive at a newsgroup or download its messages to your computer, messages appear in the top of the window, as shown in Figure 7.6. To read a message, click it and read the text in the bottom of the window, or, to open the message in its own window and read it more comfortably, double-click the message. A plus sign appears beside messages to which others have responded. To read the responses, click the plus sign (+) next to a message and view the responses.

Outlook Express offers three ways to register your opinion in a newsgroup and either post a message or send a message directly to

Click a message
to read it

Click the plus sign to
read responses to
a message

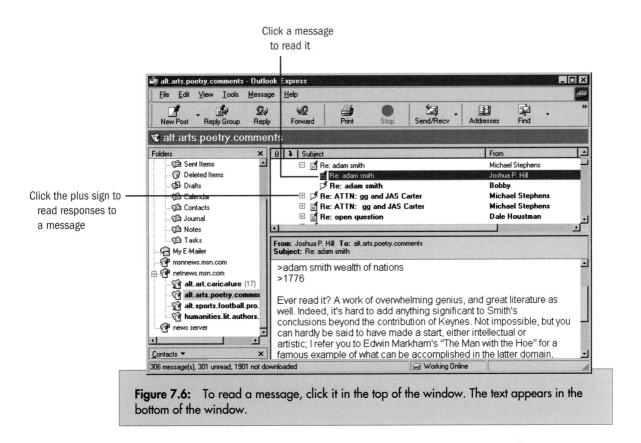

Figure 7.6: To read a message, click it in the top of the window. The text appears in the bottom of the window.

another author. Click the message that deserves a reply and follow
these steps:

- **Post a New Message for the Newsgroup to Ponder**   Click the
  New Post button. You see the New Message window with the
  newsgroup's address where the To box usually is. Enter a subject
  for your post, type the message, and click the Send button.

- **Post a Reply to a Message Someone Else Wrote**   Click the
  message you want to reply to and then click the Reply Group
  button. The New Message window opens with the text of the
  message to which you are replying. A subject is already entered
  in the Subject box. Type your reply and click the Send button.
  Be sure to erase the text in the message to which you are
  replying before you write your reply.

- **Reply Personally to the Author of a Message** Click the Reply button. The New Message window opens with the author's e-mail address in the To box and the text of the original message. Enter your reply and click the Send button. Your message goes straight to the person named in the To box—it is not posted on the newsgroup.

All About Printing

In Chapter 4 "Installing a New Printer" explains how to install a printer.

Fifteen years ago, paper company executives were wringing their hands over the coming of the paperless office. Paper was supposed to become obsolete. The paperless office, however, is still a pipe dream. Despite the Internet and e-mail, most communication is done on paper. This section describes how to print a file, choose which printer to use if you have more than one printer, and cancel or change the order of print jobs. You also learn some tried-and-true techniques for handling a printer that doesn't do its job right.

Printing All or Part of a File

Most computer programs offer a Print button that you can click to print a file in its entirety. Printing an entire file is fine and dandy, but suppose you want to print part of a file, several copies, or print the file on your color printer instead of your black-and-white model. Figure 7.7 shows how to do just that.

The fastest way to print an entire file is to find it in My Computer or Windows Explorer and simply drag it to a printer shortcut icon on the desktop. Figure 7.8 demonstrates how to do that. "Create the Shortcut Icons You Need" in Chapter 2 describes how to create a shortcut. To get to the Printers folder and create a shortcut to a printer, click the Start button and choose Settings | Printers.

The figure shows a File menu and Print dialog box with numbered callouts 1-5.

- File menu: New, Open..., Edit with Microsoft, Save, Save As..., Page Setup..., Print..., Send, Import and Export.., Properties, ✓ Work Offline, Close

- Print dialog box:
  - Printer Name: HP LaserJet IIIP — Properties
  - Status: Default printer; Ready
  - Type: HP LaserJet IIIP
  - Where: LPT1:
  - Comment: ☐ Print to file
  - Print range: ○ All ⊙ Pages from: 1 to: 3 ○ Selection
  - Copies: Number of copies: 2 ☐ Collate
  - OK Cancel

1 Open the file and choose File | Print or press CTRL-P. You see the Print dialog box.
2 Under Print Range, choose which part of the file to print.
3 Under Copies, enter the number of copies to print.
4 If your computer is attached to more than one printer, open the Name drop-down list and choose which printer to send the file to.
5 Click OK.

Figure 7.7: To print part of a file or more than one copy, choose File | Print or press CTRL-P to open the Print dialog box.

EXPERT ADVICE

You can change a printer's default settings and save yourself the trouble of always having to choose options in the Print dialog box. Perhaps you work in a law office, for example, and you always print on legal-size paper. To change a printer's default settings, click the Start button and choose Settings | Printers. In the Printers folder, right-click a printer and choose Properties. On the six tabs of the Properties dialog box, select default settings and then click OK.

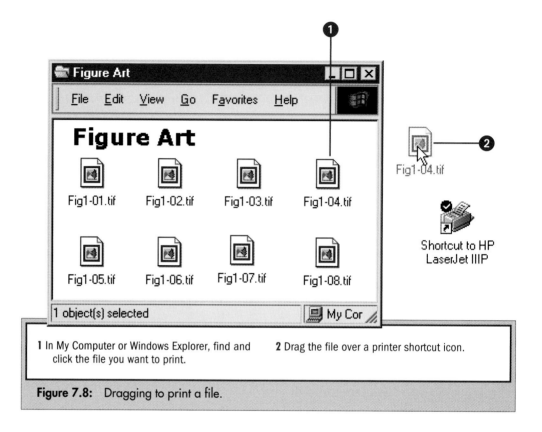

1 In My Computer or Windows Explorer, find and click the file you want to print.

2 Drag the file over a printer shortcut icon.

Figure 7.8: Dragging to print a file.

Canceling a Print Order or Changing the Order of Print Jobs

Suppose you give the order to print a file or a bunch of files but then you want to keep a file from being printed or change the order in which files are printed. Follow these steps to control how files are printed:

1. Double-click the Printer icon in the lower-right corner of the screen (next to the clock) or else click the Start button and choose Settings | Printers.

2. In the Printers folder, double-click the icon of the printer you are using. You see a Printer window similar to the one in Figure 7.9. Files are shown in the order in which they will be printed.

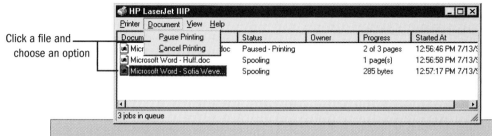

Click a file and
choose an option

Figure 7.9:   In the Printer window, you can stop printing documents or change the order in which they are printed.

3. Do the following to change the order in which files are printed or stop printing a file:

- **Change the Print Order**   Click a file at the top or near the top of the list and choose Document | Pause Printing. As shown in Figure 7.9, the word "Paused" appears in the Status column. Files further down the list will now be printed before the one that has been "paused." To resume printing the file, click it and choose Document | Pause Printing again.

- **Stop Printing a File**   Click the file and choose Document | Cancel Printing. The file is removed from the list.

- **Stop Printing All Files**   Choose Printer | Purge Print Documents.

SHORTCUT

To stop printing files without having to go to the Printer window, click the Start button and choose Settings | Printers. Then right-click the printer icon in the Printers folder and choose Purge Print Documents.

What to Do When You Can't Print Anything

Few things are more frustrating than not being able to get a printer to work correctly. When you get one of those "There was a problem sending your document to the printer" messages, try these techniques to solve the problem:

- See if the printer is turned on. Is paper in the paper tray? Is the right size paper in the paper tray?

- Find out if the power cord that connects your computer to the printer is plugged in correctly on both ends. For that matter, is the printer plugged in a wall socket?
- Make sure you are sending the file to the right printer if more than one printer is connected to your computer.

CHAPTER 8

Creating Web Pages with FrontPage Express

INCLUDES

- Creating a Web page from scratch or from a template

- Formatting and laying out the text

- Putting graphic images on Web pages

- Choosing a color background

- Creating hyperlinks to the Web and to other places in your Web site

- Uploading your Web pages to an Internet service provider

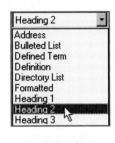

Create a Web Page ➥ pp. 196–197

1. Click the New button or choose File | New and create the page from a template.
2. Click the Save button, enter a title for your Web page in the Save As dialog box, click the As File button, and save and name the file in the Save As File dialog box.

Format Text on the Web Page ➥ pp. 198–200

- Choose a style on the Change Style drop-down menu.
- Choose a font from the Change Font drop-down menu, and click the Increase Text Size or Decrease Text Size buttons to change the size of letters.
- Click the Bold, Italic, Underline, or Text Color button.

Align and Indent Text ➥ p. 199

- Click the Align Left, Align Right, or Center button to change the alignment of a paragraph.
- Click the Increase Indent or Decrease Indent button to move text further from or closer to the right side of the page.

Put a Graphic Image on Your Web Page ➥ pp. 201–202

1. Click the Insert Image button and then click the Browse button in the Image dialog box.
2. Locate and select the graphic file, and click the Open button.
3. Click the image to select it.
4. To change its size, drag a corner of the image. To place the image, right-click, choose Image Properties, click the Appearance tab, and choose Alignment and Spacing options.

Choose a Background Color for Your Web Page ➡ p. 203

1. Choose Format | Background.
2. On the Background tab of the Page Properties dialog box, open the Background drop-down menu, choose an option, and click OK.

Insert a Hyperlink to a Page on the Internet ➡ pp. 205–206

1. Select a word, phrase, or graphic and choose Insert | Hyperlink (or press CTRL-K).
2. Click the World Wide Web tab in the Create Hyperlink dialog box.
3. In the URL box, enter the address of the Web page you want to link to in the URL box.

Insert a Hyperlink to Another Place on Your Web Page or Web Site ➡ pp. 206–207

1. Select the words or graphic that will form the hyperlink and choose Insert | Hyperlink.
2. On the Open Pages tab of the Create Hyperlink dialog box, open the Bookmark drop-down menu and choose a bookmark to link to a place on the same Web page. To link to a different page, click its name in the Open Pages list; open the Bookmark drop-down menu and choose a bookmark as well if you want to link to a place on the page other than the top.

Send Your Web Pages to Your ISP ➡ pp. 210–211

1. Click the Start button and choose Programs | Accessories | Internet Tools | Web Publishing Wizard.
2. Click Next and fill in the Web Publishing Wizard dialog boxes.

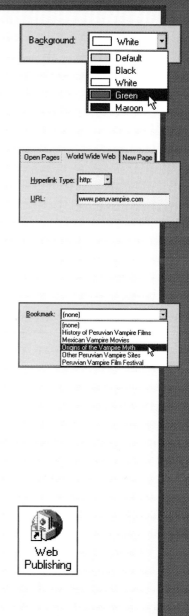

In the future, everyone will be famous for 15 minutes, and everyone will have a Web page. Chapter 8 explains how to use FrontPage Express to create your own corner of the World Wide Web. In this chapter, you learn how to create a page, lay out the text, include images on a Web page, and include background sounds as well. This chapter also describes how to post Web pages on the Internet so that others can enjoy them.

What You Need to Know Before You Begin

DEFINITION

Frame:
A part of a Web site, usually found on the left side, with hyperlinks that you can click to go from place-to-place on a Web site.

DEFINITION

HTML codes:
The codes that tell browsers such as Internet Explorer how to display text and graphics onscreen. Also called HTML tags.

Before you know anything about FrontPage Express, you need to know that the program is not particularly sophisticated. Web pages made with FrontPage Express can't include frames or other fancy gizmos. The pages that you can create with the program are utilitarian and do a good job if you want to post a simple page on the company intranet or create an appealing page for friends, like-minded hobbyists, and afficionados. However, if you want to engage in selling on the Web, or if you want to promote a business, your pages should have a professional look, and you should opt for a more sophisticated program or else let someone else create the page for you.

So much for the bad news. The good news is that FrontPage Express is not hard to learn. You don't have to concern yourself with the dreaded HTML (HyperText Markup Language) codes to create a Web page. The coding is done in the background. All in all, FrontPage Express works like a word-processing program. You lay out the page, write the words, and stick the images on the page, and what you see is pretty much what others will see when they view your Web pages over the Internet.

Figure 8.1 shows a page with and without the HTML codes showing. The codes are scary, aren't they? In the old days, you had to know codes like these to lay out and present a Web page. Nowadays, for simple pages at least, you don't have to worry about HTML codes.

However, if you want to see the codes or you want to enter them by hand, choose View | HTML. (Next time you're admiring a Web page in Internet Explorer, try choosing View | Source in that program to see the HTML codes that make the Web page what it is.)

Before you create any Web pages, create a new folder to keep them in (Chapter 3 explains how). When you send your Web page or pages to an Internet service provider (ISP) so they can be displayed on the Web, you will send the contents of the folder you create. Keep all files you need for your Web site—graphic files and sound files as well as hypertext files—in one folder to make uploading the files easier.

And before I forget, here's how to start FrontPage Express: Click the Start button and choose Programs | Internet Explorer | FrontPage Express. Why the program got buried so deep in the menu system, I don't know.

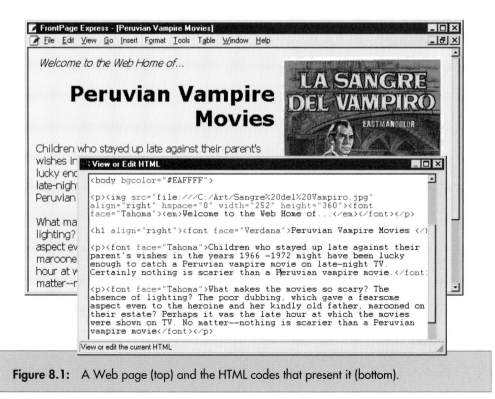

Figure 8.1: A Web page (top) and the HTML codes that present it (bottom).

EXPERT ADVICE

In many computer programs, you can save a file as an HTML file and thereby code the file with HTML tags. In Microsoft Word, for example, choose File | Save As Web Page (in Word 2000) or File | Save As HTML (in Word 97). After a file has been coded in HTML format, you can copy the parts of the file you need into your FrontPage Express file and in so doing spare yourself a lot of trouble. To insert an entire file into FrontPage Express, choose Insert | File.

Creating Web Pages

Later in this chapter, "Hyperlinking Your Page to the Internet" explains how to link Web pages to form a Web site.

A Web page is a file that can be viewed through a Web browser. A Web site can include one page or many pages. To get from page to page in a Web site, visitors click hyperlinks. Before you create your first Web page, create a folder to hold the Web page and all the material it requires—the graphic images, sound files, and so on. Then follow these instructions to create the Web page:

- **Creating a Blank Web Page**   Either click the New button, or choose File | New, select the Normal Page template in the New Page dialog box, and click OK.

- **Creating a Page from a Template**   Choose File | New, choose a template or wizard in the New Page dialog box, click OK, and fill in the wizard dialog boxes. The Form options are for creating online forms that visitors to your Web page can fill out. Choose Personal Home Page Wizard to set up a generic Web page.

After you create your Web page, give it a title. And be sure to choose a descriptive title. Lycos, Yahoo, and other search engines keep careful track of the words on Web pages, and the word or words in the title are given a lot of weight. If you enter **Madagascar** in the title, for example, a Web surfer who enters they keyword **Madagascar** in order to conduct a search of the Web is more likely to find your page than he or she is if you enter **Greenland** for the title.

To give your page a title, choose File | Page Properties, enter the title in the Title text box on the General tab of the Page Properties dialog box, and click OK. When others visit your Web page, they will see the title you enter in the title bar along the top of their browser windows. You can always change the title by choosing File | Page Properties and entering a different title.

General | Background | Margins | Custom |

Location: file:///C:/Collwin/Busy/Busy Art 2/madagasc.htm|

Title: Madagascar

Madagascar - Microsoft Internet Explorer

The next step after giving the page a title is to save it. You prepared a new folder for your Web page, right? To save the page there, click the Save button, enter a title in the Save As dialog box (if you haven't already given your page a title), and click the As File button. In the Save As File dialog box, locate and select the folder you prepared for your Web page, and click the Save button. FrontPage Express names the file after the first eight letters of the title, but you can enter a new name if you want in the File Name text box. Make sure the name isn't longer than eight characters, however, because ISPs prefer it that way.

Save As

Page Title:
Madagascar

Page Location:
http://default/madagasc.htm

Tip
Please be sure your page has a title.
Click OK to save this page to the web.

OK

Cancel

Help

As File.

EXPERT ADVICE

You can save all the Web pages you are working on, if you are working on more than one, by choosing File | Save All. The Save All command is convenient. Instead of visiting each Web page and saving it, you can save all the pages at once. To switch back and forth between Web pages, choose a page name from the Window menu.

Entering and Formatting the Headings and Text

When it comes to entering headings and text, FrontPage Express works like a word processor. Anyone who has worked in WordPad or Microsoft Word will recognize the buttons on the Standard toolbar for aligning and formatting text—those buttons work the same way in FrontPage Express. To enter text, all you really have to do is press ENTER until you reach the part of the page where you want text to go, and then start typing. Forthwith are instructions for formatting text, indenting text, aligning text, and creating lists.

Changing the Look of Text

Select the text and then choose a formatting command to change the text's appearance—or choose a formatting command and then start typing. To select text, drag the pointer over it. Here are the different ways to change the look of text:

• **Choosing a Format Style** Make a choice from the Change Style drop-down menu, or choose Format | Paragraph and make a choice in the Paragraph Properties dialog box. Choosing a style is the best way to make sure that headings and text look the same from page to page on a Web site. By choosing a style, you give your Web site a professional look, because pages share a similar appearance. A *style* is a bundle of formatting commands—for changing text size and aligning text, for example.

• **Choosing a Font for Text** Open the Change Font drop-down menu and choose a font. You can also choose Format | Font and make a choice in the Font dialog box.

• **Changing the Size of Letters** Click the Increase Text Size button or Decrease Text Size button. Each time you click, you enlarge or shrink the letters by 2 points. A *point* equals 1/72 of an inch. You can also choose Format | Font and make a choice in the Font dialog box to change the size of letters.

- **Boldfacing, Italicizing, or Underlining Text**   Click the Bold, Italic, or Underline button to **boldface,** *italicize,* or underline text.

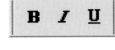

- **Changing the Color of Text**   Click the Text Color button and choose a new color in the Color dialog box.

EXPERT ADVICE

Sometimes FrontPage Express stubbornly refuses to show a format change onscreen. After you make a format change, click the Refresh button to update your Web page and force FrontPage Express to display it.

Laying Out Text on the Page

Align and indent text to lay out the text on the page. *Aligning* refers to how lines of text fall on the page—flush left, flush right, or across the center. *Indenting* means to move text away from or toward the left margin. Figure 8.2 demonstrates the ways to align text. Play with the aligning and indenting commands until you get an interesting layout for your page. Here are instructions for aligning and indenting:

- **Aligning Text**   Click anywhere in the paragraph you want to realign and then click the Align Left, Center, or Align Right button. To align several paragraphs at once, select them before clicking a button.

- **Indenting Text**   Click anywhere in the paragraph you want to indent and click the Decrease Indent or Increase Indent button. Each click moves the text further from or closer to the left side of the page.

EXPERT ADVICE

Press SHIFT-ENTER to break a line without starting a new paragraph. FrontPage Express puts a large blank space between lines, but if you want to end one line and start the next without the large blank space appearing, press SHIFT-ENTER.

Aligned left ———

Aligned right

Centered ———

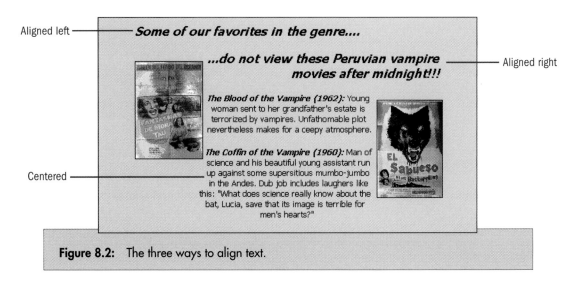

Figure 8.2: The three ways to align text.

Entering a Bulleted or Numbered List

Numbered lists are great for ranking items or presenting step-by-step instructions. As for bulleted lists, use them when you want to present alternatives to the viewer of your Web page. A *bullet* is a black filled-in circle or other character. Follow these instructions to enter a bulleted or numbered list:

1. Type the list. For now, don't worry about the bullets or the numbers.
2. Select the list. To do so, drag the pointer over it.
3. Click the Bulleted List or Numbered List button on the Standard toolbar.

Decorating a Web Page

It goes without saying, but visitors to a colorful Web page are bound to stay longer than visitors to a drab Web page without any decorations on it. In the interest of making the Internet a more colorful place to visit, the pages that follow explain how to draw horizontal lines on pages, put images on pages, change the background color, and play sounds for visitors.

Drawing a Line Across the Page

Draw a line across the page to separate one part of a Web page from another. In this illustration, for example, the horizontal line divides the hyperlinks at the top of a Web page from the main text below:

History of Peruvian Vampire Movies § Mexican Vampire Movies
Peruvian Vampire Film Festival § Other Peruvian Vampire Movie
Sites
Origins of the Vampire Myth

To draw a line across the page like the one in the illustration, click where you want the line to be and choose Insert | Horizontal Line.

Putting an Image on the Page

What is a Web page without one or two graphics? It's like an emperor without any clothes. Two types of images can appear on Web pages: .jpg and .gif. Some browsers can read other kinds of graphic files, but all can read those two, so you are wise to stick with .jpg and .gif files. Figure 8.3 shows how to place a graphic image in a Web page. Before you put the image on the page, however, make a copy and put the copy in the folder where you keep all your Web materials. Click an image and press the DELETE key if you change your mind and decide you don't need it.

After you land the image on your Web page, you probably need to change its size. To do so, click the image. Square selection handles appear on the corners and sides. Carefully move the pointer over a corner selection handle, and, when you see the double-headed arrow, click and drag. Be sure to drag a selection handle in a corner. Doing so changes the size of the image but keeps its proportions. If you drag a side handle, the image gets distorted.

For a sophisticated layout, make text appear beside graphics. To tell FrontPage Express where to put text in relation to a graphic, double-click the graphic. You see the Image Properties dialog box. On the

---

CAUTION

In the lower-right corner of the FrontPage Express window is a number that shows roughly how many seconds others need to download your Web page. As you load your Web page with images, sounds, and other gizmos, make sure that number doesn't grow too high.

TIP

Before putting an image on the page, click where you want the image to go. You can't drag an image to change its position, so where the cursor is located when you insert the image matters a lot.

Figure 8.3 content (dialog boxes):

Image

Other Location | Clip Art

⦿ From File

Browse...

○ From Location

http://

Image

Look in: Art

Name	Size	Type	M
Elvis.jpg	23KB	JPEG Image	1
eye.gif	4KB	GIF Image	5
Farlessvamp.jpg	23KB	JPEG Image	7
Giants logo.gif	6KB	GIF Image	5
itseasy.gif	3KB	GIF Image	5
kissme3.gif	70KB	GIF Image	7

File name: Farlessvamp.jpg   Open

Files of type: GIF and JPEG (*.gif, *.jpg)   Cancel

1 Click the Insert Image button or choose Insert | Image.

2 In the Image dialog box, make sure the From File option button is selected, and then click the Browse button.

3 In the second Image dialog box, go to the folder where you keep files for your Web site, and select the image file. (Click the Details button in the dialog box to see which type of files you are dealing with.)

4 Click the Open button.

Figure 8.3: Putting a graphic image on a Web page.

TIP

Others will be able to download your Web page faster if you check the Specify Size check box on the Appearance tab. With the box checked, browsers know exactly how much space to allot to the graphic, and they can display it faster.

Appearance tab of the dialog box are these options for running text beside a graphic and for putting borders around graphics:

- **Alignment** Specifies where the image goes on the page. Choosing Left, for example, places the graphic against the left margin and runs text around the right side.

- **Horizontal and Vertical Spacing** Puts blank space between the image and nearby text so that the text is easier to read and the page looks less crowded.

- **Border Thickness** Draws borderlines around the graphic. The higher the number of pixels, the wider the border.

Choosing a Background Color for Web Pages

Figure 8.4 explains how to choose a background color for a Web page. Choosing a background color is the easiest way to decorate a Web page. But be careful about choosing colors. Dark colors make the text hard to read. On the other hand, if you are in an experimental mood, you might choose a dark background and a pale color for the letters.

Playing Background Sounds or Music for Visitors to Your Web Page

Before you think about playing sounds or music for visitors to your Web site, remember that tinny sound can be annoying. In your adventures on the Internet, how often have you heard an annoying sound when you arrive at a Web site? More than once, I venture. Keeping that in mind, follow these steps to play a wave (.wav), Midi (.mid and .rmi), or Sun audio format (.au) sound for visitors to your Web site:

1. Choose Insert | Background Sound.
2. Click the Browse button in the Background Sound dialog box.
3. In the second Background Sound dialog box, go to the folder where you store your Web materials and select the sound file.

CAUTION

Copy the sound file you intend to use to the folder where you keep your Web page. That way, it will be uploaded successfully to the Internet.

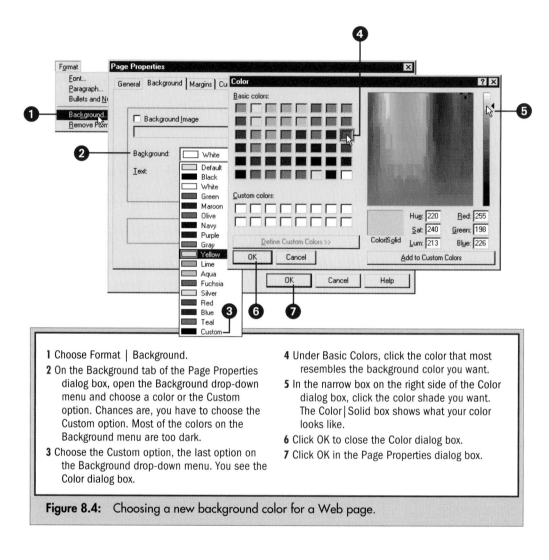

1 Choose Format | Background.
2 On the Background tab of the Page Properties dialog box, open the Background drop-down menu and choose a color or the Custom option. Chances are, you have to choose the Custom option. Most of the colors on the Background menu are too dark.
3 Choose the Custom option, the last option on the Background drop-down menu. You see the Color dialog box.

4 Under Basic Colors, click the color that most resembles the background color you want.
5 In the narrow box on the right side of the Color dialog box, click the color shade you want. The Color | Solid box shows what your color looks like.
6 Click OK to close the Color dialog box.
7 Click OK in the Page Properties dialog box.

Figure 8.4: Choosing a new background color for a Web page.

4. Click the Open button. You return to your Web page, but you're not done yet. You still have to tell FrontPage Express whether to play the sound file once or continuously.

5. Choose File | Page Properties.

6. On the General tab of the Page Properties dialog box, enter a number in the Loop box to play the sound a certain number of times, or check the Forever check box to play it over and over and over again.

7. Click OK.

Background Sound

Location: file:///C:/WINDOWS/MEDIA/Logoff.wav   Browse...

Loop: 1   ☐ Forever

Hyperlinking Your Page to the Internet

As you know if you spent any time on the Internet or in Chapter 6 of this book, a *hyperlink* is an electronic shortcut between two Web pages. You know when you have encountered a hyperlink on a Web page because the pointer changes into a hand. By clicking when the hand appears, you go to a different Web page.

    These pages explain how to include hyperlinks on a Web page. Creating hyperlinks takes only a few steps and is easy to do. Read on to find out how to link to other places on a Web page, to other pages on your own Web site, and to other Web sites on the Internet.

In Chapter 6, "Clicking Hyperlinks to Go Here and There" explains what hyperlinks are.

Creating a Hyperlink to a Page on the Internet

The easiest way to create a hyperlink between your Web page and a page on the Internet is to start Internet Explorer and go to the page you want to link to. That way, you don't have to enter or know the address of the Web page when you create the link, because FrontPage Express will already know it. Anyhow, Figure 8.5 explains how to link your page to a page on the Internet so that visitors to your page can click the link and go straight to the other page.

TIP

Each page on the Internet has an address, also known as a URL, or *uniform resource locator*. You can tell the address of a Web page by looking in the Address box in a Web browser.

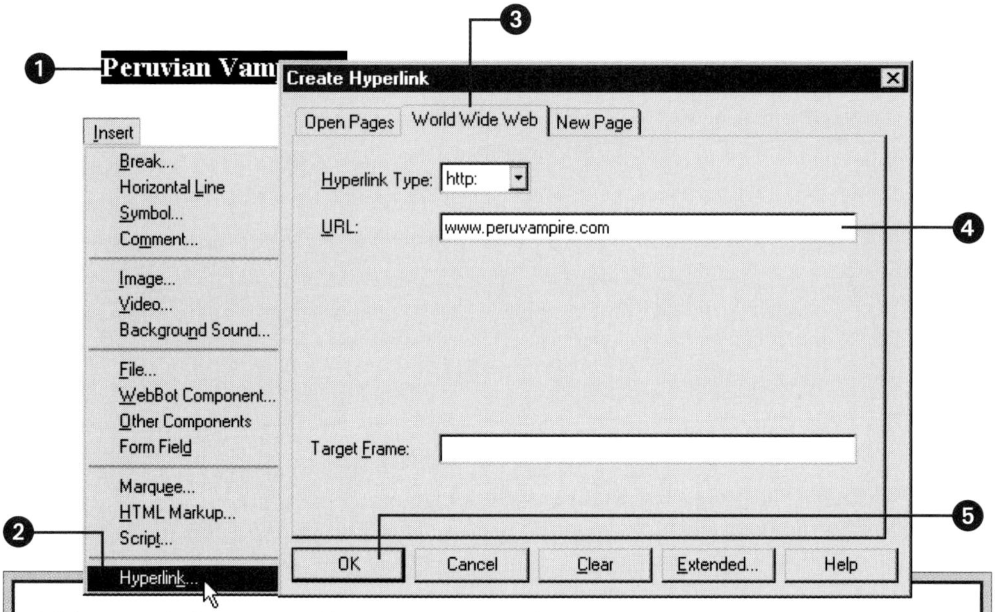

Figure 8.5:   Creating a hyperlink to another Web page on the Internet.

1 Select a word, phrase, or graphic to serve as the hyperlink. When visitors to your Web page click the words or graphic, they will go to another site on the Internet.

2 Choose Insert | Hyperlink or press CTRL-K. You see the Create Hyperlink dialog box.

3 Click the World Wide Web tab.

4 In the URL box, enter the address of the Web page you want to link to. If the page is open in Internet Explorer, its address is already listed in the URL box.

5 Click OK.

Inserting a Hyperlink to Another Place in Your Web Site

Creating a hyperlink to the top of a different Web page on your site is easy. However, before you can create a link to a different place on the same page or a specific place on another page in your Web site, you have to bookmark the place. By bookmarking, you establish the target of your hyperlink.

Follow these steps to bookmark a place on a Web page:

1. Click where you want the bookmark to go. In other words, click the place you want visitors to come to when they click a hyperlink you intend to create in the future.

2. Choose Edit | Bookmark. You see the Bookmark dialog box.

3. Enter a name for the bookmark in the Bookmark Name box and click OK. Be sure to choose a descriptive name you will recognize later on.

After you have created the bookmarks, follow these steps to insert a hyperlink to a different location on the same page, the top of another page, or a different location somewhere inside another page:

1. Select the word, phrase, or graphic that will form the hyperlink.

2. Choose Insert | Hyperlink or press CTRL-K. You see the Open Pages tab of the Create Hyperlink dialog box, as shown in Figure 8.6. The tab lists other pages in your Web site. The page you are working on is highlighted.

3. Create the link to a place on the same Web page, to the top of a different Web page, or to the middle of another Web page:

   - **To the Same Web Page**   Open the Bookmark drop-down menu and choose the bookmark that marks the place you want to link to.

   - **To the Top of a Different Web Page**   Click the name of the page in the Open Pages list.

   - **To a Location on a Different Web Page**   Click the name of the page in the Open Pages list. Then open the Bookmark drop-down menu and choose a bookmark name.

4. Click OK to insert the hyperlink.

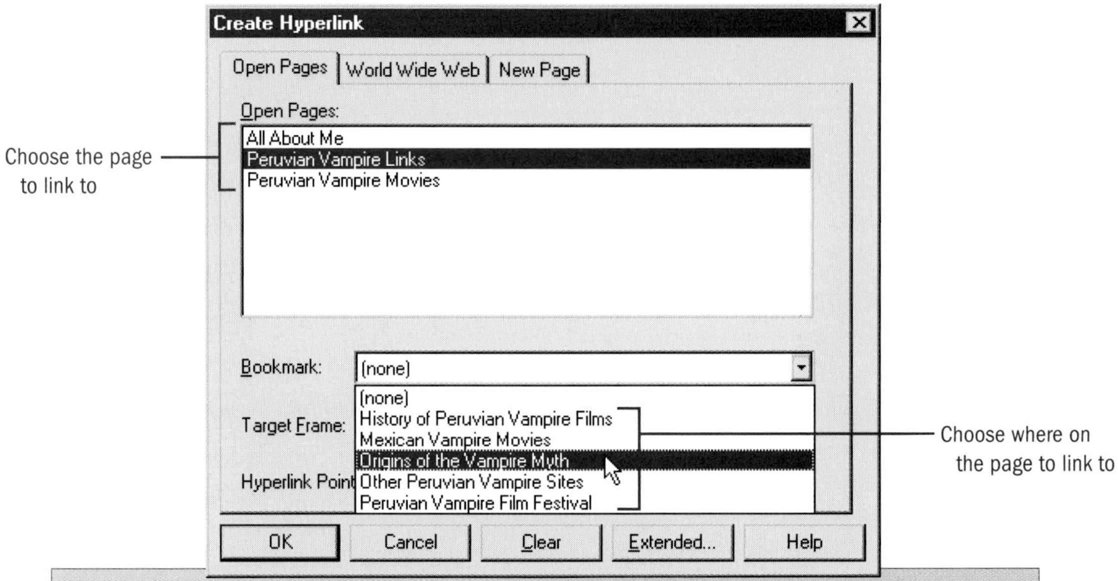

Choose the page to link to

Choose where on the page to link to

Figure 8.6: Creating a hyperlink to another Web page.

Editing and Maintaining Hyperlinks

To edit or maintain a hyperlink, right-click it and then choose
Hyperlink Properties (or press ALT-ENTER). You see the Edit Hyperlink
dialog box, which looks and works much like the Create Hyperlink
dialog box (see Figure 8.6). Here's how to handle hyperlinks in the
Edit Hyperlink dialog box:

- **Removing a Hyperlink**   Click the Clear button. The text or
  graphic that used to be the launching pad for the link remains
  on your Web page, but it is no longer a hyperlink.

- **Changing the Destination of a Hyperlink**   For a link to
  another part of your Web site, make new choices on the Open
  Pages tab (and see the previous section of this chapter if you
  need help). For a link to another Web site, go to the World
  Wide Web tab and enter a new Web page address in the URL
  text box.

Test-Driving Your Web Page

Before you put your Web page on the Internet, test-drive it. Open Internet Explorer and see what the thing looks like and whether the hyperlinks really work. Follow these steps to test-drive a Web page or Web site you created in FrontPage Express:

1. Start Internet Explorer and connect to the Internet.

2. Choose File | Open (or press CTRL-O). You see the Open dialog box.

3. Click the Browse button.

4. In the Microsoft Internet Explorer dialog box, find the folder in which you keep your Web site materials.

5. Select the HTML file where your Web page is and click the Open button.

6. Click OK in the Open dialog box. Your Web page appears in the Internet Explorer screen, as shown in Figure 8.7.

Chapter 6 explains Internet Explorer.

In Chapter 2, "Learn the Ways to View Folders and Files" explains how to find and open a file.

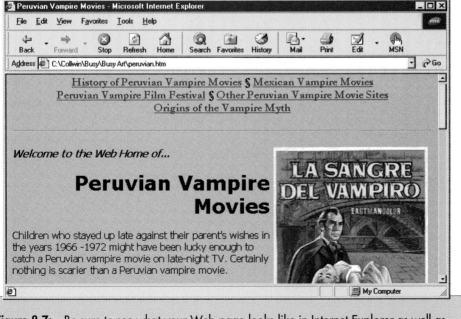

Figure 8.7: Be sure to see what your Web page looks like in Internet Explorer as well as FrontPage Express.

In Internet Explorer, click all the hyperlinks to make sure they work correctly. While you're at it, change the size of the Internet Explorer window to see how the text and graphics move onscreen as the window's size is changed. Suppose you come upon an error? In that case, open the Web page in FrontPage Express, correct it there, and click the Refresh button to save the changes you made. Then go back to Internet Explorer and click the Refresh button there to update your Web page.

Web Publishing Wizard: Uploading Your Web Page to the Internet

TIP

To upload a Web page to your ISP, you need a program called the Web Publishing Wizard, but the program is not installed as part of a standard Windows 98 installation. To install it, you probably need to reinstall Windows, as explained in Appendix A. When you reinstall, go to the Internet Tools category and select Web Publishing Wizard as a component to install.

Uploading means to send Web pages across the phone lines to an Internet service provider so the pages can be made available on the Web. ISPs store Web pages on a dedicated computer called a *server*. You need an account with an ISP or an online service like America Online in order to post pages on the Web.

Before you start uploading your Web pages, you need to know the following:

- Your user name or user ID (the part of your e-mail address that appears before the at @ symbol).
- The password you use to log in.
- The URL (uniform resource locator) address of your Web site.
- The name of your Internet service provider's Web server and the path for uploading files to your ISP's Web server.

TIP

If you are unsure in any way, shape, or form of what you need to do to upload Web pages, call your ISP. Any ISP worth the name is required to help its customers upload pages to the Internet.

Follow these steps to upload Web pages to your ISP with the Web Publishing Wizard:

1. Click the Start button and choose Programs | Accessories | Internet Tools | Web Publishing Wizard.

2. Click Next in the first wizard dialog box.

3. In the Select a File or Folder dialog box, click the Browse Folders button if you are uploading files to your Web site for the first time; if you changed some of your Web pages, choose Browse Files to upload just a few files.

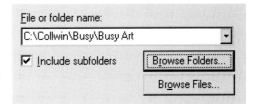

4. In the Browse dialog box, find the folder or file on your computer that you want to upload and double-click it. You return to the Select a File or Folder dialog window. The name of the folder or file appears in the File or Folder Name box.

5. Click the Next button. You see the Name the Web Server dialog box.

6. Type the name of your ISP in the Descriptive Name box and click the Next button.

7. In the Specify the URL and Directory dialog box, type the address to which you are supposed to upload Web pages in the URL or Internet Address box. Only your ISP knows for sure what the address is, but you probably type something like **ftp.***YourISPName.*

8. Click the Next button.

9. In the Connect dialog box, enter your user ID and password, and click Connect to go on the Internet.

CAUTION

Make sure the Include Subfolders box is checked if you are uploading your site for the first time or you are uploading new pages with graphics subfolders.

Shortly, you'll see the Publishing Files window and its familiar image of paper files being tossed from place to place. As long as the Web Publishing Wizard doesn't encounter any glitches, a dialog box tells you, "Web Publishing Wizard has successfully published your files to the Web server."

CHAPTER 9

Maintaining Your System and Making It Run Better

INCLUDES

- Surveying the Windows 98 system tools
- Maintaining your system and making it run better
- Compressing files and drives to get more free disk space
- Updating your copy of Windows from the Internet
- Scheduling maintenance and backup programs
- Backing up important files and folders

Disk Cleanup

Get More Disk Space by Removing Temporary Files ➡ pp. 218–219

1. Click the Start button and choose Programs | Accessories | System Tools | Disk Cleanup.
2. Make sure Temporary Internet Files and Temporary Files are checked in the Disk Cleanup dialog box, and then click OK.

Disk Defragmenter

Defragment the Hard Disk to Make Your Computer Run Faster ➡ pp. 219–220

1. Click the Start button and choose Programs | Accessories | System Tools | Disk Defragmenter.
2. Choose a disk to defragment and click OK.

Energy saving features of monitor

Tell Windows How and When to Switch into Standby Mode ➡ p. 221

1. Right-click the desktop, choose Properties, and click the Screen Saver tab in the Display Properties dialog box.
2. Under Energy-Saving Features of Monitor, click the Settings button.
3. In the Power Management Properties dialog box, choose your settings.

ScanDisk

Check for and Repair Damage to Files on Disk ➡ pp. 221–223

1. Click the Start button and choose Programs | Accessories | System Tools | ScanDisk.
2. Choose a disk to check, choose whether you want to do a Standard or Thorough scan, and click the Start button.

Make Sure Your Copy of Windows 98 is Up-to-Date ➥ p. 230

1. Click the Start button and choose Windows Update or Settings | Windows Update.
2. Go to the Windows Update site on the Internet and follow the instructions for downloading the latest edition of windows.

Run Maintenance Programs While You Are Away from Your Computer ➥ pp. 231–232

1. Click the Start button and choose Programs | Accessories | System Tools | Scheduled Tasks.
2. Double-click Add Scheduled Task in the Scheduled Tasks window (the first icon in the window) and answer the questions in the Scheduled Task Wizard dialog boxes.

Back Up Important Files and Folders ➥ p. 236

1. Click the Start button and choose Programs | Accessories | System Tools | Backup.
2. Click Close in the Microsoft Backup dialog box.
3. On the Backup Job drop-down menu, choose the name of a backup job and click the Start button.

Retrieve and Use the Backup Copy of a File ➥ pp. 236–237

- Open the drive to which you made the backup copies in Windows Explorer or My Computer, and copy the files to their original locations.
- Run the Backup program and click the Restore tab in the Backup window. In the Select Backup Sets dialog box, click the name of the backup job with the files and folders that need restoring, and then click OK. Then check the files and folders that need restoring and click the Start button.

A computer is like a high-strung English sports car. If you don't take the time now and then to maintain your computer, it starts to slow down. And if you ignore those strange noises and weird flickering lights, eventually your computer starts crashing. Then you have a real problem on your hands. When you need your computer most, it fails and stops running altogether.

Lucky for you, Windows 98 offers a bunch of different ways to diagnose computer problems, maintain your computer, and make it run smoothly. This chapter explains how to play garage mechanic with Windows 98. You also learn how to acquire more disk space by compressing files and drives, back up files, schedule maintenance tasks so they can be done in your absence, and update Windows 98 by visiting a Web site on the Internet.

Introducing the Windows 98 System Tools

Windows 98 offers many utility programs for making sure that your computer runs well. Most are found on the Programs | Accessories | System Tools menu. The programs that matter to most users (not network administrators or technicians) are explained throughout this chapter. Table 9.1 lists the programs, briefly explains what they do, and tells you how often to use them.

System Tool	What It Does	When to Use It
Backup	Makes backup copies of important files and folders to a tape or zip drive.	Daily, weekly—depending on how important data is
Compression Agent	After running DriveSpace, lets you compress selected files.	Once, if ever

Table 9.1: The Windows 98 System Tools.

System Tool	What It Does	When to Use It
Disk Cleanup	Removes temporary files and files downloaded from the Internet from the hard disk.	Every week or so
Disk Defragmenter	Reassembles parts of each file on disk so that each file is stored more efficiently in one place on disk.	When the computer runs slowly
Drive Converter (FAT32)	Converts a hard disk from the FAT16 to the FAT32 format.	Once, if ever
DriveSpace	Compresses files on disk to allow more free space for storing additional files.	Once, if ever
Power Management	Switches the monitor and computer into standby mode.	Make these settings once
ScanDisk	Checks for and repairs damaged files and warped areas on the hard disk.	After a computer crash, frequent program failures, or a "bad sector" or "unable to read" error
Scheduled Tasks	Allows you to schedule maintenance and backup programs so they can be run automatically in your absence.	Daily, weekly—depending on which tasks are scheduled
System Information	Presents information about your computer, its components, and its resources.	When you talk to a technician
Windows Tune-Up	Allows you to run Defragmenter, Disk Cleanup, and ScanDisk automatically according to a schedule.	Make these settings once
Windows Update	Takes you to a Web site where you can copy up-to-date Windows drivers and system files to your computer.	Periodically

Table 9.1: The Windows 98 System Tools *(continued)*.

Maintaining Your System

Windows 98 offers several different ways to maintain your system and make it run more smoothly. You can remove temporary files and other unneeded files, defragment a disk so files can be accessed faster, arrange for the monitor and computer to be turned off in your absence, and repair corrupted files. Better read on.

Disk Cleanup: Uncluttering the Hard Disk

Disk Cleanup

Certain kinds of files have a habit of cluttering the hard disk and making the computer run slowly. *Temporary files,* for example, are a big culprit. When a computer crashes, Windows 98 turns all unsaved files into temporary (.tmp) files. After a while, the number of temporary files adds up. And if you surf the Internet, thousands of temporary Internet files (especially .gifs) collect like barnacles on your hard disk.

Lucky for you, Windows offers a special command for purging these files. Follow these steps:

1. Click the Start button and choose Programs | Accessories | System Tools | Disk Cleanup. (If you see the Select Drive dialog box, choose the drive that you want to clean up.) A message says "Disk Cleanup is calculating how much space you will be able to free," and then you see the Disk Cleanup dialog box.

2. Select which kinds of files to remove (click the View Files button if you want to see which files will be deleted):

    *   **Temporary Internet Files**   Definitely remove these. Your personalized Web-surfer settings remain intact when you remove these files.

    *   **Downloaded Program Files**   Get rid of them. These Java applets and ActiveX controls are just jet trash from the Internet.

    *   **Offline Web Pages**   Keep them, more than likely. These are Web pages you stored for viewing when

Disk Cleanup | More Options | Settings |

You can use Disk Cleanup to free up to 231.52 MB of disk space on (C:).

Files to delete:

☑	Downloaded Program Files	0.00 MB
☐	Offline Web Pages	0.04 MB
☐	Recycle Bin	20.00 MB
☑	Temporary files	0.36 MB
☐	Delete Windows 98 uninstall information	172.90 MB

Total amount of disk space you gain: 38.57 MB

you are not connected to the Internet (see "Making Web Pages Available for Offline Viewing" in Chapter 6).

- **Recycle Bin**   You can empty the Recycle Bin here if you want (see "Recycle Bin: Recovering Deleted Files and Folders" in Chapter 3 to learn about the Recycle Bin).

- **Temporary Files**   Yes, yes, yes. Delete 'em.

- **Delete Windows 98 Uninstall Information**   When you upgraded from an earlier version of Windows, Windows 98 stored this information in case you want to go back to Windows 95 or Windows 3.11. If you are in Windows 98 to stay, remove these files.

3. Click OK and then click Yes when Windows asks if you really want to delete this stuff.

Disk Defragmenter: Loading Files and Programs Faster

When you save a file, the new data you recently added gets placed on the hard disk wherever Windows can find room for it. Consequently, a file is stored in many different places on disk. If you've used your computer for a long time, files become fragmented—the bits and pieces are spread all over the disk and your computer has to work hard to assemble all the pieces when you open a file.

Disk
Defragmenter

   To make your computer work faster, you can *defragment* the files so that the various parts of each file are run together in one place on disk. Defragment your hard disk if your computer is running slowly. Defragmenting can take upwards of an hour, depending on how fast

EXPERT ADVICE

Before you defragment a disk, remove the files and computer programs you don't need anymore. That way, you make defragmenting go faster. And while you're at it, you might run the ScanDisk utility as well to make sure that files after they are defragmented aren't copied to bad sectors on the computer's hard disk. ScanDisk is explained later in this chapter.

your computer is and how crowded the disk is. I recommend doing it while you eat lunch.

Figure 9.1 shows how to defragment a hard disk. Be sure to close all open computer programs before you start defragmenting.

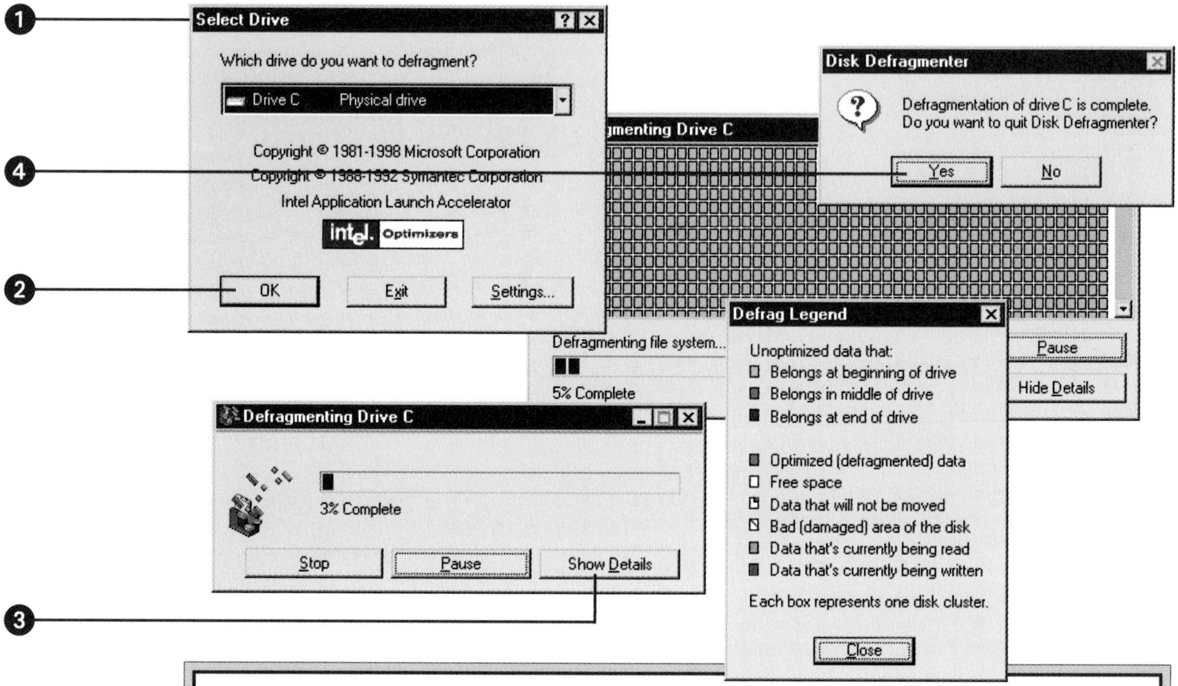

1 Click the Start button and choose Programs | Accessories | System Tools | Disk Defragmenter.

2 In the Select Drive dialog box, click OK to defragment drive C (the hard disk) or choose another disk from the drop-down menu before clicking OK. You see the Defragmenting dialog box, which shows by percentage how much of the hard disk has been defragmented.

3 Click the Show Details button if you like being freaked out. You see a map that shows parts of files being stitched together. Click the Legend button if you want to see what the little squares mean in the Defrag Legend dialog box.

4 Click Yes in the message box that tells you that the disk has been defragmented.

Figure 9.1:   Defragmenting takes a while, but it can really make a computer work faster.

Power Management: Saving Energy and Resting Your Computer

Most computers come with an energy-saving feature whereby the monitor and hard disk switch into standby mode after a certain amount of idle time has elapsed. In standby mode, the screen turns gray, the computer uses less electricity, and the computer gets a rest. To switch the monitor and computer out of standby mode, jiggle the mouse or press a key on the keyboard.

Figure 9.2 shows how to tell Windows 98 when to switch the monitor into standby mode, when to turn off the monitor automatically, and when to shut down the hard disk as well.

ScanDisk: Repairing Damage to Files and the Hard Disk

Chances are you have already seen ScanDisk in action. If your computer crashes and you have to shut down by turning off the power switch, ScanDisk runs the next time you start the computer. The program checks the computer for damaged files and warped areas on the hard disk. It looks for files and parts of files that the computer has lost track of, files that were supposed to have been deleted, files that occupy the same space on the disk, and other anomalies. After ScanDisk finds these errors, it fixes them.

ScanDisk

Run ScanDisk if a program fails frequently, if you see a "bad sector" or "unable to read" error, or if you see a bunch of gibberish after you open a file. Depending on which type of check you want—Standard or Thorough—ScanDisk can take a long time to search for and rectify errors. However, you can run the program in the

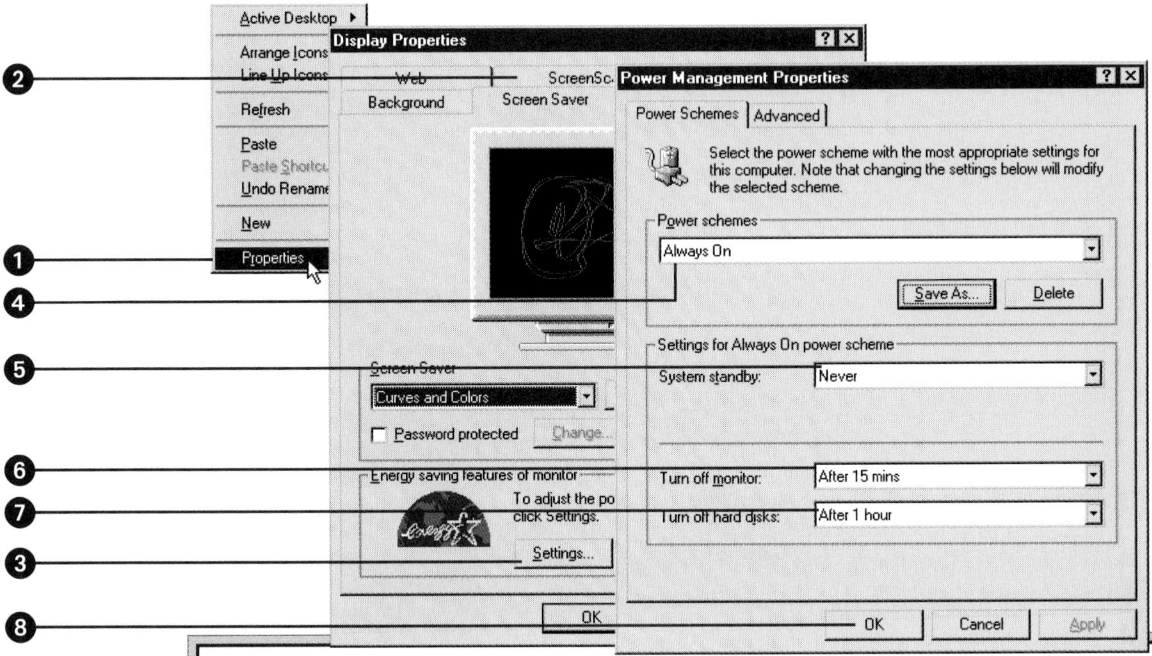

1 Right-click an empty place on the desktop and choose Properties from the shortcut menu.

2 Click the Screen Saver tab in the Display Properties dialog box.

3 Under Energy Saving Features of Monitor, click the Settings button. You see the Power Management Properties dialog box.

4 On the Power Schemes drop-down menu, choose Portable/Laptop if yours is a laptop computer.

5 On the System Standby menu, choose how much time should elapse before the monitor switches to standby mode.

6 On the Turn Off Monitor menu, say how much time should pass before the monitor is turned off.

7 On the Turn Off Hard Disks menu, declare how many minutes should pass before the hard disk is shut down.

8 Click OK and then click OK again in the Display Properties dialog box.

Figure 9.2: In the Power Management Properties dialog box, tell Windows when to switch into Standby mode.

background while you do other work. Follow these steps to run ScanDisk:

1. Click the Start button and choose Programs | Accessories | System Tools | ScanDisk. You see the ScanDisk dialog box shown in Figure 9.3.

ScanDisk - (C:)

Select the drive(s) you want to check for errors:

3½ Floppy (A:)

(C:)

Type of test

○ Standard
(checks files and folders for errors)

● Thorough
(performs Standard test and scans disk surface for e

☑ Automatically fix errors

Scanning disk surface (data area)...

Start   Cancel   Advanced...

ScanDisk Results - (C:)

ScanDisk found errors on this drive and fixed them all.

2,103,566,336 bytes total disk space
0 bytes in bad sectors
4,378,624 bytes in 779 folders
217,915,392 bytes in 360 hidden files
1,565,851,648 bytes in 23,368 user files
315,420,672 bytes available on disk
4,096 bytes in each allocation unit
513,566 total allocation units on disk
77,007 available allocation units

Close

Figure 9.3: Use the ScanDisk program to check for damaged files and warped areas on the hard disk.

2. In the ScanDisk dialog box, select a disk to check (probably your hard drive, [C:]).

3. Choose which type of test to run:

   • **Standard** Checks for file errors and file-allocation errors.

   • **Thorough** Does what the Standard test does and also checks the actual surface of the disk for damaged areas that can't be relied upon for storing data. Run this test periodically, but not as often as the Standard test.

4. Make sure that the Automatically Fix Errors check box is checked and then click the Start button. When the test is done, the ScanDisk Results dialog box tells which errors, if any, were found and how the test was conducted.

5. Click Close in the ScanDisk dialog box.

 TIP
If you want to see the ScanDisk Results dialog box, click the Advanced button, click the Always option button under Display Summary, and click OK.

Windows Tune-Up: Running Maintenance Programs Automatically

Windows
Tune-Up

Windows Tune-Up is not really a program—it's a task scheduler. The program is actually a way to run three utility programs—Disk Defragmenter, ScanDisk, and Disk Cleanup—on a daily basis or other schedule. All three programs are explained earlier in this chapter. To make Windows Tune-Up work, you have to leave your computer on overnight. Windows Tune-Up runs the three utility programs in your absence.

Follow these steps to schedule Disk Defragmenter, ScanDisk, and Disk Cleanup tune-ups of your computer system:

1. Click the Start button and choose Programs | Accessories | System Tools | Windows Tune-Up. You see the first Windows Tune-Up Wizard dialog box.

2. Click Next to use the common tune-up settings.

3. In the next dialog box, choose when you want tune-ups to occur and click Next.

4. Click the Finish button (click the When I Finish check box as well to see exactly what a tune-up does).

The Task Scheduler icon appears in the lower-right corner of the screen so you know that

> Task Scheduler is ready.

Windows Tune-Up is ready to pounce on your system and repair stuff while you are away. You can tell which is the Task Scheduler icon because the words "Task Scheduler is ready" appear when you move the pointer over the icon. Double-click the icon to change settings or quit using it.

SHORTCUT

To choose a specific tune-up schedule for each of the three utilities or to quit using Windows Tune-Up, double-click the Tasks Scheduler icon in the lower-right corner of the screen. You see the Scheduled Tasks window. Click the name of a maintenance program on the list and choose File | Delete to cancel it or choose File | Properties, click the Schedule tab, and enter a new schedule. Later in this chapter, "Scheduled Tasks: Running Programs in Your Absence" explains more about scheduling tasks.

Getting Information About Your System

If your system goes south and you have to call a technician, he or she will ask all sorts of personal questions about your computer. How much RAM does it have? What kind of hard-disk controller does it have? You can answer these questions and even find out from Windows 98 if a device on your computer is not working by following these steps:

1. Click the Start button and choose Programs | Windows Explorer.

2. Scroll to the top of the folders side of the window and click My Computer.

3. Either choose File | Properties or right-click and choose Properties. You see the System Properties dialog box.

4. Visit each tab on the dialog box to see what you can see:

   • **General**   Not much here that you wouldn't know already. The bottom of the tab lists how much RAM (random access memory) your system can draw upon.

   • **Device Manager**   This tab is the interesting one. Click the plus sign (+) next to each device type, as shown in Figure 9.4, to find out more about it. You see manufacturer names and device types. By clicking a device and then clicking the

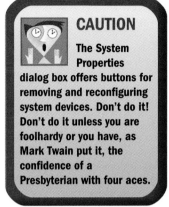

CAUTION

The System Properties dialog box offers buttons for removing and reconfiguring system devices. Don't do it! Don't do it unless you are foolhardy or you have, as Mark Twain put it, the confidence of a Presbyterian with four aces.

Figure 9.4: From the System Properties dialog box, you can tour the insides of your computer.

Properties button, you can learn more about it. As the right side of Figure 9.4 shows, you can also learn from the Device Status box whether the device is working properly.

- **Hardware Profiles**   This is an advanced tab that has to do with system configurations and drivers. It's for professionals only.
- **Performance**   Here you see how much memory and virtual memory your system employs, among other things.

5. Click Cancel to close the System Properties dialog box.

Compressing Files and Drives to Gain More Disk Space

This part of the chapter explains two programs you can use to acquire more space on a crowded hard disk: Drive Converter (FAT32) and DriveSpace. The first switches the computer from the FAT16 system for allocating file space to the FAT32 system. The FAT32 system is far more efficient, allows more files to be saved on disk, and carves out more disk space. The second program, DriveSpace, is for compressing files. After files are compressed, they take up less space on disk, which allows more room for new files.

Besides running the file and disk compression programs described in the following pages to gain more disk space, try using these techniques:

CAUTION

Converting to the FAT32 format is definitely the best way to acquire more disk space. However, you can't go back to the FAT16 format after you run Drive Converter (FAT32), you have to reinstall Windows 98 after the conversion, you can't compress files after your system has adopted the FAT32 format, and you can't switch to FAT32 if files on your computer have been compressed.

- Uninstall software programs that you don't need anymore. See "Removing Unwanted Software Programs" in Chapter 4.
- Delete files that you no longer need. See "Deleting Files and Folders" in Chapter 3.
- Remove Windows 98 components that you don't need or want. See Appendix A.
- Run Disk Cleanup to delete unneeded files, Windows 98 uninstallation files, and files in the Recycle Bin. See "Disk Cleanup: Uncluttering the Hard Disk" earlier in this chapter.
- Run Disk Defragmenter to store files on disk more efficiently. See "Disk Defragmenter: Loading Files and Programs Faster" earlier in this chapter.

- Run ScanDisk to repair errors that cause files to be stored inefficiently. See "ScanDisk: Repairing Damage to Files and the Hard Disk" earlier in this chapter.

Drive Converter (FAT32): Converting to the More Efficient FAT32 Format

On PCs, the *file allocation table* (FAT) controls how space is allocated to files on the hard disk. Under the old FAT16 format, a minimum of 32KB of space was needed to store each file, no matter how small it was, but FAT32 decreases the minimum amount of space per file to 4KB, one-eighth the amount of space that FAT16 needs. By converting to FAT32, you shrink files significantly and thereby acquire more free space on the hard disk.

Your hard disk may use the FAT32 format already. Figure 9.5 explains how to find out which format is in use on your system.

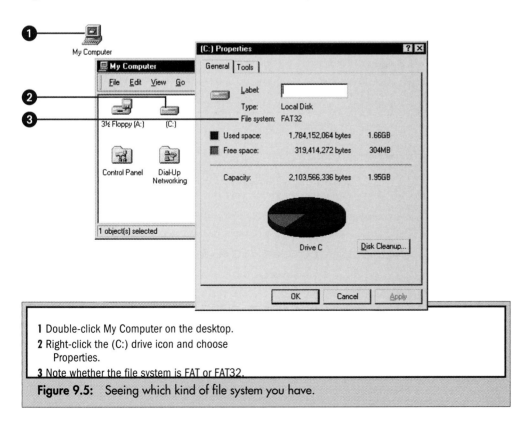

1 Double-click My Computer on the desktop.
2 Right-click the (C:) drive icon and choose Properties.
3 Note whether the file system is FAT or FAT32.

Figure 9.5: Seeing which kind of file system you have.

Follow these steps to convert to the FAT32 format from the FAT16 format:

1. Close all programs if any are running.

2. Click the Start button and choose Programs | Accessories | System Tools | Drive Converter (FAT32).

3. Click Next in the first Drive Converter dialog box.

4. If necessary, select the drive that you want to convert to FAT32 and click Next.

5. Click Next in the dialog box that explains what Drive Converter does.

6. Negotiate the various warning screens that tell you how anti-virus programs work under FAT32 and that FAT32 doesn't work with the Windows NT operating system.

7. Click Next and wait while the Converter restarts your computer and completes the conversion.

As part of the conversion, Windows runs the Disk Defragmenter, which can take many minutes to run. Wait until Disk Defragmenter is finished doing its job before you start working again.

EXPERT ADVICE

If anti-virus software has been installed on your computer, the software might detect what it thinks is a virus after you convert to FAT32. The anti-virus software might think that the partition table and boot record have changed and offer to repair these items. *Do not* instruct the anti-virus software to repair the partition table and boot record. If you do, you won't be able to access your hard drive.

DriveSpace: Compressing a Drive to Get More Disk Space

DriveSpace

Use DriveSpace to compress the files on a disk so they take up less space. By compressing files, you gain more space for new files. DriveSpace increases the amount of free space on the disk by 50 to 100 percent. That's the good news. The bad news is that you take a risk by compressing files. DriveSpace is a "ten pounds in a five-pound sack" means of getting more disk space on your computer. After files are compressed, it is harder for the computer to open and display them onscreen. Computers sometimes run slowly when they have to manage compressed files.

In my experience, compressing files is far more trouble than it's worth. If you're running out of disk space, consider installing a larger disk drive on your computer—disk drives are getting cheaper by the day. Instead of running DriveSpace, run the Drive Converter (FAT32) program to gain more disk space if your disk uses the outmoded FAT16 format.

Earlier in this chapter, "Drive Converter (FAT32): Converting to the More Efficient FAT32 Format" explains the FAT32 format.

Compressing a drive can take an hour or more, depending on how fast your computer is. Follow these steps if you disregard my advice and decide to run DriveSpace:

1. Back up all the important files on the disk.

2. Shut down all programs if any are running.

3. Click the Start button and choose Programs | Accessories | System Tools | DriveSpace. You see the DriveSpace dialog box.

4. Select the drive you want to compress and choose Drive | Compress. If Windows can compress the drive, you see the Compress a Drive dialog box, which shows how much free space is on the drive now and how much will be available when the drive is compressed.

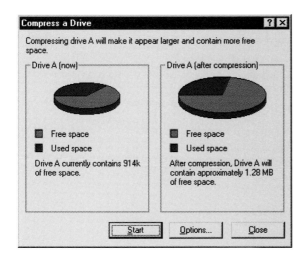

5. Click the Start button.

6. Click Compress Now in the "Are you sure?" message box.

7. Go to lunch. When you come back, click the Close button in the Compress a Drive dialog box and the DriveSpace dialog box.

   In order to compress a drive, Windows creates a new drive, Drive H, to store files that pertain to compressing. You can just ignore Drive H. To uncompress a drive, open the DriveSpace dialog box and choose Drive | Uncompress.

Windows Update: Getting an Up-to-Date Copy of Windows

Windows Update

Registered users of Windows 98 can go on the Internet and download the most up-to-date edition of Windows 98 from the Windows Update site, a Web site that Microsoft maintains. At the site, you answer a few questions, learn what parts of Windows 98 need updating, and get the opportunity to download new drivers and system files. Follow these steps to update your copy of Windows 98:

1. Click the Start button and choose Windows Update or Settings | Windows Update. Your Web browser starts so you can connect to the Internet.

2. Click the Connect button to go on the Internet. Soon you arrive at the Windows Update site (**http://windowsupdate.microsoft.com**).

3. Follow the instructions on the Web site for updating your copy of Windows 98.

Scheduled Tasks: Running Programs in Your Absence

To make sure that files get backed up and important maintenance tasks are done on a regular basis, you can schedule a program to run in your absence. For the plan to work, you have to leave your computer on overnight so the programs run when they won't distract you. Schedule tasks for the wee hours of the morning. I suggest choosing one night a week to run scheduled tasks. Turn off the monitor but make sure the computer is left on during "Scheduled Tasks Night."

Scheduled
Tasks

Follow these steps to schedule a program to run in your absence:

1. Either double-click the Scheduled Tasks icon in the lower-right corner of the screen or click the Start button and choose Programs | Accessories | System Tools | Scheduled Tasks. You see a Scheduled Tasks window similar to this one:

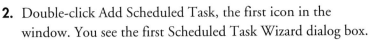

Earlier in this chapter, "Windows Tune-Up: Running Maintenance Programs Automatically" explains how to use Windows Tune-Up to put Disk Defragmenter, ScanDisk, and Disk Cleanup on the Scheduled Tasks list.

2. Double-click Add Scheduled Task, the first icon in the window. You see the first Scheduled Task Wizard dialog box.

3. Click Next. You see a list of the programs that are installed on your computer.

4. Scroll down the list, click the program that you want to run automatically, and then click Next. Obviously, you have to

TIP
Choose When My Computer Starts to run the program each time you start your computer.

choose a program that can run without your assistance, since you will be napping when the program runs. Prime candidates for scheduling are Backup, Disk Cleanup, Disk Defragmenter, ScanDisk, and anti-virus programs.

5. Choose when to run the program and click Next.

6. Enter the time of day, weekly frequency, and day of the week for the program to run, and then click Next.

7. Make sure your settings are correct in the last dialog box and then click Finish. A new task is entered in the Scheduled Tasks window. The window says when the program is to run and when it will run next.

8. In the window, click the task you just scheduled and choose File | Run to make sure the task you created can indeed be run correctly.

Suppose you decide not to run a program automatically. For that matter, suppose you want to change schedules. Double-click the Scheduled Tasks icon in the lower-right corner of the screen (or click the Start button and choose Programs | Accessories | System Tools | Scheduled Tasks) and do one of the following in the Scheduled Tasks window:

- **"Unschedule" a Task**   Click the program's name in the window and choose File | Delete.

- **Change Schedules**   Click the program's name and choose File | Properties. Then click the Schedule tab and enter new schedule settings.

- **Stop Running All Programs**   Choose Advanced | Stop Using Task Scheduler. Choose this option, for example, when you go on vacation for a few weeks and turn your computer off. When you come back from Firenze, click the Start button and choose Programs | Accessories | System Tools | Scheduled Tasks. Then choose Advanced | Start Using Task Scheduler.

Backup: Backing Up Files and Folders on the Hard Disk

To make backing up files easier, Windows 98 offers a program called Backup. Instead of backing up files and folders by copying them one at a time to a zip drive, tape drive, or floppy disk, you can back up several dozen files at once with the Backup program. To do so, you tell the Backup program what your most important files and folders are. Then you give those items a name. When you want to back up the files, you choose the name from a drop-down menu. With the Backup program, you can be sure that all the important data on your hard disk gets backed up. The program also makes it easier to retrieve backup copies.

The following pages explain how to tell the Backup program which files need backing up, give those files a name, and copy the files to a zip drive, tape drive, or floppy disk. You also learn how to retrieve the backup copy of a file and put it back on your hard disk.

In Chapter 2 "Decide When and How to Back Up Files" examines how to formulate a strategy for backing up important files. "Making Backup Copies to a Floppy Disk" in Chapter 3 explains how to back up one or two files at a time.

Telling Backup Which Files and Folders Need Backing Up

Follow these steps to create a "backup job"—a list of important files and folders that need backing up—and give the backup job a name:

Backup

1. Click the Start button and choose Programs | Accessories | System Tools | Backup. You see the Microsoft Backup dialog box.

2. Click Close in the dialog box instead of OK. (If you click OK, you use the Backup Wizard to choose which files need backing up, but you are a grown-up and you don't need to rely on a wizard.) You see the Backup window shown in Figure 9.6.

3. Click the Maximize button (the square in the upper-right corner of the window) to make the window fill the screen.

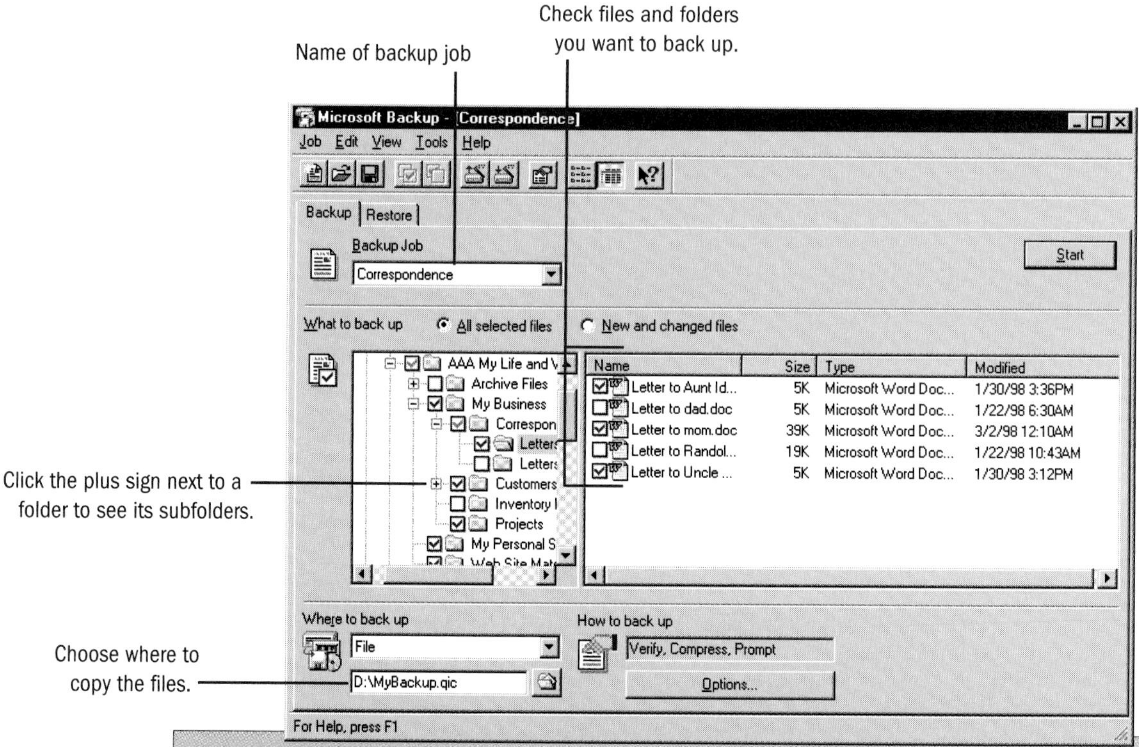

Name of backup job

Check files and folders
you want to back up.

Click the plus sign next to a
folder to see its subfolders.

Choose where to
copy the files.

Figure 9.6: Check off the folders and files that you want to back up, then choose Job |
Save and give a name to the "backup job."

4. In the window, click the check box beside each folder and file
   you want to back up. Use these techniques to locate and select
   the items that need backing up.

   • **To See a Folder** Click the plus sign beside the folder's
     name. Its subfolders and files appear on the right side of the
     window. Click a minus sign to "collapse" the folder and
     keep its contents from being displayed.

   • **To Back Up a Folder's Contents** Click the check box
     beside the folder's name. When you select a folder, all the
     subfolders and files inside it are backed up.

- **To Back Up Some of a Folder's Contents**   Select a folder on the left side of the window and click check boxes next to the files and folders you want to back up on the right side.

5. Under Where to Back Up, click the folder button to tell the Backup program where to copy the files. The folder button is kind of hard to find. Look for it below and to the right of the Where to Back Up box. When you click the folder button, you see the Where to Back Up dialog box.

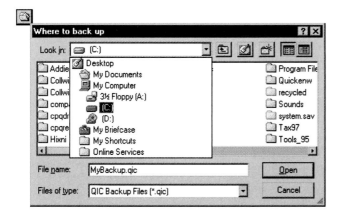

6. Click the down arrow to open the Look In drop-down menu, choose the drive to which the files and folders will be copied, and click the Open button. The path to the drive appears in the text box.

7. Choose Job | Save. You see the Save Backup Job As dialog box.

8. Enter a descriptive name in the Job Name text box and click the Save button. In the Backup window, the name you entered appears in the Backup Job drop-down menu.

In the Backup window, create another backup job and give it a name, if you want to. Click the Close button (the X) when you are done telling the Backup program which of your precious files need backing up. You can always revisit the Backup window and check or uncheck files and folders to include or exclude items from a backup job.

arlier in this chapter, "Scheduled Tasks: Running Programs in Your Absence" explains how to run the Backup program automatically by putting it on the Scheduled Tasks list.

Giving the Order to Back Up the Files

After you have gone to the trouble to tell the Backup program which files and folders to back up, backing up the files is as easy as counting to five. Follow these steps:

1. Click the Start button and choose Programs | Accessories | System Tools | Backup. (If ever a program needed a shortcut icon, it's the Backup program. See "Creating a Shortcut Icon" in Chapter 2.)

2. Click Close in the Microsoft Backup dialog box. The Backup window appears (see Figure 9.6).

3. On the Backup Job drop-down menu, choose the name you gave to the folders and files you want to back up.

4. Make sure the backup device is turned on and then click the Start button. You see the Backup Progress dialog box as backup copies of the files are made.

5. Click OK in the Operation Completed and Backup Progress dialog boxes.

SHORTCUT

If you have to back up a lot of files, click the New and Changed Files button in the Backup window. That way, backup copies are made only of files that were altered since the last backup.

Retrieving the Backup Copies of Files

The beauty of the Backup program is that it lets you restore many backed-up files at once. Follow these steps to restore a file:

1. Click the Start button and choose Programs | Accessories | System Tools | Backup.

2. Click Close in the Microsoft Backup dialog box.

3. In the Backup window, click the Restore tab.

4. Click Yes when you are asked if you want to refresh the current view.

5. In the Select Backup Sets dialog box, click the name of the backup job with the files and folders that need restoring, and then click OK.

DEFINITION

Restore: To replace the original copy of a file with its backup copy.

6. Using the same techniques you used to include a file in a backup job, click plus signs (+) until you reach the files or folders that need restoring, and then click the check boxes beside their names.

7. Click the Start button.

8. Make sure the backup device is on and the right tape or disk is loaded in the backup device, and then click OK in the Media Required dialog box.

9. Click OK in the Operation Completed and Restore Progress dialog boxes.

CHAPTER 10

Sights and Sounds

INCLUDES

- Adjusting the volume of the sounds you play
- Playing a CD on your computer
- Playing sound files
- Recording sounds of your own
- Including a sound file or video clip in another file
- Playing video clips onscreen

FAST FORWARD

Control the Volume of Speakers and Other Sound-Producing Devices ➥ pp. 241–242

- Turn the volume knob on your computer monitor.
- Click the Speaker icon and drag the slider up or down.
- Double-click the Speaker icon and change settings in the Speaker dialog box.

Play Your Favorite CD on Your Computer ➥ pp. 243–244

1. Put the CD in the CD-ROM drive or click the Start button and choose Programs | Accessories | Entertainment | CD Player.
2. Click the Play button.
3. Click the Next Track button or choose a song from the Track drop-down list to hear a different song.
4. Click the Stop button to stop playing the CD.

Play a Sound File on Your Computer ➥ p. 244

1. Click the Start button and choose Programs | Accessories | Entertainment.
2. Choose either Sound Recorder or Windows Media Player.
3. Choose File | Open and open a sound file.
4. Click the Play button.

Play a Video Clip on Your Computer ➥ pp. 249–250

- Find an .avi or .mpeg file in Windows Explorer or My Computer and double-click it.
- Click the Start button and choose Programs | Accessories | Entertainment | Windows Media Player. Then choose File | Open and, in the Open dialog box, find and double-click the .avi or .mpeg file.

It might interest you to know that the computer and the television are slowly merging into one device. In ten years, you will be able to watch movies and TV on computer monitors. Instead of visiting the local video rental store, you will download movies from the Internet when you want to watch a movie. You will be able to surf the Internet and watch television at the same time.

This chapter explains what you can do today to play video and sounds on your computer. As long as speakers are attached to your computer and your computer has a sound card and video capabilities, you can record sounds and play short videos and sound clips. This chapter describes how to do that; how to include video clips and sound clips in files; and how to use Imaging to view, print, and annotate PC-based image files.

CAUTION

Sound and video clips consume a lot of space on disk. For example, a 60-second .mpeg video clip that includes sound and music consumes about 7MB of disk space. If you want to experiment with video clips and sound files, make sure your computer has enough disk space to handle them.

Volume Control: Adjusting the Volume Levels

These days, most computer monitors have a knob that you can turn to adjust the volume of sound coming from the speakers. And if the speakers aren't built into the monitor, you can usually control the volume of the speakers themselves. However, if your monitor and speakers don't have a knob, you can adjust the volume by clicking the Speaker icon in the lower-right corner of the screen (next to the clock). This icon looks like a bullhorn. When you click it, you see the Volume slider shown on the left side of Figure 10.1. Drag the slider up or down to adjust the volume.

Volume Control

You can also choose a volume level for the different sound and video devices installed on your computer. To do so, either

TIP

If you don't see the Speaker icon, click the Start button and choose Settings | Control Panel. Then double-click the Multimedia icon and, on the Audio tab of the Multimedia Properties dialog box, click the Show Volume Control on Taskbar check box.

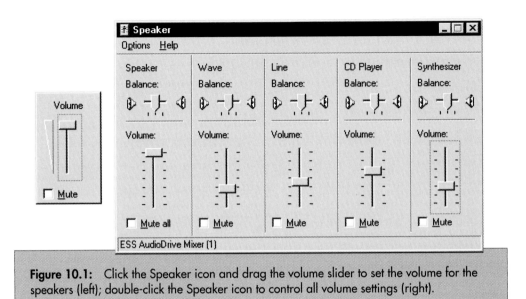

Figure 10.1: Click the Speaker icon and drag the volume slider to set the volume for the speakers (left); double-click the Speaker icon to control all volume settings (right).

double-click the Speaker icon or click the Start button and choose Programs | Accessories | Entertainment | Volume Control. You see the Speaker dialog box shown on the right side of Figure 10.1. Drag the sliders up or down to decide how loud the CD Player and other sound-producing devices on your computer should be.

EXPERT ADVICE

Sometimes the Volume Control dialog box doesn't offer sliders for controlling all the sound-producing devices on your computer. If that is the case, choose Options | Properties in the Volume Control dialog box. In the Properties dialog box, check the names of sound-producing devices you want to see in the Volume Control dialog box, and click OK.

Playing and Recording Sounds on Your Computer

As long as speakers and a sound card are installed in your computer, you have the makings of a wee little recording studio. And if you have a CD-ROM drive as well, you can play CDs at your desk. These pages explain how to play CDs, play sound files, and record sounds of your own.

CD Player: Playing CDs on Your Computer

People whose computers have CD-ROMs and speakers can whistle while they work. Actually, they can have someone else do the whistling—they can play CDs from the computer. To be sure, a Nina Simone or Mozart CD doesn't sound as good on a computer as it does on a stereo system, but an Eagles or Jackson Browne CD doesn't sound any worse, either.

CD Player

Do the following to play a CD:

- Insert the CD in the CD-ROM drive. The CD starts playing. Click the CD Player button on the Taskbar to see the dialog box shown in Figure 10.2.
- If the CD is already loaded in the drive, click the Start button and choose Programs | Accessories | Entertainment | CD Player. You see the CD Player dialog box shown in Figure 10.2. Click the Play button.

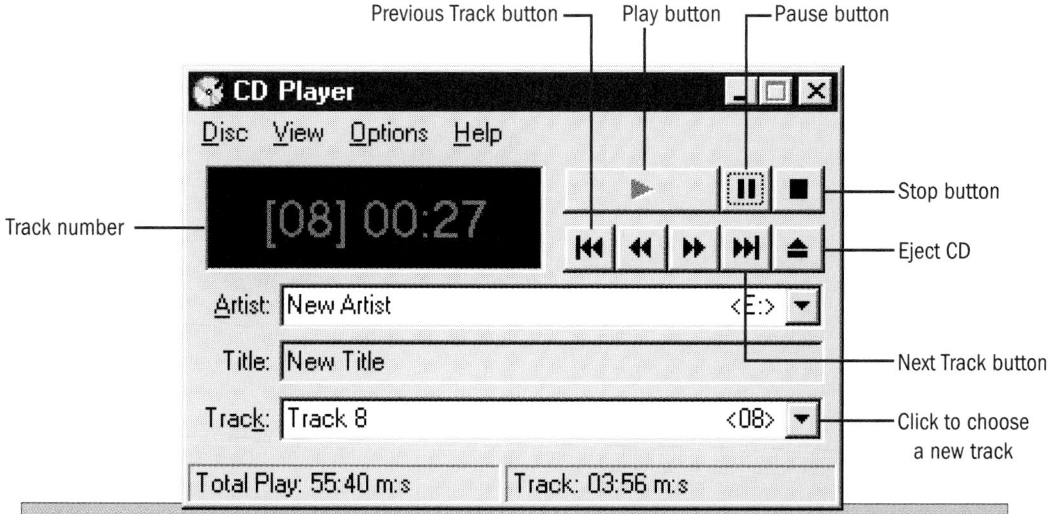

Previous Track button — Play button — Pause button

Track number — [08] 00:27

Stop button

Eject CD

Artist: New Artist <E:>

Title: New Title

Next Track button

Track: Track 8 <08>

Click to choose a new track

Total Play: 55:40 m:s   Track: 03:56 m:s

Figure 10.2: As long as a CD-ROM drive, speakers, and a sound card are installed on your computer, you can play CDs.

Figure 10.2 explains what the various buttons do. Tracks are played from first to last, but you can change the order in which songs are played by following these steps:

- **Play Randomly**   Choose Options | Random Order to let your computer decide which track is played next.
- **Choose a Track**   Click the Previous Track or Next Track button, or click the down arrow to open the Track drop-down list and choose another track.

Choose Disc | Edit Play List if you have a half hour on your hands and you want to permanently change the order in which songs are played or even type the names of songs on the play list.

Playing Sound Files

Sound
Recorder

Windows
Media Player

Two Windows 98 accessory programs can play sounds: Sound Recorder and Windows Media Player (the Media Player also plays video clips). Use Sound Recorder to play wave (.wav) sound files and Windows Media Player to play wave as well as MIDI (.mid and .rmi) sequences.

The easiest way to play a sound file is to find and double-click it in Windows Explorer or My Computer. Windows 98 opens either the Windows Media Player or Sound Recorder and plays the sound. Figure 10.3 shows the Windows Media Player and Sound Recorder. You can also open these programs by clicking the Start button and choosing Programs | Accessories | Entertainment and either Windows Media Player or Sound Recorder. Open a file you want to hear by choosing File | Open in either program.

TIP

If you would like to experiment with sound as you read the following pages, open My Computer or Windows Explorer and go to the C:\Windows\Media folder. In that folder are several sound files.

In both programs, you can drag the slider to move forward or backward in the sound file. The buttons are self-explanatory and work much the same as buttons on tape recorders. Both programs also offer commands for cutting out part of a sound file and saving it under a new name (a subject not covered in this book). The Sound Recorder offers a neat command, Effects | Reverse, for playing a sound file backwards to see if it masks a subliminal or satanic message.

To Be or Not to Be.wav - Windows Media Player _ □ X

File   View   Play   Favorites   Go   Help

⬅ ➡   🎬 Web Events

▶ ❚❚ ■ | ⏮ ⏪ ⏩ ⏭ | ☰ | ◁ ／￣

Show:
Clip:
Author:
Copyright:
Playing

To Be or Not to Be.wav - Sound... _ □ X

File   Edit   Effects   Help

Position:		Length:
19.99 sec.	▬▬▬▬▬▬	99.15 sec.

⏪ | ⏩ | ▶ | [■] | ●

Figure 10.3: Use Windows Media Player (top) or Sound Recorder (bottom) to play sound files. These programs are found on the Programs | Accessories | Entertainment menu.

Recording Sounds of Your Own

To record live sound, a microphone as well as speakers must be connected to your computer. Sounds you record with Sound Recorder are saved as wave (.wav) files. Follow these steps to record a sound:

Sound Recorder

1. Click the Start button and choose Programs | Accessories | Entertainment | Sound Recorder. The Sound Recorder dialog box opens (see the bottom of Figure 10.3).

2. Choose File | Properties. You see the Properties dialog box shown in Figure 10.4.

3. From the Choose From drop-down menu, choose Recording formats.

4. Click the Convert Now button. The Sound Selection dialog box opens (see Figure 10.4).

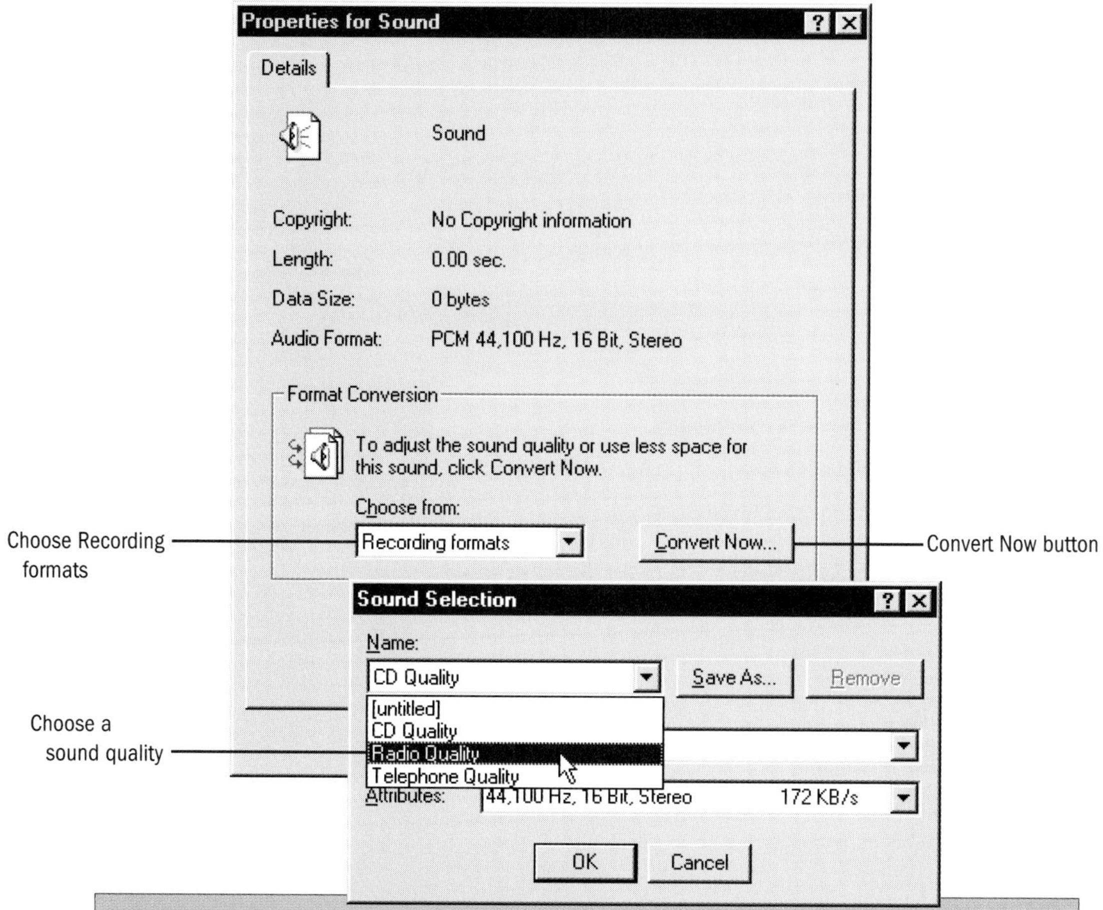

Choose Recording formats

Choose a sound quality

Convert Now button

Figure 10.4:   Before you record a sound, tell Sound Recorder how you want to record it by making choices in these dialog boxes.

5. From the Name drop-down list, choose a sound quality:

- **CD Quality**   The highest quality sound, with the largest amount of space (172KB per second) required to store the sound on disk.

- **Radio Quality**   Medium-quality sound, with less disk space required (22KB per second).

- **Telephone Quality**   Low-quality sound with the least amount of disk space required (11KB per second).

6. Click OK to close the Sound Selection dialog box.

7. Click OK in the Properties for Sound dialog box.

8. In the Sound Recorder dialog box, click the Record button and start yapping, yammering, whistling, cooing, or making whatever sound you want to record.

9. Click the Stop button when you are finished.

10. Choose File | Save and, in the Save As dialog box, choose a folder in which to save the file, give the file a name, and click the Save button.

Editing a Wave File

In Sound Recorder, wave (.wav) sound files can be cut and edited like video tape. In fact, with a couple of good wave files, you can pretend very easily that you are a record producer. Here are instructions for editing wave files in Sound Recorder:

- **Cutting out the Start or End of a File**   Either play the sound or move the slider to the point before which or after which you want to delete the file. Then open the Edit menu and choose either Delete Before Current Position or Delete After Current Position.

- **Inserting One File into Another**   Move the slider to the point where you want to insert the file, choose Edit | Insert File, find and select the file in the Insert File dialog box, and click the Open button. It goes without saying, but you can only insert a wave file into a wave file.

- **Mixing Sound Files**   Open one file and move the slider to the point where you want the second file to start. Then choose Edit | Mix with File, locate and select the other file in the Mix With File dialog box, and click the Open button.

- **Changing the Volume**   To make a sound file louder or softer, choose Effects | Increase Volume (by 25%) or Effects | Decrease Volume.

- **Changing the Speed (and Pitch)**   To make voice recordings higher or lower, choose Effects | Increase Speed (by 100%) or Effects | Decrease Speed.
- **Adding an Echo Effect**   Choose Effects | Add Echo.
- **Reversing a Sound**   Choose Effects | Reverse.

Including (and Playing) a Sound File or Video Clip in a File

Figure 10.5 explains how to put a sound file or video clip in a file and how to play sounds and videos in files. Before you get excited about burdening your files with sights and sounds, remember that a sound bite and especially a video clip can make a file grow astronomically in size.

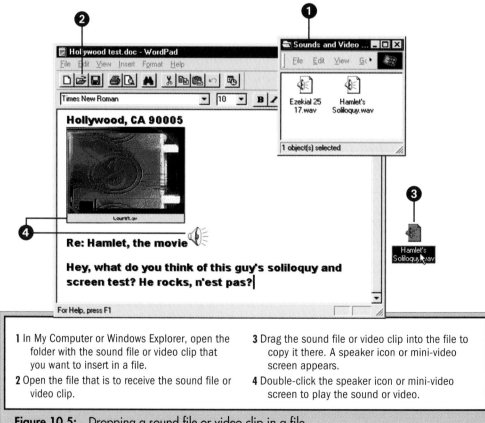

1 In My Computer or Windows Explorer, open the folder with the sound file or video clip that you want to insert in a file.

2 Open the file that is to receive the sound file or video clip.

3 Drag the sound file or video clip into the file to copy it there. A speaker icon or mini-video screen appears.

4 Double-click the speaker icon or mini-video screen to play the sound or video.

Figure 10.5:   Dropping a sound file or video clip in a file.

Windows Media Player: Playing Video Clips

However momentarily, you can pretend you are at the movies while you stare at your computer screen. Windows 98 can play .mpeg and .avi video clips. To play a video clip, find and double-click it in Windows Explorer or My Computer. You can also click the Start button and choose Programs | Accessories | Entertainment | Windows Media Player to open the movie file in Windows Media there. Figure 10.6 shows an .avi movie being played in Windows Media Player.

Click the Play button to start playing the video. Figure 10.6 describes what the other buttons and controls do. When you are finished watching the movie, please carry your popcorn boxes and soft drink containers to the lobby and dispose of them there.

In Chapter 2, "Decide How to List Files in Folders and Dialog Boxes" explains how to display file extensions such as .mpeg and .avi in windows. See "Looking for Files and Folders with the Find Command" to search for .mpeg and .avi files on your computer (hint: enter *.mpeg or *.avi).

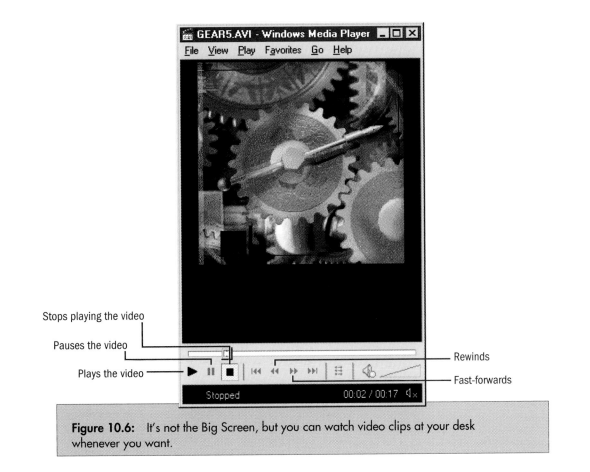

Figure 10.6: It's not the Big Screen, but you can watch video clips at your desk whenever you want.

When you play a video clip, it appears onscreen in its "original size"—the size at which the maker of the video clip wanted it to appear. However, you can change the size of the video window onscreen by clicking a window border and dragging. You can also choose View | Full Screen or View | Zoom and then select a zoom setting to change the size of the window. To change the size of the window once and for all, click the Start button and choose Settings | Control Panel. In the Control Panel, double-click the Multimedia icon, and then click the Video tab in the Multimedia Properties dialog box. From there, choose Window settings—Double original size, 1/2 of screen size, and so on—or click the Full screen button. At full-screen size, however, most videos look grainy and a bit crude.

Imaging: Annotating and Viewing Images

Imaging

Use Imaging to view and manipulate scanned images and image files you've copied from the Internet. The program works with the graphic files listed in Table 10.1. Imaging is a fun little toy. On the menu bar are commands for zooming in and out, rotating images, and cropping images. You are invited to experiment with Imaging to your heart's content. As you experiment, click the Best Fit button or choose View | Full Screen to get a better look at images.

File Extension	Format
.bmp	Windows Paint
.gif	Graphics Interchange Format
.jpg	JPEG File Interchange Format
.pcx	PC Paintbrush
.tif	Tagged Image File Format

Table 10.1: Types of Graphic Files That Work with Imaging.

Click the Start button and choose Programs | Accessories | Imaging to start the program. Following are instructions for annotating an image:

1. Open the image you want to annotate and click the Annotation Toolbar button. The Annotation toolbar appears along the bottom of the screen, as shown in Figure 10.7.

2. Click the Text button on the Annotation toolbar.

3. Click where you want the annotation to go and drag to create a text box to put the annotation in.

4. Type the annotation text.

5. Click the Straight Line button.

6. Drag to draw a line from the annotation to a part of the image.

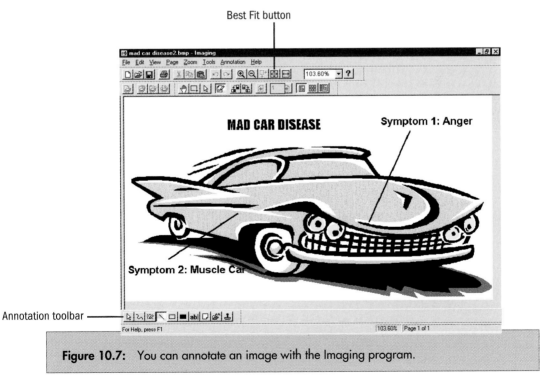

Figure 10.7: You can annotate an image with the Imaging program.

7. To change the font or font size of the letters in an annotation or the thickness of a line, right-click the annotation or line and choose Properties. In the Properties dialog box, choose new settings.

To move an annotation or line, click the Annotation Selection button, click the thing you want to move, and start dragging.

Installing and Reinstalling Windows 98

This appendix explains how to install Windows 98 as well as how to reinstall it when you want to add or remove some of the program's components.

To run Windows 98, your system must meet these requirements:

- At minimum, a 386 machine, although to run Windows well you should have a 486, Pentium, or faster processor.
- At least 24MB (megabytes) of RAM.
- 240MB to 400MB of free disk space, depending on which parts of Windows 98 you install.
- A CD-ROM or DVD-ROM drive.

Installing Windows 98 for the First Time

Installing Windows 98 is actually very simple. You need a blank floppy disk with at least 1.2MB of disk space and about 30 to 60 spare minutes, depending on how many Windows 98 components you want to install and how fast your computer is. The first time you install Windows 98, you get a standard installation with the default components. Later, you can reinstall the operating system and remove or add components (later in this appendix, "Reinstalling Windows to Add or Remove System Components" explains how). Follow these steps to install Windows 98:

1. Close all programs if any are running.
2. Insert the Windows 98 CD in the CD-ROM drive. A message box tells you that the CD contains a newer version of Windows and asks if you want to install Windows 98.
3. Click Yes. You see the Windows 98 Setup dialog box.

If you don't see the message box or the Windows 98 Setup dialog box, either click Add/Remove Software in the Windows 98 CD-ROM window or click the Start button and choose Settings | Control Panel, double-click the Add/Remove Programs icon in the Control Panel window, and click Install in the Add/Remove Programs Properties dialog box. Then click Next and click Finish.

4. Click Continue in the Windows 98 Setup dialog box. Windows runs some tests on your computer to see how much disk space you have.

5. Keep answering questions and clicking Next or OK.

In the course of the installation, you are asked to do the following:

- Tell Windows 98 which country you live in.
- Insert a blank floppy disk in your machine in order to create an emergency startup disk.
- Restart your computer three times (be sure to take the emergency startup disk out of the disk drive before you restart the computer). Restarting your computer takes considerably longer than usual when you install Windows 98. Be patient.

When the ordeal is over, you can take a tour of Windows 98, although you don't have to take it right away. Take the tour whenever you want by clicking the Start button and choosing Programs | Accessories | Tips and Tour.

At the end of Chapter 2, "Create an Emergency Startup Disk" explains what an emergency startup disk is.

EXPERT ADVICE

As part of the installation procedure, Windows 98 saves your old Windows 95 system files in case you want to abandon Windows 98 and go back to using the older version of Windows. See "Disk Cleanup: Uncluttering the Hard Disk" in Chapter 9 to learn how to remove old system files and save on disk space.

Reinstalling Windows to Add or Remove System Components

After you have used Windows 98 for a while, you might discover that you need system components that weren't installed the first time around. Or perhaps you don't need some components and you would like to remove them to save on disk space.

Table A.1 lists all the Windows 98 component categories and component options. When you install the program, the components in the table with check marks (✔) next to their names were installed. The remainder of this appendix explains how to add or remove the Windows 98 system components in Table A.1. To do so, you reinstall Windows 98.

Component/Component Options	Size with Default Installation (MB)	Size with All Options Installed (MB)
Accessibility ✔ Accessibility Options Enhanced Accessibility	0.4	4.2
Accessories ✔ Calculator ✔ Desktop Wallpaper ✔ Document Templates ✔ Games ✔ Imaging ✔ Mouse Pointers ✔ Paint ✔ Quick View ✔ Screen Savers ✔ Windows Scripting Host ✔ WordPad	17.7	17.7

Table A.1:   The Windows 98 System Components.

✔ Indicates component was installed at initial installation.

Component/Component Options	Size with Default Installation (MB)	Size with All Options Installed (MB)
Address Book	1.5	1.5
Communications	7.0	10.1
Dial-Up ATM Support		
✔ Dial-Up Networking		
Dial-Up Server		
✔ Direct Cable Connection		
✔ HyperTerminal		
Microsoft Chat 2.5		
✔ NetMeeting		
✔ Phone Dialer		
Virtual Private Networking		
Desktop Themes	0.0	31.7
Internet Tools	.2	11.9
Internet Connection Sharing		
Microsoft Wallet		
✔ Personal Web Server		
Web Publishing Wizard		
Web-Based Enterprise Mgmt		
Multilanguage Support	0.0	1.1
Baltic		
Central European		
Cyrillic		
Greek		
Turkish		
Multimedia	5.0	11.6
✔ Audio Compression		
✔ CD Player		
DVD Player		
✔ Macromedia Shockwave		
✔ Macromedia Shockwave Flash		
✔ Media Player		
Microsoft NetShow Player 2.0		
Multimedia Sound Schemes		
✔ Sample Sounds		
✔ Sound Recorder		
✔ Video Compression		
✔ Volume Control		

Table A.1: The Windows 98 System Components *(continued).*

✔ Indicates component was installed at initial installation.

Component/Component Options	Size with Default Installation (MB)	Size with All Options Installed (MB)
Online Services ✔ America Online ✔ AT&T WorldNet Service ✔ CompuServe ✔ Prodigy Internet	1.2	1.2
Outlook Express	4.7	4.7
System Tools ✔ Backup ✔ Character Map ✔ Clipboard Viewer ✔ Drive Converter (FAT 32) Group Policies NetWatcher ✔ System Monitor ✔ System Resource Meter	5.9	6.2
WebTV for Windows	0.0	31.4

Table A.1:   The Windows 98 System Components *(continued)*.

✔ Indicates component was installed at initial installation.

Follow these steps to reinstall Windows 98 and add or remove some of its components:

Add/Remove Programs

1. Close all programs if any are running.
2. Click the Start button and choose Settings | Control Panel.
3. Double-click the Add/Remove Programs icon.
4. Click the Windows Setup tab in the Add/Remove Programs Properties dialog box. As shown in Figure A.1, the dialog box lists all component categories (these are the categories in Table A.1). You can tell how many component options in each category are installed on your computer by looking at the check boxes:
   - **Check with No Shading**   All component options in this category are installed on your computer.
   - **Check with Shading**   Some component options in the category are installed.

- **Empty Check Box**   No component options in this category are installed.

5. Click a component category and then click the Details button. As shown in Figure A.1, you see a list of the component options in the category.

6. Scroll down the list and check or uncheck boxes to add or remove component options, and then click OK.

7. Repeat steps 5 and 6 to add or remove more component options from your computer.

8. Click OK in the Add/Remove Programs Properties dialog box.

9. Insert the Window 98 CD and click OK in the Insert Disk message box.

10. Follow the onscreen directions to reinstall Windows 98.

TIP

Read the description of the component options to see what they are or do.

Check or uncheck component options to add or remove them

Select a component category

Description of component

Click Details

Figure A.1: Adding and removing Windows 98 system components.

Index

The Computer Books You
Love to Read Are
Even Better Than Ever!

With the release of Office 2000, Osborne presents a fresh new line of Busy People™ books…

"Well-organized and illustrated and aimed directly at working people who need to get specific jobs done quickly."
—LIBRARY JOURNAL

"Entertaining enough to be read over lunch and relaxing enough to take to bed."
—WACO TRIBUNE-HERALD

"About as far from the old dry textbook-style computer books as you can get with good navigational aids, lots of illustrations and shortcuts."
—COMPUTER LIFE

500,000+ Busy People Books Sold!

Office 2000 for Busy People
Peter Weverka
ISBN: 0-07-211857-1 $19.99

Word 2000 for Busy People
Christian Crumlish
ISBN: 0-07-211982-9 $19.99

Excel 2000 for Busy People
Ron Mansfield
ISBN: 0-07-211988-8 $19.99

Access 2000 for Busy People
Alan Neibauer
ISBN: 0-07-211983-7 $19.99

FrontPage 2000 for Busy People
Christian Crumlish
ISBN: 0-07-211981-0 $19.99

OSBORNE